Espionage, Diplomacy & the Lodge

Espionage, Diplomacy & the Lodge

Charles Delafaye and The Secret Department of the Post Office

RIC BERMAN

THE OLD
STABLES
PRESS

• Oxfordshire •

First published 2017 in Great Britain by
The Old Stables Press, Goring Heath, Oxfordshire RG8 7RT
theoldstablespress@gmail.com

British Library Cataloguing in Publication Data
A CIP catalogue record for this book is available from the British Library

Library of Congress Cataloguing-in-Publication Data
Berman, Ric
Espionage, Diplomacy & the Lodge. Charles Delafaye and The Secret Department of the Post Office/Ric Berman.
p. cm.
Includes biographical references.

ISBN: 0995756805
ISBN 13: 9780995756809

1.   Freemasonry - Great Britain - History - 18th century.
2.   Freemasonry - Europe - History - 18th century.
3.   Espionage - History - 18th century.
I. Title

For Caroline, Jonathan,
Jacob, Camilla and Gabriel

Other titles by the author

The Foundations of Modern Freemasonry —
The Grand Architects: Political Change and the
Scientific Enlightenment, 1714-1740

Schism: the Battle that Forged Freemasonry

Loyalists & Malcontents:
Freemasonry & Revolution in the Deep South

The Prestonian Lecture:
Foundations - new light on the formation and early years of
The Grand Lodge of England

Contents

Acknowledgments

I would like to express my gratitude to the Department of History, Philosophy and Religion at Oxford Brookes University, and the librarians and archivists at the British Library, the Institute of Historical Research, the University Library at the University of Cambridge, the Bodleian Libraries at the University of Oxford, and the Library and Museum of Freemasonry at the United Grand Lodge of England. Thank you for your assistance.

Many people have given their time to read and comment on early drafts of this work including Professors William Gibson, Paul Monod and Susan Sommers, Emeritus Professor Aubrey Newman, and Dr Marsha Keith Schuchard. Others have helped with the thankless task of proof reading. Thank you all for your support and patience.

Finally, I would like to thank a long-standing friend, Professor Jeremy Black, for his advice and guidance when I first stepped out on this then-unknown road a decade ago.

As always, any errors within this work should be regarded entirely as my own.

Richard Berman
March, 2017
Oxfordshire

Abbreviations

1723 *Constitutions*	James Anderson, *The Constitutions of the Freemasons* (London: John Senex & John Hooke, 1723).
1738 *Constitutions*	James Anderson, *The New Book of Constitutions of the Antient and Honourable Fraternity of Free and Accepted Masons* (London: Cæsar Ward and Richard Chandler, 1738)
ADC	Aide-de-Campe, or senior aide
ADM	Admiralty
AQC	*Ars Quatuor Coronatorum*, the *Transactions* of Quatuor Coronati Lodge, No. 2076, London
BH	British History Online
BL	British Library
Burney	Burney Collection of 17th and 18th century newspapers, British Library
CUP	Cambridge University Press
CUL	Cambridge University Library
f./ff.	folio/folios
Foundations	Ric Berman, *The Foundations of Modern Freemasonry. The Grand Architects: Political Change and the Scientific Enlightenment, 1714–1740* (Brighton: Sussex Academic Press, 2012)
FRS(s)	Fellow(s) of the Royal Society
GM/DGM	Grand Master/Deputy Grand Master

Grand Lodge *Minutes*	*The Minutes of the Grand Lodge of Freemasons of England, 1723-1739*, QCA (London, 1913), Volume X
Grand Lodge *Minutes II*	*The Minutes of the Grand Lodge of Freemasons of England, 1740-1758*, QCA (London, 1960), Volume XII
	In each case page references are to *QCA Masonic Reprints, volumes X and XII*, published in 1913 and 1960, respectively
HMC	Historic Manuscripts Commission
HMSO	His/Her Majesty's Stationery Office
HPO	History of Parliament Online: www.historyofparliamentonline
IHR	Institute of Historical Research
Lane's *Masonic Records*	John Lane, *Masonic Records, 1717–1894*, version 1.0 www.hrionline.ac.uk/lane
LCC	London County Council
LL	*London Lives 1690-1800*: www.londonlives.org
LMA	London Metropolitan Archives
Loyalists & Malcontents	Ric Berman, *Loyalists & Malcontents: Freemasonry and Revolution in the Deep South* (The Old Stables Press, 2015).
MP	Member of Parliament
MS[S]	Manuscript[s]
MUP	Manchester University Press
NA	National Archives
n.s.	new series

ODNB	*Oxford Dictionary of National Biography* (Oxford: OUP); 2004 edition unless stated otherwise.
o.s.	old series
OUP	Oxford University Press
PRO	Public Record Office
QC	Quatuor Coronati Lodge, No. 2076, London
QCA	Quatuor Coronatorum Antigrapha
Schism	Ric Berman, *Schism: The Battle that Forged Freemasonry* (Brighton: Sussex Academic Press, 2013)
SP	State Papers
TCD	Trinity College Dublin
UL	University of London
V&A	Victoria & Albert Museum, London
YUP	Yale University Press

INTRODUCTION

During the first half of the eighteenth century, the threat posed to Hanoverian Britain, principally England, by the exiled James Stuart - 'the Pretender' - and his followers was thought existential. One consequence was a drive to expand Britain's intelligence capabilities. Secret service funds were deployed to enhance existing resources, not least an expansion of mail intercepts and decoding capabilities, and extend the networks of formal and informal agents at home and overseas. The material sourced through these channels was passed to an inner circle within Whitehall via a handful of senior under-secretaries among whom the main conduit for monitoring anti-Jacobite intelligence was Charles Delafaye.

Unarguably one of the government's most trusted officials, Delafaye served as a senior under-secretary of state and secretary to the Lords Justices through to 1734.[1] He was a Huguenot, one of tens of thousands of French Protestant refugees who had found sanctuary in England, and a freemason, a member of the influential Horn Tavern lodge in Westminster. And under his aegis fragments of the Huguenot diaspora and elite freemasonry would be positioned to support the government's political and diplomatic objectives.

The Horn Tavern was by far the largest and most important of London's masonic lodges. Its master was the charismatic and well-connected Duke of Richmond and its members comprised a cross-section of the Whig establishment, a mix of politicians, aristocrats, soldiers, scientists and prominent members of London society. The lodge was the principal force behind freemasonry's remoulding and politicisation, with a kernel of members who

---

[1] Government officials were servants of the crown and at a senior level lacked permanent tenure. They were appointed by the secretary of state and generally left with them. The small number of officials who were retained in office were the exception not the rule, and this remained the case until the mid-eighteenth century when the problems caused by the absence of continuity in administration led slowly to the introduction of a permanent civil service. 'Lords Justices' is the correct spelling, cf., for example, NA SP 63/373/208.

exercised almost unimpeded sway within the Grand Lodge of England in 1717 through to the 1730s.[2]

The Horn dominated the masonic hierarchy at Grand Lodge, providing five grand masters between 1719 and 1726, and a deputy grand master in every year bar two from 1720 until 1735. And its members held other pivotal offices, including that of grand secretary and grand treasurer, and served as grand wardens throughout.[3] Perhaps as importantly, the lodge also supplied at least half of the *de facto* standing committee of Grand Lodge: the Grand Charity Committee.[4]

The Horn's influence was prodigious and eighteenth-century English freemasonry was restructured largely at its bidding. It was because of the Horn that Grand Lodge and much of English freemasonry established and maintained an alliance with successive Whig administrations. And it was the Horn's members, Charles Delafaye among them, who ensured that freemasonry's mediaeval ritual and oaths and charges would be altered to endorse Enlightenment beliefs and embrace Whig political principles. It is not possible to conceive that this was other than intentional and in part a response to the perceived Jacobite threat.[5]

---

[2]   The Grand Lodge of England was known initially as the Grand Lodge of London & Westminster.

[3]   Cf., *Foundations*, esp. chapter three. Appendix one provides a list of principal grand officers.

[4]   Cf., appendix four.

[5]   'Jacobite' is derived from 'Iacomus', the Latin form of James. It refers to James Stuart's supporters but was also used as a derogatory term to describe anyone opposing the policies and approach of the Hanoverian establishment.

James Anderson's 1723 *Constitutions of the Freemasons*,

Frontispiece

The Duke of Montagu is shown presenting the Constitutional
scroll and a set of compasses to the Duke of Wharton. Each Grand
Master is supported by his respective Grand Officers.

Desaguliers is on the far right dressed in clerical robes.

THE CHARGES OF A FREEMASON — A NEW ORDER

The Grand Lodge of England's alterations to the stonemasons' mediaeval
charters, *The Old Charges*,[6] created a new masonic liturgy that expressed

---

[6]   Records from the mediaeval period comprising *inter alia* the regulations
governing stonemasons' lodges. Examples include the *Regius* MS (*c.*1400) and the
Cooke MS (*c.*1450). Cf., *Foundations*, appendix two.

different sentiments. Freemasonry was re-configured to advocate religious toleration and constitutional government, and to promote obedience to the civil powers – Parliament and the magistracy – rather than blind compliance with royal authority. The themes are expressed overtly in James Anderson's 1723 *Constitutions*, a collaborative work co-authored by Dr Jean Theophilus Desaguliers, a cleric, scientist and Huguenot émigré, and George Payne, a masonic colleague at the Horn and the lodge's deputy master.[7]

The first masonic charge - *Concerning God and Religion* - replaced the traditional invocation to the Trinity and formal declaration of Christian belief.[8] As amended, the charge obliged freemasons only to 'obey the moral law' within a framework of 'that Religion in which all Men agree'.[9] It would no longer be the case that a mason should 'be of the religion of that country or nation' where he resided, but necessary only to believe in God and be a 'good man and true'.

The charge was not an avowal of support for a specific religious canon or church. Christian belief may have been implied but as written the new masonic oath was a simple declaration of faith in a divine being without a stated preference for any given form of worship. It was openly latitudinarian, if not deist, and represented a denial of the importance of doctrine and of ecclesiastical organisation.

> A Mason is obliged … to obey the Moral Law … But tho' in ancient times
> Masons were charged in every Country to be of the Religion of that
> Country or Nation, whatever it was, yet 'tis now thought more expedient
> only to oblige them to that Religion in which all Men agree, leaving their
> particular Opinions to themselves; that is, to be good Men and true, or
> Men of Honour and Honesty, by whatever Denominations or Persuasions

---

[7] George Payne (1685?-1757), one of Desaguliers' closest masonic collaborators. Although Anderson claimed sole authorship of the 1723 *Constitutions*, the work was a joint effort with the pivotal *Charges* and *Regulations* drawn-up by Desaguliers and Payne. Cf., *Foundations*, pp. 64-70

[8] For example, the *William Watson* MS at York (*c*.1530): 'The first Charge is that you be [a] true man to God, and the Holy Church'.

[9] 1723 *Constitutions*, p. 50.

they may be distinguished; whereby Masonry becomes the Centre and Union, and the means of conciliating true Friendship and Persons that must have remained at a perpetual Distance.

The charge gave backing to the principle of religious tolerance, not least the right to hold to Protestant beliefs in a Catholic country. This had been a long-standing part of Huguenot philosophy and was an Enlightenment sensibility shared by many Whigs. It became a core masonic tenet.

Desaguliers, then deputy grand master, was a strong advocate of this approach. His views were shared by many of his colleagues at the Royal Society, including Martin Folkes, later its president, a member of the Bedford's Head Tavern lodge in Covent Garden. For such freemasons there was no inherent conflict between a belief in God, 'the All-wise and Almighty Architect of the Universe',[10] and the Newtonian natural order, a world interpreted through rational observation:[11]

Natural Philosophy is that Science which gives the Reasons and Causes of the Effects and Changes which naturally happens in Bodies…We ought to call into question all such things as have an appearance of falsehood, that by a new Examen we may be led to the Truth.[12]

The idea became part of the masonic mainstream:

As Masons we only pursue the universal Religion or the Religion of Nature. This is the Cement which unites Men of the most different

---

[10] J.T. Desaguliers, *The Newtonian System of the World* (London, 1728), *Dedication*, pp. iii-iv.

[11] Cf., *Foundations*, chapter two.

[12] J.T. Desaguliers, *Lectures in Mechanical and Experimental Philosophy* (London, 1717), *Foreword*. Delafaye's 'inclination to mechanicks' places him in the same set: BL: MSS Add. 32689, f. 373, 20 October 1732, quoted in Margaret C. Jacob, *The Radical Enlightenment* (Lafayette, LA: Cornerstone, 2006), 2nd rev. edition), p. 105.

Principles in one sacred Band and brings together those who were most distant from one another.[13]

The second Masonic charge - *Of the Civil Magistrate Supreme and Subordinate* - addressed less than obliquely the Jacobite threat to the Hanoverian succession and the supremacy of parliamentary and judicial governance.

A Mason is a peaceable Subject to the Civil Powers … is never to be concerned in Plots and Conspiracies against the Peace and Welfare of the Nation … if a Brother should be a Rebel against the State, he is not to be countenanced in his Rebellion, however he may be pitied as an unhappy Man; and, if convicted of no other Crime, though the loyal Brotherhood must and ought to disown his Rebellion, and give no Umbrage or Ground of political Jealousy to the Government for the time being; they cannot expel him from the Lodge, and his Relation to it remains indefeasible.[14]

The charge advanced the novel concept that a freemason could be 'a Rebel against the State'. And although he 'is not to be countenanced in his Rebellion' and his views are to be disowned by 'the loyal Brotherhood', rebellion alone would not offer adequate grounds for expulsion from freemasonry 'if convicted of no other Crime'. The intellectual logic follows from the first masonic charge where 'Masonry [is] the means of conciliating… persons that must have remained at a perpetual distance'. Even so, the obligation to be obedient to the state was stated in the ritual and in his admission to the lodge each new member or Entered Apprentice was obligated to 'behave as a peaceable and dutiful Subject, conforming cheerfully to the Government under which he lives'.[15]

---

[13]   William Smith, *A Pocket Companion for Freemasons* (London, 1735), pp. 43-5.

[14]   1723 *Constitutions*, p. 50.

[15]   Smith, *A Pocket Companion for Freemasons*, pp. 43-5.

At a deeper level, the second charge echoed the changes to England's constitutional structure in the wake of the 1688 Glorious Revolution. Where allegiance to the crown – 'to be a true liege man to the king' - was core to the *Old Charges*, the 1723 *Constitutions* stated that freemasons were subject to the 'supreme legislature' and the civil powers. For Desaguliers and his circle the ideal political structure was that 'which does most nearly resemble the Natural Government of our System'.[16] Grand Lodge and hence freemasonry was supportive of constitutional monarchy and parliamentary government, a sentiment expressed allegorically in Desaguliers' *Newtonian System of the World*:

> The Primaries lead their Satellites,
> Who *guided, not enslav'd*, their Orbits run,
> Attend their Chief, but still respect the Sun,
> Salute him as they go, and his Dominion own.[17]

The implication was that resistance to the crown could be justified where a king was in breach of his Lockean moral contract with those he governed. This had been the basis of the Glorious Revolution and the justification for replacing James II with William and Mary. It was no longer obligatory for freemasons to be bound to 'be true liegemen to the King of England without any treason or falsehood'.[18] They would instead 'attend' and 'respect', but be 'guided, not enslaved'.

---

[16] Desaguliers, *The Newtonian System of the World*, pp. iii-iv.

[17] Ibid., p. 27. My italics.

[18] *Watson* MS.

The Rev. Dr John Theophilus Desaguliers (1683-1744)
Grand Master, 1719; Deputy Grand Master 1722, 1723, 1725

The third masonic charge - *Of Lodges* - emphasised that although masonic membership was open it was nonetheless selective.[19]

The persons admitted Members of a Lodge must be good and true Men, free-born, and of mature and discreet Age, no Bondmen, no Women, no immoral or scandalous men, but of good Report.[20]

---

[19] In practice, 1720s and 1730s freemasonry was restricted largely to those who could afford it.

[20] 1723 *Constitutions*, p. 51.

The sentiment was reinforced by the next charge - *Of Masters, Wardens, Fellows and Apprentices* - which offered a convention-defying approach to preferment in an age when precedence, rank and patronage almost always determined promotion and position.

> All preferment among Masons is grounded upon real Worth and personal Merit only; that so the Lords may be well served, the Brethren not put to Shame, nor the Royal Craft despised ... no Master or Warden is chosen by Seniority, but for his Merit.[21]

A catechism later summarised and reinforced these and other masonic obligations.[22] It remains in place today. Sworn by each incoming master of a lodge, the declarations were and are designed to strengthen the moral and masonic authority of the Grand Lodge of England and ensure compliance with and obedience to the established civil order.

> *I agree to be a good man and true, and strictly to obey the moral law.*
>
> *I agree to be a peaceable subject and cheerfully to conform to the laws of the country in which I reside.*
>
> *I promise not to be concerned in plots and conspiracies against government but patiently to submit to the decisions of the supreme legislature.*
>
> *I agree to pay a proper respect to the civil magistrate, to work diligently, live creditably and act honourably by all men.*
>
> *I agree to hold in veneration the original rulers and patrons of the Order of Masonry and their regular successors, supreme and subordinate, according to their stations; and to submit to the awards and resolutions of my brethren when convened,*

---

[21] Ibid.

[22] The precise date at which the full catechism was first in use in the eighteenth century is not known. Cf. William Preston, *Illustrations of Masonry* (London, 1775), 2nd edn., pp. 114-9.

in every case consistent with the constitutions of the Order. I agree to avoid private piques and quarrels, and to guard against intemperance and excess.

I agree to be cautious in carriage and behaviour, courteous to my brethren and faithful to my Lodge.

I promise to respect genuine brethren and to discountenance impostors and all dissenters from the original plan of Masonry.

I agree to promote the general good of society, to cultivate the social virtues and to propagate the knowledge of the art.

I promise to pay homage to the Grand Master for the time being, and to his officers when duly installed; and strictly to conform to every edict of the Grand Lodge or general assembly of Masons that is not subversive of the principles and ground-work of Masonry.

I admit that it is not in the power of any man, or body of men, to make innovations in the body of Masonry.[23]

I promise a regular attendance on the committees and communications of the Grand Lodge, on receiving proper notice, and to pay attention to all the duties of Masonry on convenient occasions.

I admit that no new Lodge shall be formed without permission of the Grand Lodge; and that no countenance be given to any irregular Lodge, or to any person clandestinely initiated therein, being contrary to the ancient charges of the Order.

I admit that no person can be regularly made a Mason in, or admitted a member of, any regular Lodge, without previous notice and due inquiry into his character.

I agree that no visitors shall be received into the Lodge without due examination and producing proper vouchers of their having been initiated in a regular Lodge.

---

[23] Introduced by the Grand Lodge of England on 24 June 1723 in response to the Duke of Wharton's attempt to advance his own interests and hijack the Grand Lodge: 'And the Question was moved. "That it is not in the Power of any person or Body of men, to make any Alteration or Innovation in the Body of Masonry without the Consent first obtained of the Annual Grand Lodge." And the Question being put accordingly, [it was so] Resolved.'

Viewed holistically, the purpose of the catechism, charges and regulations was not simply to provide a stringent moral and social compass but to affirm support for the political *status quo* and to demonstrate and reinforce obeisance to the masonic authorities.

The alterations made to the *Old Charges* were wholesale and not a trivial reworking of the traditions of the mediaeval guilds. But despite the change to the substance, the 1723 *Constitutions* nonetheless adopted the same format as the *Old Charges*. It was a means of demonstrating or implying that the new freemasonry was a seamless continuation of established practice that reached back to time immemorial. In this regard, the 1723 *Constitutions* were designed in part to validate the new Grand Lodge and give it credibility in a tradition-based society, an integrity that was reinforced by the social and financial standing of its first noble grand masters.

English freemasonry proved highly attractive in its reinvented form. Membership in London climbed to around 3,000 in the early 1730s, and up to a fifth and possibly as many as a quarter of London's professional and upper middling became members. Their ranks included lawyers, apothecaries and physicians, bankers and merchants, and aspirational artisans and traders. Many were government supporters and a minority were of sufficient loyalty and status to be selected as justices of the peace as successive Whig lord chancellors remade the magistracy in their own political image. Around a quarter of those appointed to the Middlesex and Westminster benches were freemasons, and their number included a majority of the more active magistrates.[24]

---

[24] *Foundations*, esp. chapter three. The position differed elsewhere, notably in the Tory strongholds of the North East, Yorkshire, Wales and the West Country, where central government influence was less pervasive and freemasonry more a function of financial status and social aspiration.

CHAPTER OUTLINE

Espionage, Diplomacy & the Lodge is broadly Anglo-centric in character. The book concentrates principally on members of the Grand Lodge of England, the Horn Tavern, and a handful of French Huguenot lodges, none of which should be regarded as representative of eighteenth-century English freemasonry as a whole. Despite their importance, Irish, Scottish and French freemasonry are considered only as tangents to the book's main theme. This is not because they lacked significance – French freemasonry in particular was interwoven with Jacobitism – but because it is not intended that this book provide a comprehensive account of European freemasonry and European politics. The focus instead is on the connections that linked freemasonry and the Huguenot diaspora to Britain's intelligence services and to British diplomacy.

It is also important to emphasise that the influence of Whig politicians and their supporters over English freemasonry was never absolute. Nor should it be considered as a moral positive. Whiggism was in the ascendancy in eighteenth-century Georgian England, and its institutions, the Grand Lodge of England included, responded to and mirrored that fact. Political allegiance was largely a function of self-interest and those seeking preferment and betterment flocked towards sources of patronage. The political and social reality was that the might of patronage was in the gift of those in power.

Espionage, Diplomacy & the Lodge examines the development of Britain's intelligence capabilities in the first half of the eighteenth century and provides biographical information on a number of pivotal figures. The book identifies the several bridges that link the Hanoverian establishment to freemasonry,[25] and seeks to show how the lodge and masonic connectivity were used to facilitate espionage and diplomacy. The evidence suggests that the bonds between successive Whig administrations and freemasonry were

---

[25] Cf., *Foundations.*

developed purposefully rather than by accident, and that this policy was shaped and facilitated by Delafaye, who exploited freemasonry's capacity to provide a cross-over into British and European polite society.

The first chapter begins with a short biography of Delafaye and examines the factors that moulded him and connected him to the English establishment. The second covers the last decade and a half of his work in Whitehall when he was at the peak of his powers and the effective head of the administration's anti-Jacobite spy network.

Chapters three and four explore two of the avenues through which the government obtained its intelligence: the Secret Department of the Post Office and the code breakers and cryptanalysts who comprised its Deciphering Branch. The chapters frame the history and operations of the Secret Department and lead the reader through the networks and associations of those involved.

It would be commonplace to suggest that the main figures in the Secret Department were chosen for their ability and loyalty but perhaps less obvious to comment that many were Huguenots and freemasons. Both factors spoke to their allegiance to the state and both offered channels for potential influence. The head of the Department, a position disingenuously described as the 'Foreign Secretary of the Post Office', was John Lefebure, a Huguenot member of the King's Head lodge in Pall Mall.[26] Lefebure had joined the Post Office in 1715 and been promoted to departmental head in 1718, shortly after Delafaye had returned to London from Dublin as under-secretary of state at the Northern Department. Lefebure would remain as Foreign Secretary and head of the Secret Department for three decades.

Although reporting formally to the postmaster general, the Secret Department in practice served the secretaries of state for the Northern and Southern Departments in whom responsibility for domestic and foreign policy resided. The two departments split the foreign brief between

---

[26] An Anglicisation of 'Jean Le Fèvre'. The English spelling 'Lefebure' is used throughout other than in direct quotations.

them but shared domestic affairs. Delafaye was a principal conduit between the secretaries of state and the Secret Department. He served as under-secretary at the Northern Department until 1724 and was thereafter under-secretary at the Southern Department until his retirement a decade later. A parallel channel was via John Wace, Delafaye's brother-in-law. Delafaye had obtained a position for Wace as a clerk at the Northern Department in 1711 and secured his promotion to chief clerk in 1717; Wace was later promoted to acting under-secretary of state.

Chapter five offers specific examples of how freemasonry was used as a part of the intelligence gathering process. It should be accepted and understood that part of what is offered as evidence can be regarded as no more than anecdotal, but this is in the nature of the subject matter. Sensitive communications in the eighteenth century were often verbal rather than written, and there is evidence, not least from Delafaye in his letters to Waldegrave, that where it was necessary to commit sensitive material to writing such letters were on occasion intentionally destroyed.[27] In addition, intelligence and counter-intelligence material is intrinsically problematic to pin down, and what might appear at first to be conclusive evidence may in reality imply the opposite. Finally, the difficulty in identi-fying specific individuals in the eighteenth century is well-known. Among the many complications are the use of different phonetic spellings with respect to the same name, the misspelling of names, and the use of assumed and code names.

Chapter five also points to the role of London's Huguenot lodges: Solomon's Temple in Hemming's Row; the King's Head in Pall Mall; the French Lodge at the Swan Tavern, Long Acre; and the lodge at Prince Eugene's Head Coffeehouse in St Albans Street. The last had relocated to the Duke of Lorraine's Head in Suffolk Street, a hundred yards to the east,

---

[27] SP 78/199/43, f. 93: Waldegrave to Delafaye. James Waldegrave (1684-1741), a member of the Horn Tavern and ambassador to Austria (1727/8-30) then France (1730-40), promises to burn Delafaye's letters as requested, 28 February 1731.

when the events described in chapter seven took place.[28] Lodge members feature in the narrative, with Delafaye one of several common links.[29] The argument is that the Huguenot network and certain elite masonic lodges provided Delafaye and thus the administration with a potentially valuable resource that could be deployed for diplomatic and intelligence gain. There is a direct parallel in the manner in which similar lodges in continental Europe were used for the same purpose by Jacobite supporters of James Stuart, something touched on briefly in the final chapters.

Although increasingly under the centralising rubric imposed by its new Grand Lodge, English freemasonry in the early and mid-eighteenth century comprised tens, then hundreds, of independent lodges. They were in essence private clubs and although not always secretive as to their activities and the names of those who were members or attendees, there are, understandably, few records of the conversations that took place in individual lodges. Nonetheless, it *is* the case that inferences can be drawn from the milieu in which certain lodges met and from the nature, status and inter-relationships of those in attendance.

Freemasonry came to be regarded as an especially attractive association, in Europe in particular, not only because it blended Enlightenment thinking with deemed mediaeval ritual but also *because* its inner workings were private. The lodge room was (perhaps misguidedly) considered a space for conversations that might otherwise be more constrained, with confidentiality deemed to be reinforced by masonic oaths and elite fraternalism.

The final two chapters focus on freemasonry in the context of European diplomacy and intelligence gathering. Chapter six examines how the Duke of Richmond's Horn Tavern in London and his lodges in Paris and Aubigny were used to advance British foreign policy objectives. It also discloses the

---

[28] Cf., John Lane's *Masonic Records*: https://www.hrionline.ac.uk/lane/index. php, accessed 8 October 2016.

[29] Appendix two provides the complete lists of members of the four lodges as submitted to the Grand Lodge of England.

names of several of Walpole's spies. Richmond's masonic activity was not simply a function of his pro-Hanoverian politics but also a reaction to the creation of pro-Jacobite masonic lodges in Paris, in particular the politicking of the exiled Lord Derwentwater.[30] The social and political influence of those attending France's pro- and anti-Jacobite lodges point to the opportunities available for diplomatic networking and intelligence gathering, and how political bias might be strengthened or modified via the fraternal camaraderie and gravitas of a masonic lodge.

Chapter seven assesses freemasonry's links to Anglo-Austrian diplomacy, a key aspect of British foreign policy in the second quarter of the eighteenth century and beyond. The initiation and raising of Francis Stephen, the Duke of Lorraine,[31] was designed expressly to court a potential diplomatic and military ally and cement a strategic relationship. Francis Stephen had been chosen by Charles VI, the Holy Roman Emperor, to be Maria Theresa, his daughter's future consort, and it was accepted across Europe that this would lead in due course to his election and coronation as Holy Roman Emperor. As London tilted away from a political accord with Paris towards an alliance with Vienna, Lorraine was an obvious target for a government-sanctioned masonic embrace, a soft diplomatic component of a far broader political engagement.

The initiation in London of Prince Anton Esterházy, the head of one of the Habsburg Empire's wealthiest families, and that of a colleague, a nobleman, a 'relative of the Elector of Maintz', occupies the final section of chapter seven. Their visit to the lodge at the Duke of Lorraine's Head in 1733 can be understood best when placed within the context of the impending War of the Polish Succession and the Habsburgs' search for military allies.

---

[30] Charles Radcliffe [sometimes written 'Radclyffe'] (1693-1746), titular 5th Earl of Derwentwater. A Jacobite, Radcliffe had fought in the 1715 Rising. He was condemned to death for treason but escaped from the Tower of London and fled to the continent.

[31] The initiation and raising took place in 1731 at The Hague and Houghton Hall, Norfolk, respectively.

With significant opposition within Parliament precluding overt backing for Austria, the unofficial visit and venue points to an attempt to use clandestine diplomacy to secure assistance from Walpole's government.

POLITICS AND RELIGION – IT'S ALL 'TO DO WITH THESE'

From 1721 when it first stepped onto the public stage, English freemasonry evolved rapidly. Multiple links were forged to Parliament, the judiciary, and polite society writ large, and membership of a leading masonic lodge and Grand Lodge was viewed as bringing cachet and an opportunity for select social interaction. But although popular verse may have testified to freemasonry's broad appeal,[32] diplomacy and espionage were reserved less for the middling lodges than those of the elites.

The lodge was not simply a forum for 'ancient' ritual, drinking and dining, networking, and well-publicised benevolence, although each of these played a role. It also represented the leading edge of eighteenth-century English society through its close association with prominent Newtonian scientists and commitment to education. As freemasonry gained a national then international reputation, the lodge was used overtly as a vehicle to promote a political and diplomatic agenda, and covertly to gather intelligence. In this context and in direct contrast to what is often posited, from the mid-1720s through to the 1740s it was not freemasonry that influenced the government but rather the opposite: that the administration, and perhaps most notably Delafaye, found it expedient to work with freemasons and freemasonry.

Perhaps the key to understanding English freemasonry in the first half of the eighteenth-century is to appreciate the backdrop against which it flourished. In simple terms, the organisation came to be pro-Hanoverian and

---

[32] *A Gentleman, Love's last shift: or, the mason disappointed* (London, c.1722): *We make for five guineas, the price is but small, and then Lords and Dukes, you your Brothers may call; have gloves, a white apron, get drunk and that's all.*

to promote Whig ideas as a function of its leaders' political and religious insecurities. There were two main drivers: first, the Jacobite *qua* Catholic threat to the Hanoverian succession; and second, the fall-out of more than a century of persecution by Catholic France of its Protestant Huguenot minority – a set of actions that had verged on genocide.

There were of course many other influences. And it has been argued that any fear of Protestant persecution was misplaced and that the Pretender would have favoured religious toleration and remained in accord with his father's Declaration of Indulgence.[33] But while this is a possibility, it is not unreasonable to believe that many contemporaries would have found it difficult to disregard the influence of France and Spain, James Stuart's main supporters, and given significant weight to the ongoing persecution of their non-Catholic subjects.[34] Both the Whig establishment and the émigré Huguenot community feared justifiably that the consequences of a Jacobite rebellion and Stuart restoration would be the demolition of their political and financial capital and penal sanction.

Politically there were legitimate reasons for anxiety. The constitutional foundations on which the Elector of Hanover, George Louis,[35] was crowned George I of Great Britain and Ireland in October 1714 were viewed by many as ambiguous and morally unsafe. And George I made what was a delicate

---

[33] The irony was that James II while on the throne had assisted Huguenot refugees in England and protested to Louis XIV against their maltreatment in France. But his and his son's later dependence on French and Spanish support made any resumption of such a policy less believable and those Huguenots who had settled in England saw the retention of the Protestant Hanoverian succession as a bulwark against further persecution.

[34] James's proclamations were issued with respect to Scotland on 12 February 1687 and England on 4 April 1687. In brief, the declarations suspended penalties for not attending the established Church of England and not receiving communion; they also permitted worship other than in the Established Church and ended the obligation to take a religious oath before obtaining civil or military office.

[35] George Louis (1660-1727), Elector of Hanover (Brunswick-Lüneburg); from 1714, king of Great Britain and Ireland.

situation materially worse by dismissing the Tories from government and national power the following year, alienating a large and powerful political segment.

Political and religious opposition to the House of Hanover was rooted in the Glorious Revolution that had swept Catholic James II[36] from the throne to be replaced a year later by two co-monarchs: the Protestant William III, Prince of Orange and Stadtholder of the Low Countries, and his wife, James II's daughter, Mary.[37]

Whether James II had abdicated or whether the monarchy had been abandoned, and its corollary, the basis on which William and Mary had been invited by Parliament to succeed, was disputed and the way forward was at best opaque. James and William's respective supporters debated the issues in the Convention Parliament that met in London in January 1689. Perhaps surprisingly the discussions were relatively balanced, especially in the Lords.

James II had tried to ensure the return of compliant MPs to the Commons from the mid-1680s and in 1689 many in Parliament remained supporters.[38] He had also moved to broaden his appeal and attempted to reach out to a constituency that included Whigs and Protestant dissenters.[39]

---

[36] James II (1633-1701), was king of England and Ireland as James II, and king of Scotland as James VII; he was the last Roman Catholic monarch.

[37] William III (1650-1702). He had succeeded his father as Prince of Orange. Mary Stuart (1631-1660), his mother, the Princess Royal, was the eldest daughter of Charles I. William's wife, also Mary (1662-1694), his first cousin, was James II's daughter.

[38] Robert Beddard, *A Kingdom without a King* (Oxford: Phaidon, 1988). Cf., also, J.H. Plumb, 'The Elections to the Convention Parliament of 1689', *Cambridge Historical Journal*, 5.3 (1937), 235-54.

[39] J.R. Jones, 'James II's Whig Collaborators', *Historical Journal*, 3.1 (1960), 65-73; and Scott Sowerby, 'Group Hunting: Religion, Politics, and Ideology in Later Stuart Britain', *Historical Journal*, 58.4 (2015), 1191–204; 'Forgetting the Repealers: Religious Toleration and Historical Amnesia in Later Stuart England', *Past and Present*, 215 (2012), 85–123; and 'Tories in the Whig Corner: Daniel Fleming's Journal of the 1685 Parliament', *Parliamentary History*, 24.2 (2005), 157–201.

There were however parts of the electorate that he found hard to attract, especially where stakeholders had become disaffected by his attempts to force new charters on towns and purge their corporations. And while James's effort to obtain the support of dissenters with an offer of religious toleration may have been genuine,[40] it was subsequently trumped by William and Mary who allied religious toleration to constitutional liberty.

The Convention Parliament's compromise settlement brought together a spectrum of divergent religious and political interests. New constitutional parameters were agreed, a declaration of ancient rights drawn up, and a list proclaimed of those rights deemed to have been violated by James II. William and Mary were invited to become king and queen of England on 13 February, and a parallel Convention of Estates gave them the crown in Scotland.[41] Their coronation took place in London at Westminster Abbey on 11 April and they recognised parliamentary sovereignty openly with an oath to uphold all its laws.

The Declaration of Rights was passed into law as the Bill of Rights and followed in 1701 by the Act of Settlement which restricted the succession to James I of England's (James VI of Scotland) Protestant heirs alone. Scotland declined to pass its own version of the Act, a decision that initiated five years of acrimonious negotiations. From England's standpoint, the key imperative to bring Scotland into line was to obviate the risk that the legal basis for a Protestant succession in England could be challenged by a competing Scottish monarch. The need to avoid what would be a potentially mutually

---

[40]   Sowerby, 'Of Different Complexions: Religious Diversity and National Identity in James II's Toleration Campaign', *English Historical Review*, 124.506 (2009), 29–52.

[41]   Although the Scottish Convention of Estates declared the throne vacant, it did not accept that James VII had abdicated but had forfaulted through misgovernment. William III was accepted as the *de facto* sovereign by right of conquest. Cf., Tim Harris, *Revolution: The Great Crisis of the British Monarchy 1685-1720* (London: Allen Lane, 2006).

destructive contest became the principal driver behind England's push for an Act of Union.[42]

Understandably, political union and the loss of parliamentary sovereignty was opposed by many north of the border. They found voice in the Scottish Act of Security, passed in 1704, in which Scotland set down its objections to the same royal succession as in England. London's response was a package of blackmail and bribery. The Alien Act of 1705 - 'An Act for the Effectual Securing the Kingdom of England from the apparent Dangers that may arise from several Acts lately passed in the parliament of Scotland' - stated that Scotland must either accept the Hanoverian succession or negotiate to unite the English and Scottish parliaments. If Scotland failed to do so its main exports to England - cattle, linen and coal - would be banned, and Scots would forfeit their privileges under English law:

> That from and after the 25 day of December 1705, no Person or Persons being a Native or Natives of the Kingdom of Scotland... shall be capable to inherit any Lands... within this Kingdom of England ... or to enjoy any Benefit or Advantage of a natural-born Subject of England: But every such Person shall be from henceforth adjudged and taken as an Alien born out of the allegiance of the Queen of England, until such time as the Succession to the Crown of Scotland, be declared and settled by an Act of Parliament in Scotland.[43]

At the same time the elites who dominated Scotland's parliament were courted with cash and honours. Some £400,000 was distributed, nominally to compensate for the future liabilities that would be assumed in relation to

---

[42] The Union was enacted by two parliamentary Acts: one passed by the English Parliament and a second by the Scottish Parliament.

[43] The Alien Act, 1705. National Records of Scotland, Hamilton Papers, GD406/M1/247/1. Cf., also, Brendan Bradshaw & Peter Roberts (eds), *British Consciousness and Identity. The Making of Britain, 1533–1707* (Cambridge: CUP, 2003), eps. pp. 322-4.

the English national debt but in practice directed at those who had invested in the Company of Scotland's failed Darien Land Scheme.[44] This had cost its mainly Scottish shareholders around £500,000, a vast sum that had almost bankrupted the country.[45] Other funds were scattered alongside, including £20,000 personally by David Boyle, newly created Earl of Glasgow,[46] one of the commissioners for the Union. James Douglas, Duke of Queensberry,[47] received half - some £10,000 - and adopted pro-Union political views accordingly. Following passage of the Acts of Union he was created Duke of Dover, Marquess of Beverley and Earl of Ripon, and sworn to the Privy Council. He was not alone. Robert Burns's comment that 'we're bought and sold for English gold' had resonance, and the blatant corruption that accompanied that passage of the legislation by the Scottish parliament was heavily resented. It found expression in support for the Stuarts and the Jacobite cause.

THE JACOBITE THREAT

The Pretender, James Stuart, was the son of the exiled James II and his second wife, Mary of Modena.[48] He was without question Queen Anne's closest relative, her half-brother,[49] but as a Catholic he was excluded from the succession. Prince George of Hanover's claim on the crown was more

---

[44] The Darien Scheme was a plan to establish a trading settlement and colony - 'Caledonia' - on the isthmus of present-day Panama.

[45] The financial loss would be in the order of £1 billion in current money.

[46] Earl of Glasgow (*c.*1666-1733).

[47] Douglas, 2nd Duke of Queensberry (1662-1711), Keeper of the Privy Seal of Scotland (1705-1709), Lord High Commissioner (1707) and secretary of state for Scotland (1709-1711).

[48] James Francis Edward Stuart (1688-1766).

[49] Anne and Mary, her older sisters, were the product of James II's first marriage to Anne Hyde (1638-1671).

convoluted but equally legitimate. A great-grandson of James I and as such James Stuart's second cousin, George's father was Ernst Augustus, Prince Elector of Hanover (1629-1698), and his mother, Sophia of Hanover, the daughter of Elizabeth Stuart, the second child and eldest daughter of James I.[50] It is a Stuart myth that there were between thirty and fifty Catholic contenders who had more direct links to Queen Anne than Prince George. There were six, and all were foreign. But the Jacobite fable of un-entitlement was assisted by George having been born in Hanover with German as his first language and limited spoken English.[51]

George I's supporters may have argued accurately that his succession was justified by law and hereditary right but the political reality was that he was crowned as a function of parliamentary edict - the Act of Settlement.[52] And this was not without opposition both in Westminster and nationally. The riots that marked the coronation in October 1714 were instigated and supported not only by James Stuart's Jacobite followers but by Tories and High Church Anglicans, Henry Sacheverell among them.[53] The revelries of Hanoverian loyalists were disrupted by protests in more than twenty towns and cities across England from Canterbury to Shrewsbury and Taunton to

---

[50]   Sophia of Hanover (1630-1714). Elizabeth Stuart (1596-1662), had married Frederick V of Bohemia, Elector of Palatine (1506-1632).

[51]   Cf., William Gibson, *How Closely Related Were George I and Queen Anne?*, comment added 29 July 2014 at https://thehistoryofparliament.wordpress.com/2014/07/29/how-closely-related-were-george-i-and-queen-anne/, accessed 2 September 2016.

[52]   The Sophia Naturalisation Act of 1705 confirmed that Sophia of Hanover was a naturalised British citizen. The Act also granted that right to her direct heirs and styled such heirs 'prince' or 'princess'.

[53]   Henry Sacheverell (1674-1724), an English High Church Anglican clergyman, achieved prominence in 1709 with sermons promoting a union between church and state and an attack on 'false brethren'. He was impeached, found guilty, but received only a light punishment – a three-year suspension. He was a popular figurehead in the country and characterised the coronation of George I as 'an unparalleled insolence and a vile trampling upon royal ashes'.

Norwich.[54] It is significant that local Tory magistrates were acquiescent and failed to disperse the 'tumults and riot ... universally fomented'.[55] Their inaction was noted, and the disturbances led within days to a declaration suppressing 'Riot, Assembly or Rout of People against the Law'[56] and the passage in Parliament of a Riot Act.[57]

Protests in London were initially restrained. Many leading Tories had given up on a Stuart restoration and self-interestedly recognised George I. Even the Tory Lords Oxford and Bolingbroke were in attendance when the new king's reign was proclaimed formally, with Oxford organising a public bonfire to celebrate the event. But the concord would be brief. Later the same month defiant protesters obstructed the king's return from the Lord Mayor's banquet and rioting broke out at Whitechapel on the eastern fringe of the City.[58]

Periodic public disturbances continued into 1715 and grew in scope after the parliamentary elections in March in which the Whigs obtained a crushing majority in the Commons.[59] A purge of virtually all Tories in central government followed and was replicated on a lesser scale at county and city level. The political exodus triggered further anti-Hanoverian riots and

---

[54] Paul Kleber Monod, *Jacobitism and the English People. 1688-1788* (Cambridge: CUP, 1989), esp., 174-9.

[55] *An Address of Thanks to the King* in *History and Proceedings of the House of Commons* (London: Chandler, 1742), volume 6, 1714-27 (London, 1742), 9 January 1715, pp. 47-68.

[56] *British Mercury*, 27 October - 3 November 1714; *Post Boy*, 30 October - 2 November 1714 et al; *London Gazette*, 2 - 14 November 1714.

[57] The Riot Act - 'An Act for preventing tumults and riotous assemblies, and for the more speedy and effectual punishing the rioters' - was approved by Parliament in 1714 and came into force on 1 August 1715: (1 Geo.1 St.2 c.5).

[58] Abel Boyer (ed), *The Political State of Great Britain* (London: J. Baker, 1711-40), volume 8, p. 439; cf., also, BL Add. MSS 22202, ff. 200-12.

[59] The parliamentary elections were held between 22 January and 9 March 1715; the dates on which voting took place were determined by the returning officer in each constituency.

demonstrations that swept across England from Bristol and Gloucester to Oxford, Manchester and Leeds.

For George I and his government worse was to come. Taking advantage of the popular discontent and building on an existing support base, the Earl of Mar raised James Stuart's royal standard at Braemar in September to foment a rebellion in Scotland.[60] He met with initial success and a swathe of Scotland went over to the Pretender within the month, as did parts of Durham, Northumberland and Cumberland. At the same time, Mar's revolt was emulated on a lesser scale with riots in the Tory-dominated West of England.

London reacted promptly. Troops were despatched to Bristol, Plymouth and Southampton to curtail any insurgency, and intelligence resources exploited to arrest the ringleaders in the West and Wales. Acts of Attainder were passed against the principal leaders of the opposition, including Bolingbroke.[61] Habeas corpus was suspended. And detachments of the army were hurried north to reinforce the military garrisons in Scotland and protect the North of England and the Midlands.

Hanoverian and Jacobite forces engaged in battles at Sherrifmuir and Inverness, but they were indecisive. They also clashed at Preston in Lancashire which had fallen to the Jacobites. Loyalist troops surrounded the town and prevailed when the arrival of reinforcements forced the Jacobites to agree an unconditional surrender.

In December 1715 James Stuart finally landed in Perth to stake his claim personally. He was too late. The Jacobite army stood at less than 5,000 men when Mar led them the following month. He was defeated and the rebel army fell back to Perth, then retreated, demoralised, north-east to

---

[60] John Erskine, Earl of Mar, KT (1675-1732). He had been secretary of state for Scotland but was deprived of the office by George I.

[61] Cf., for example, *Post Man and the Historical Account*, 20 - 23 August 1715. Henry St John, 1st Viscount Bolingbroke (1678-1751), secretary of state under Queen Anne. He fled to France where he served the Pretender but later recanted and was permitted to return in 1723.

Dundee and Montrose. In early February James Stuart abandoned his supporters and sailed from Scotland to return to exile. He was joined by Mar, Drummond[62] and other leading figureheads. Deserted by its leadership, the Jacobite uprising collapsed and its army scattered.

Although the uprising had been unsuccessful, the Indemnity Act passed by Parliament in 1717 recognised a need for reconciliation.[63] Many of those captured were pardoned or reprieved, including Lords Carnwath,[64] Nairne[65] and Widdrington.[66] And large numbers of prisoners held at Newgate, Carlisle, Edinburgh and Stirling, were freed, as were around 200 rebels captured at Preston. But this was not the only story. The Jacobite leaders in the Borders and Northumberland, Lords Derwentwater[67] and Kenmure,[68] were found guilty of treason and sentenced to death, and at least fifty more suffered the same fate.[69] Several hundred other rebels were exiled to the American colonies.

Despite defeat the Jacobite threat endured. Although described variously as real, imagined, and a contrivance wheeled out by Whig politicians to maintain political power, the reality was a mix of all three. The hazard may have waxed and waned but protecting Britain and Ireland against

---

[62] James Drummond, 1st Duke of Perth (1648-1716), 4th Earl of Perth and 7th Lord Drummond.

[63] 'The Act of Grace and Free Pardon': 4 Geo. I. The Act was not absolute; many attainders were not cancelled and certain higher value estates were not restored. The general pardon granted by the Act also excluded *inter alia* Robert Harley, 1st Earl of Oxford, and Lord Harcourt, as well as the Clan MacGregor.

[64] Robert Dalzell, 5th Earl of Carnwath, (1687-1737).

[65] William Murray, 2nd Lord Nairne (*c*.1665-1726).

[66] William Widdrington, 4th Baron Widdrington (1678-1743).

[67] James Radclyffe, 3rd Earl of Derwentwater (1689-1716).

[68] William Gordon, 6th Viscount of Kenmure and Lord Lochinvar (*c*.1672-1716).

[69] Cf., for example, Daniel Szechi, *1715: The Great Jacobite Rebellion* (New Haven, CN: YUP, 2006).

another Jacobite Rising coupled to a French or Spanish-backed invasion remained a core tenet of government policy until the 1750s.

The danger posed by the Pretender - the 'king over the water' - was not exclusively military; there was also a philosophical and religious element. James Stuart's claim to the throne was considered valid by a large minority, and not only Jacobites.

Two rival constitutional arguments competed for dominance. The ascendant view held that England was governed by a constitution rooted in established custom that could be traced back to Anglo Saxon times. From this perspective constitutional governance was the product of a notional balance between the legislature - the king, the Lords and the Commons - and the subjects of the realm, who enjoyed an implicit right to resist autocracy and tyranny. The structure had checks and balances to prevent royal absolutism and examples of popular resistance seeded a narrative that stretched from before Magna Carta to encompass the Glorious Revolution.

John Locke extended the thesis. His *Two Treatises of Government*[70] argued that an absolute monarchy by definition made slaves of its subjects and that a legitimate government was established by consent and served to secure the rights to life, liberty and property. In Locke's analysis, a government exercised power legitimately only if it did not encroach on the natural rights of the governed. Where such rights had been breached 'the people' had the moral authority to resist and the legal right to dismiss the government and establish a successor:

> The great end of men's entering into society being the enjoyment of their properties in peace and safety and the great instrument and means of that being the laws established in that society, the first and fundamental positive law of all commonwealths is the establishing of the legislative power...[71]

---

[70] John Locke, *Two Treatises of Government* (London, 1689).

[71] Ibid., chapter 11, section 134.

To this end it is that men give up all their natural power to the society they enter into and the community put the legislative power into
such hands as they think fit with this trust that they shall be governed by
declared laws or else their peace, quiet, and property will still be at the
same uncertainty as it was in the state of Nature...[72]

The legislative cannot transfer the power of making laws to any other
hands, for it being but a delegated power from the people, they who have
it cannot pass it over to others. The people alone can appoint the form of
the commonwealth which is by constituting the legislative and appointing in whose hands that shall be. And when the people have said 'We will
submit and be governed by laws made by such men and in such forms',
nobody else can say other men shall make laws for them, nor can they be
bound by any laws but such as are enacted by those whom they have chosen and authorised to make laws for them.[73]

Locke's definition of the nature of government was radical and inevitably had
only narrow support in its unvarnished form.[74] It was disavowed by those
in power who were disinclined to support any theory that could encourage
a challenge to their authority. And in the late 1680s it was of course never
intended or asserted that the consent of the public at large was required to
approve the transfer of the crown to William and Mary, nor that ultimate
sovereignty rested with the general population. Both were alien concepts in
a society where the franchise was restricted and based on narrowly defined
property rights. This - in effect the mainstream Whig historical perspective
on constitutional history - was encapsulated by Edmund Burke towards the
end of the eighteenth century when he noted that the Glorious Revolution

---

[72] Ibid., section 136.

[73] Ibid., section 141.

[74] Locke's approach was nonetheless central to the drafting of America's
Declaration of independence.

was to be celebrated precisely *because* it had limited political change to the minimum needed to reinstate the 'ancient constitution'.[75]

A contrarian argument was advanced by James Stuart's supporters. Notwithstanding their obvious political self-interest, the Jacobite starting point was that there was only one legitimate basis for a constitution: the divine right of kings. From this standpoint the authority to govern was derived solely from God and a king ruled his nation by virtue of God's direct command. Hereditary succession was the only means by which a king could and should be replaced and it had thus been unlawful for the Convention Parliament to have interfered with what was an inalienable right of succession. The unavoidable result of such an analysis was that George I's coronation was neither legally binding nor morally valid.

Such thinking had been a central plank of conventional Catholic teaching for centuries. It was expressed by Dante in *Inferno* where the Ninth Circle of Hell was reserved for those who had committed regicide, the ultimate sin of treachery against God being the slaughter of one he had anointed.[76] It was for precisely this reason that Brutus and Cassius were condemned to the Ninth Circle alongside Judas Iscariot.[77]

Support for the Pretender's entitlement to the crown was not restricted to Catholics. The doctrine of hereditary succession was favoured by non-jurors whose influence belied their relatively modest numbers. Sections of the Protestant clergy whose support for James Stuart flowed from the oath of loyalty they had originally sworn to the crown also

---

[75] H.T. Dickinson, 'The British Constitution' in Dickinson (ed.), *A Companion to Eighteenth-Century Britain* (Oxford: Blackwell, 2002), pp. 3-18.

[76] Dante Alighieri (*c.*1265-1321), 'il Sommo Poeta' — Catholicism's Supreme Poet.

[77] Dante, *Inferno* [*The Vision of Hell*], Canto XXXIV: '*That upper spirit, Who hath worse punishment,' so spake my guide, 'Is Judas, he that hath his head within And plies the feet without. Of th' other two, Whose heads are under, from the murky jaw Who hangs, is Brutus: lo! how he doth writhe And speaks not! Th' other Cassius*'. Excerpt from Henry Cary (trans.), (London: Cassell, 1892).

opposed George I.[78] The issue led to a schism within English and Irish Anglicanism, while in Scotland many Episcopalians refused to swear allegiance to George I or accept that William and Mary had ruled other than as co-regents.[79] And James Stuart had other devotees, especially among those who stood to benefit from his return. This silo of support was not limited to Tory landowners forced from power by George I and his Whig administration. France, Spain and Sweden also favoured the Stuart cause.

Consecutive Whig governments believed that a French or Spanish invasion in tandem with domestic Jacobite insurgence posed the most serious threat to Hanoverian Britain. If successful, the combination would sever the Hanoverian line, dismember the administration, and dial the political clock back to the early 1680s. Whig concerns were broadly justified and continental European support for the Jacobites was real, not imagined. Faced with such a risk, governments from Stanhope to Walpole maintained a firm anti-Jacobite strategy, following the axiom that 'ministerial idleness where Jacobites were concerned was an unaffordable luxury'.[80]

A key component of this policy was the extension of Britain's matrix of formal and informal spy networks, which included the interception of diplomatic and private mail. Intelligence was sought by all sides but the required apparatus was arguably most advanced in England. The seizure of suspect correspondence centred on the Secret Department of the Post Office, with decoding taking place within its Deciphering Branch.

---

[78] Nonjuring, from the Latin 'non juro' - not swearing an oath to William III. William Gibson has commented that although the non-jurors were highly vocal they numbered less than 500 out of some 13,000 clergy.

[79] Although some of those who fell within this category could be categorised correctly as Jacobites, relatively few intrigued actively in support of the Pretender.

[80] Paul S. Fritz, 'The Anti-Jacobite Intelligence System of the English Ministers, 1715-1745', *Historical Journal*, 16.2 (1973), 265-89; quote from 265.

Although under the nominal authority of the postmaster general, the Secret Department was financed by secret service funds and reported to the secretaries of state.[81] From 1717 until the 1730s, the government's anti-Jacobite intelligence operations fell largely within the remit of Charles Delafaye, one of several Huguenot émigrés given senior positions within the administration. They were trusted, not least for sharing a pro-Hanoverian perspective that was the consequence of 150 years of oppression by France of its Protestant minority.

PROTESTANT PERSECUTION AND EXODUS

The Protestant Reformation began in Germany in the second decade of the sixteenth century and spread rapidly. Its first French martyr, Jean Vallière, was executed in 1523 and state persecution was stepped-up as Protestantism became synonymous with opposition to the established order. 'L'affaire des placards' in October 1534, a Protestant protest in Paris against the perceived abuses of Roman Catholicism, was accompanied by demonstrations in Blois, Rouen, Tours, Orléans and other cities. The authorities responded immediately with the arrest and execution of twenty-four deemed heretics while others were driven into exile. The latter included John Calvin who fled to Basel and then Geneva, before moving to join Martin Bucer's community of French Protestants in Strasbourg in 1538.

Calvin's teaching and his *Institutes of the Christian Religion*[82] encouraged a few French émigrés to return home and a small Calvinist community was established at Meauz in the mid-1540s. A church was founded in Paris a decade

---

[81]   With respect to foreign affairs, the Southern Department was responsible for Ireland, the American colonies and Britain's relations with the Roman Catholic states of Europe; the Northern Department was responsible principally for relations with Europe's Protestant states.

[82]   John Calvin, *Christianae Religionis Institutio* (Basel, 1536). The volume was published in French as *Institution de la Religion Chrétienne* (Basel, 1541); a Latin edition was published in Geneva in 1559.

later and notwithstanding harassment by the Catholic Church, Calvinism expanded. In 1559, fifteen churches attended a synod in Paris to establish a French Reformed Church and within two years the number of affiliated churches approached two thousand. Rapid growth brought the movement into direct conflict with the French Catholic aristocracy and the Catholic Church hierarchy in France, whose power it threatened. And the reaction was violent. The Duke of Guise[83] sanctioned an attack on Calvinist - Huguenot - congregants at Vassy in March 1562, killing over sixty and wounding another hundred. The violence foreshadowed what would be a century of religious discrimination and conflict, a fight encapsulated by the Saint Bartholomew's Day Massacre a decade later in August 1572.[84]

The wedding of Margaret de Valois, the sister of Charles IX, the king of France, to Henry de Navarre,[85] a Huguenot, was the catalyst for an attempt to assassinate the Protestants' political leaders, not least Gaspard de Coligny, a charismatic aristocrat and decorated admiral.[86] The plot failed but Charles IX was nonetheless persuaded to permit Coligny's execution and that of other Huguenots following false allegations that they were plotting against him. The move sparked mob violence against the Huguenot community which spread from Paris to cities and towns across France. The word 'massacre' is appropriate; estimates of the number of French Protestants killed over the months that followed vary, but the range spans the low tens of thousands to as many as one hundred thousand.

The Catholic hierarchy regarded the carnage as having secured deliverance from heresy and France from a conspiracy to overturn the state.

---

[83]   François de Lorraine II (1519-1563), Prince de Joinville, Duc de Guise, Duc de Aumale.

[84]   Cf., James R. Smither, 'The St Bartholomew's Day Massacre and Images of Kingship in France: 1572-1574', *Sixteenth Century Journal*, 22.1 (1991), 27-46, for an overview.

[85]   Henry de Navarre (1553-1610), escaped the St Bartholomew's Day massacre. He ruled as King of Navarre from 1572-1610 and from 1589-1610 as King of France.

[86]   Gaspard II de Coligny (1519-1572), Seigneur de Châtillon.

Pope Gregory XIII sent a congratulatory symbolic golden rose to Charles IX and instructed that a *Te Deum* be sung and a celebratory medal struck. The coin depicts an angel holding a cross and sword standing to the left of a half circle of Huguenot corpses surmounted with the legend *Ugonottorum Strages - Massacre of the Huguenots.* The reverse carries an image of the Pope. Protestant countries in Europe were aghast and contemporary reports of the massacre by Walsingham, at the time Elizabeth I's ambassador to France, did much to reinforce a pro-Huguenot agenda in England.

France's Huguenot survivors' attempts to resist further repression were unsuccessful despite the later coronation of Henry de Navarre as Henry IV and his issuing the Edict of Nantes and two favourable royal brevets that offered modest protections. Henry had been obliged to convert to Catholicism. Some 85% of the French population was Catholic and he needed the support of the Catholic Church to govern.

Henry IV was assassinated in 1610 and the persecution of the Huguenots resumed under his son and successor, Louis XIII.[87] Their oppression was expressed not least in the siege of La Rochelle in 1628, during which the city's population plummeted from around 27,000 to 5,000 as a consequence of starvation and disease, leading to its unconditional surrender. Although the Huguenots were no longer a political threat, the Catholic Church maintained an anti-Protestant stance and harassment continued. Some three-quarters of France's 800 Protestant churches were razed in the three decades to 1685, and thousands of Huguenots forcibly converted to Catholicism. Those who refused faced 'insupportable violence', the destruction or confiscation of their estates, and imprisonment or death.[88]

---

[87] Louis XIII (1601-1643), king of France (1610-1643). Navarre was merged with the French crown in 1620.

[88] Robert Burton, *Martyrs in Flames: or the history of Popery Displaying the horrid persecutions and cruelties exercised upon Protestants by the Papists, for many hundred years past* (London, 1729), 3rd edn., pp. 75–6.

Under Louis XIV, Huguenot mistreatment became even more en-trenched.[89] It reached an apogee in the 1680s with the introduction of the *Dragonnades*, the billeting of French dragoons on Huguenot households. The policy was synonymous with violence, rape and theft. Compounding the Huguenots' troubles, Louis XIV rescinded the Edict of Nantes in 1685. The limited protections that had applied under its aegis were removed, ef-fectively depriving French Protestants of any remaining civil and religious liberties.

Huguenot migration from France accelerated in response. What had been a trickle of refugees from the mid-sixteenth century became a torrent. Despite the penal risks, almost a third of France's Huguenot population escaped, an estimated 250,000 people, with more leaving in later years.[90] Many migrated to the United Provinces. Others settled in the German states and Switzerland. A small number migrated to North America and Southern Africa.[91] But the most popular destination was England, with be-tween 50,000 and 80,000 refugees, the majority settling in London. There they joined an existing community which was itself the product of Huguenot flight over the preceding century.[92]

The influx had a substantial impact with the incoming refugees repre-senting around 10% of London's 500,000 population. The establishment was sympathetic however and sought to ensure that their co-religionists

---

[89] Louis XIV (1638-1715), 'the Sun King'.

[90] The French population at the time was *c.*18 million; England's population was *c.*5 million.

[91] Robin Gwynn, *Huguenot Heritage* (Brighton: Sussex Academic, 2001), 2nd revised edn., pp. 29-30.

[92] Huguenot persecution continued in France notwithstanding Louis XV's announcement in 1715 that the Protestant religion in France had ended. Despite an intensification of maltreatment in the mid-eighteenth century, public opinion began to turn and despite a rear guard action by the Catholic Church, an edict in 1787 began the process of restoring the Huguenots' civil rights. France's National Assembly affirmed liberty of religion in 1789.

received tangible support.[93] Multiple contributions were made from the Civil List, with William and Mary donating almost £40,000 between 1689 and 1693, and by the aristocracy and via parliamentary vote; charity was also provided through parish collections.[94] In total, around £100,000 was raised in the years following the Revocation, with additional monies contributed subsequently, much from the Royal Bounty Fund.

The Huguenot community in London had conformist and non-conformist branches but both shared an allegiance to their new home and the English crown. This was especially evident in the military where hundreds of Huguenot officers joined William III's army. They included Henri de Massue.[95] His success at the Battle of Aughrim in 1691 led to his promotion to commander-in-chief in Ireland and he was subsequently elevated to the Irish peerage as Viscount Galway. In 1694, as a lieutenant general, he commanded an English force alongside the Duke of Savoy against France. He was created Earl of Galway in 1697.

Five Huguenot regiments were established by William III, with three Huguenot battalions of Foot raised in 1689. Other 'trained, professional officers'[96] became supernumeraries, attached to regiments of Horse or Foot and serving on half pay until vacancies became available. They provided a reservoir of potential officers, 'proven and trustworthy'.[97] It has been estimated that up to a fifth of England's army officers were French or Low Country Huguenots, around 1,000 in total. But the actual number may

---

[93] J.M. Hintermaier, 'The First Modern refugees? Charity, Entitlement and Persuasion in the Huguenot Immigration of the 1680s', *Albion*, 32.3 (2000), 429-49. Cf., also, Jean Francois Bion, *An account of the torments the French Protestants endure aboard the galleys* (London, 1708).

[94] Gwynn, *Huguenot Heritage*, pp. 71-3.

[95] Henri de Massue (1648-1720), 2nd Marquis de Ruvigny, later Earl of Galway.

[96] John Childs, *The British Army of William III, 1689-1702* (Manchester: MUP, 1987), pp. 132-7.

[97] Ibid., p. 134.

have been higher given that around 3,000 officers left Louis XIV's service after the Revocation.

Although the 1713 Treaty of Utrecht brought three decades of peace between Britain and France, French persecution of the Huguenots continued and recognition of the Protestant faith was denied. Two years later, England's Huguenot émigrés faced danger once again: 'l'invasion d'un prétendant papist' - the 1715 Jacobite Rising. The prospect of a Catholic monarch on the British throne was regarded as an existential threat. It would remain so for more than three decades as the 1715 Rising was followed by attempted invasions of Britain in 1717 and 1719, and by the Atterbury Plot. Other alarms would follow, not least the 1745 Jacobite Rising.

Entrenched religious and political insecurities were at the root of the widespread belief among Whigs and Huguenots that the institutions that shielded them and maintained the Hanoverian *status quo* required, if not demanded their support.

The same pattern was etched onto freemasonry, with the Grand Lodge of England configured to promote and defend the philosophical legacy of the Glorious Revolution and advance a Whig agenda. It is this which provides the backdrop to *Espionage, Diplomacy & the Lodge* and explains the interconnections between Delafaye, freemasonry, and the Secret Department of the Post Office.

CHAPTER ONE

A HUGUENOT AT THE HEART OF GOVERNMENT

It is conceivable that clerks of Huguenot origin were depended
upon to make use of their close ties with France to acquire
intelligence for the English government. The two countries were,
after all, almost continually at war from 1689 to 1713.[1]

In the early 1720s, Charles Delafaye, under-secretary to the Duke of
Newcastle, secretary to the Lords Justices, and a senior magistrate on the
Middlesex and Westminster benches, stood at the pinnacle of the civil administration. Less well-known was his responsibility for managing the press
and his role as the administration's leading spymaster, privy to its secrets and
a locus for its anti-Jacobite spy networks.[2]

Delafaye's entry in the *Oxford Dictionary of National Biography* is brief and
although his seniority and efficiency is noted, the fidelity and discretion that
kept him at the heart of policy-making and at the core of the intelligence
network for more than two decades is absent.[3] His power as a political gate-
keeper, especially to Newcastle, is similarly understated, notwithstanding
that his influence was known to many of his contemporaries. But perhaps
the most telling omission is that Delafaye was not simply a neutral government official. By 1717 he had become an integral part of the policy making
matrix with a web of personal alliances within Whitehall and overseas. His
associates included Martin Bladen at the Board of Trade and Plantations,

---

[1]   J.C. Sainty, 'A Huguenot civil servant: the career of Charles Delafaye,
1677-1762', *Proceedings of the Huguenot Society*, 22 (1975), 398-413, quote 398.

[2]   NA SP 34, 36 and 42.

[3]   J.C. Sainty, 'Delafaye, Charles (1677-1762)', *ODNB*, online edn, Jan 2008,
accessed 23 January 2015. Cf. also, Sainty, 'A Huguenot civil servant', and Sainty,
'The Secretariat of the Chief Governors of Ireland, 1690-1800', *Proceedings of the
Royal Irish Academy*, 77.C (1977), 21.

with whom he had built a professional and personal relationship while in Ireland,[4] and officials in Europe, colonial America and the Caribbean. Delafaye's correspondence reveals a man whose influence was pervasive, and whose position at the centre of government was a function of astuteness, loyalty and competence.[5]

Charles Delafaye was born in Paris on 25 July 1677, the elder son of Louis (later anglicized to Lewis) and Marie (Mary).[6] The family migrated to England in the late 1670s[7] and in 1679 Louis Delafaye obtained the position of 'writer', essentially editor and translator, of the *French Gazette*, the French language version of the *London Gazette*,[8] the government's mouthpiece. The role was sensitive and the former incumbent, a Monsieur Moranville, had been dismissed for failing to include an article on Titus Oates's revelations of a Catholic conspiracy to assassinate Charles II.

Oates had trumpeted his allegations of a Jesuitical Popish Plot, causing political havoc. The product was multiple trials for treason and more than a dozen executions. Oates's assertions hardened anti-Catholic sentiment

---

[4] Martin Bladen (*c*.1680-1746), MP (Ireland) 1715-27; PC (Ireland) 1715. MP for Stockbridge, 1715-34; Maldon, 1734-41; Portsmouth, 1741-death. He is discussed below.

[5] 'If the author of *The Beggars' Opera* made Sir Robert Walpole and Lord Townshend the originals of his characters Lockit and Peachum, he must certainly have found his Filch in Mr Delafaye'. Folkestone Williams, *Memoirs and Correspondence of Francis Atterbury* (London: W.H. Allen, 1869), p. 460.

[6] The name was also written as 'de la Faye', 'de la Fay', 'de la Foy' and 'de la Haye'. It was possibly under the last version that he was recorded as a member of the Lodge at the Prince Eugene's Head Coffee House. For an alternative view cf., W.J. Songhurst, *QCA*, volume X, pp. 192-3.

[7] However, see David C.A. Agnew, *Protestant Exiles from France* (London: Reeves & Turner, 1874), p. 39.

[8] *Office-Holders in Modern Britain: Officials of the Secretaries of State 1660-1782.*

across England and were used to justify a clampdown on Catholics, including their expulsion from London; they also served as a precursor to the Exclusion Crisis.[9] That Oates's claims were false - he was arrested in August 1681 and convicted of perjury - was not known at the time, and Moranville's omission led to a political witch-hunt and suspicion as to his integrity. He was summoned to the Commons to be questioned and defended himself with the argument that the slip had been unintended and simply an unfortunate oversight.[10] Moranville was nonetheless thought a liar and compounded his problems by asserting that he was 'born a *Roman* Catholic and … am so still',[11] a statement taken as an affront to the House and additional proof that he was untrustworthy. Moranville was committed to the custody of the Sergeant-at-Arms and his lodgings searched. The discovery of sundry documents 'written in French' provided further justification for his dismissal.[12]

Louis Delafaye took over as editor a few months later.[13] His Huguenot background would have been an inevitable consideration in his recruitment. In the febrile political conditions of the last quarter of the seventeenth century, a Huguenot émigré would have been a safe choice, not only educated

---

[9]   The late 1670s were marked by substantial political division in England that laid the foundations for what became the Tory and Whig parties in Parliament. Charles II and the Tories supported the accession of the Duke of York, Charles II's brother as James II. The Whigs were opposed to the Catholic duke taking the throne and sought his exclusion from the succession. The conflict gave rise to the Glorious Revolution of 1688 and the expulsion of James II in favour of William & Mary.

[10]   *Journal of the House of Commons, volume 9, 1667-1687* (London: HMSO, 1802), pp. 533-5, 6 November and 7 November 1678.

[11]   Ibid.

[12]   *Grey's Debates of the House of Commons, volume 6* (London: T. Becket and P.A. De Hondt, 1769), pp. 148-72.

[13]   For additional background material, cf., John Childs, 'The Sales of Government Gazettes during the Exclusion Crisis, 1678-81', *English Historical Review*, 102.402 (1987), 103-6.

and linguistically proficient, but politically reliable and committed to the Protestant faith.

The *London Gazette* and *French Gazette* were published for domestic and foreign audiences respectively and produced jointly by the secretaries of state for the Southern and Northern Departments, at the time, Robert Spencer, 2nd Earl of Sunderland, and Sir Leoline Jenkins. The average sale of the *London Gazette* was around 5,000 copies per issue, although it occasionally exceeded 7,000. The paid circulation figures for the French-language *French Gazette* were trivial in comparison, running only to around 300. But the number sold was unrelated to its impact. The *French Gazette* had a vast print run and was distributed virtually free-of-charge at home and overseas for diplomatic and propaganda purposes, with distribution funded by its profitable sister paper.[14]

Louis Delafaye remained writer of the *French Gazette* until his retirement in 1710, some three decades later.[15] An indication of the value placed on his work is that the family was granted denization - the right of permanent residence - in 1684 and were naturalised the following year.[16]

Charles Delafaye's primary education is undocumented but he matriculated at All Souls College Oxford in 1692 at the age of 14.[17] His admission was probably a function of his father's Whitehall connections.[18] All

---

[14] Ibid., 104.

[15] *Office-Holders in Modern Britain: vol. 2, Officials of the Secretaries of State 1660-1782.*

[16] William A. Shaw, *Letters of Denization and Acts of Naturalization for Aliens in England and Ireland, 1603-1800* (Huguenot Society of London, 1911), vol. 18, pp. 165 & 171. Charles's brother, Lewis Delafaye, named for their father, joined the army and served and then settled in Ireland. He predeceased Charles.

[17] The date of matriculation is the date of entry to the relevant college.

[18] Robert Yard, the senior under-secretary at the Northern Department, matriculated at Wadham College on 18 May 1672, aged 16. James Vernon, the departmental secretary of state, matriculated at Christ Church in 1662, also aged 16. Cf., Joseph Foster (ed.), *Alumni Oxonienses, 1500-1714* (Oxford: Parker & Co., 1891). The Warden of All Souls from 1686 was Leopold William Finch (*c.*1663-1702), a graduate of Christ Church.

Souls has never admitted undergraduates and Charles was one of a small number of members (not Fellows) who were bible clerks, in essence servitor scholars, often the sons of former bible clerks, who were appointed by the Warden rather than elected by the Fellows.[19] The number was usually limited to four and the expense of board, lodging and education was funded by the College in return for which the bible clerks read lessons during Hall and in Chapel.

Delafaye graduated in 1696 and obtained a position almost immediately as private secretary to Sir Joseph Williamson, England's ambassador to the United Provinces.[20] The introduction was probably through Robert Yard, the senior under-secretary at the Northern Department and Williamson's main point of contact. Yard also edited the *London Gazette* and in that capacity worked closely with Louis Delafaye. The department was small, comprising two under-secretaries, a chief clerk, four or five junior clerks, two office-keepers and a housekeeper.[21] Yard's standing and influence within the

---

[19] Private communication from Gaye Morgan, Librarian in Charge & Conservator at the Codrington Library, All Souls College. All Souls' bible clerks are identified easily in *Alumni Oxonienses* with matriculation at least three years earlier than the date of their Batchelor's degree and an age at entry considerably younger than Fellows of the College. Cf., Hastings Rashdall, *The Universities of Europe in the Middle Ages* (Cambridge: CUP, 2010), vol. 2, pt. 2, pp. 511-2; also Richard Eason, *The last of their line: The Bible Clerks of All Souls College, Oxford* (Oxford: All Souls College, 1976).

[20] Sir Joseph Williamson (1633-1701), administrator, diplomat and politician. Cf., Alan Marshall, 'Williamson, Sir Joseph (1633–1701)', *ODNB*, online edn, Jan 2008, accessed 5 December 2015. In common with most other diplomats, Williamson also engaged in intelligence-gathering, something that may have given Delafaye his first exposure to that craft.

[21] Roughly the same number worked at the Southern Department. Cf., *Office-Holders in Modern Britain*, vol. 2, pp. 59-62.

administration was considerable and is underlined by his appointment as secretary to the Lords Justices in 1699[22] and again in 1701.[23]

Ambassador Williamson was involved in concluding the Treaty of Ryswick, which was signed in September 1697. The settlement marked the end of the Nine Years' War between France and the Grand Alliance.[24] Delafaye, fresh from All Souls and fluent in French, joined Williamson in the Netherlands during the final negotiations.[25] Among its provisions, the treaty secured Louis XIV's withdrawal from the pivotal ducal territory of Lorraine, and French recognition of William III rather than James Stuart as England's rightful monarch. It also confirmed that France and Britain would assume a position of mutual military neutrality.[26]

Perhaps inevitably there were wrinkles. Although Louis XIV recognised William III as the rightful English and Scottish king, he allowed James II to remain in France. And peace in Europe would be temporary, lasting only four years before the War of Spanish Succession, a conflict designed principally to prevent the fusion of Spain and its Low Country and Italian possessions into a French-dominated pan-European monarchy.

In December 1697, Yard wrote to Williamson asking that Delafaye be released from the ambassador's service to take up a position at Whitehall: 'It has been in my thoughts for some time to get Mr Lefay, who is now

---

[22]   William A. Shaw (ed), *Calendar of Treasury Books, volume 15, 1699-1700* (London: HMSO, 1933), pp. 174-93.

[23]   Shaw, *Calendar of Treasury Books, volume 16, 1700-1701* (London: HMSO, 1938), pp. 381-94, 'Warrants etc.: 14 November 1701'. Yard received a gratuity of £500 on each occasion; he was also paid for his work at the *Gazette*, e.g., '£10 15*s* to Robert Yard, Gazetteer': Shaw, *Calendar of Treasury Books, volume 17, 1702* (London: HMSO, 1939), pp. 191-203, 24 April 1702.

[24]   The Grand Alliance comprised Great Britain, the United Provinces, the Holy Roman Empire, Spain and Sweden.

[25]   There were three treaties between the various parties.

[26]   Article IV, Treaty of Ryswick, 20 September 1697.

with your Excellency, into the Duke of Shrewsbury's office, his father being an old acquaintance and having served many years. I have now obtained a vacant seat for him'.[27] Williamson side-lined Yard's request. Delafaye was too useful and was retained for another sixteen months until Williamson's retirement through ill-health brought their joint return to England in March 1699. Yard seized the opportunity and Delafaye was secured a place as the most junior of his clerks.

His position at Whitehall may have encouraged Delafaye to consider marriage and just over a year later on 30 April 1700 he wed Elizabeth Coulbourne[28] at Robert Aske's Hospital in Hoxton, Middlesex.[29]

Delafaye remained at the Northern Department for three years until May 1702, when the accession of Queen Anne and the election that followed brought wholesale changes to the departments of state. James Vernon was dismissed as secretary of state from the Northern Department and Charles, Earl of Manchester, from the Southern. Despite his junior clerical position Delafaye was also affected and relocated to the Southern Department to work for the Earl of Nottingham, Daniel Finch.[30] The transfer brought additional responsibility with Delafaye taking over from Yard as writer and

---

[27] *Calendar of State Papers Domestic, William III, 1697* (London: HMSO, 1927), p. 523.

[28] Also written as Coleborne. Cf., Sainty, 'Delafaye', *ODNB*.

[29] Cf. Victoria & Albert Collection E4841-1923.

[30] Nottingham had served in the role before, albeit briefly, in 1693. Cf. Mark Thompson, *The Secretaries of State 1681-1782* (Oxford: Clarendon Press, 1932), p. 181.

editor of the *London Gazette*, a role he held for five years working alongside his father throughout.[31]

Sainty comments on Delafaye's inexperience as editor of the *Gazette*, reflecting that his successor, Richard Steele,[32] whose annual salary of £300

---

[31] *Office-Holders in Modern Britain: vol. 2, Officials of the Secretaries of State 1660-1782.* The entry details Delafaye's positions in full: *Clerk* (Jersey) c. 1700; (Vernon) Nov. 1700-May 1702; (Nottingham) May 1702-April 1704; (Hedges) May 1704-Dec. 1706. *Chief Clerk* (Sunderland) Dec. 1706-June 1710; (Dartmouth) June 1710-Aug. 1713. *Under-secretary* (Sunderland) April 1717-March 1718; (Stanhope) March 1718-Feb. 1721; (Townshend) Feb. 1721-April 1724; (Newcastle) April 1724-July 1734. *Writer of Gazette* May 1702-May 1707. *Clerk of Signet* 28 May 1728-11 Dec. 1762. Additional notes provide attribution: appointment as clerk to Shrewsbury mentioned 21 December 1697 (*CSPD 1697*, 523); as 'Extraordinary' Clerk to Jersey 1700 (Chamberlayne, *Present State* (1700), 502); became clerk to Vernon on his transfer to Southern Department Nov. 1700; as such 1701 (Miége, *New State* (1701), pt. iii, 109); not one of Vernon's salaried clerks (BM Add. MSS 40785-6); clerk to Nottingham from 1702 to 1704 (*Compleat History* (1702), 69; Chamberlayne, *Present State* (1704), 530); clerk to Hedges on his transfer to Southern Department May 1704; as such 1707 (Chamberlayne, *Present State* (1707), 513). Appointed chief clerk by Sunderland December 1706; heads lists of clerks to Sunderland from 1708 to 1710 (Ibid. (1708), 585; Ibid. (1710), 515-16), to Dartmouth 1711 (Boyer, *Political State* (1711), 377); kept Dartmouth's accounts as secretary of state (Dartmouth MS D 1778 I, ii no. 444). Left office September 1713 on appointment as private secretary to Shrewsbury as Lord Lieutenant, Ireland (Ibid. no. 425). Appointed under-secretary by Sunderland April 1717 (*Hist. Reg. Chron.* (1717), ii, 20; SP 44/120 p. 157); under-secretary to Stanhope from 11 April 1718 to 6 Aug. 1720 (SP 44/120 pp. 316, 523), to Townshend from 17 Feb. 1721 to April 1724 (SP 44/122 p. 8; *Hist. Reg. Chron.* (1724), ix, 20); appointed under-secretary by Newcastle April 1724 (*Hist. Reg. Chron.* (1724), ix, 20). Left office July 1734 (*Gent. Mag.* (1734), iv, 392).

[32] Delafaye later assisted Steele during the latter's editorship of the Gazette. The two became friends, Steele noting in one letter that 'James [his servant] will find me at Mr Delafaye's house in Downing Street or at the Coffee House'. It is also possible that they were later connected masonically, the most obvious evidence being the Bernard Picart print of 1736. Cf. Rae Blanchard, 'Was Sir Richard Steele a Freemason?', *PMLA*, 63.3 (1948), 903-17; also, Richard Steele to Prudence (Mrs) Steele, 22 December 1708, in *The Epistolary Correspondence of Sir Richard Steele* (London, 1787), pp. 72-3.

was fivefold the £60 paid to Delafaye, was held in far higher esteem.[33] There was also an abortive effort to replace Delafaye with John de Fonvive, a successful and celebrated newspaperman.[34]

Despite a mortifying summons to the House of Lords in 1704 to explain why privileged material from the Admiralty had appeared in the *Gazette*, Delafaye was not fired.[35] But his longevity was not a function of political patronage. When Nottingham resigned as secretary of state in April 1704, Delafaye was retained under Sir Charles Hedges, a Tory MP. And when the Earl of Sunderland, a Whig, replaced Hedges in 1706, Delafaye again kept his position. Notwithstanding his earlier mistake, Delafaye's durability can be explained by his administrative competence, something given credence by his promotion to chief clerk under Sunderland, 'a position of special trust',[36] a job he retained when William Legge, Earl of Dartmouth, succeeded Sunderland in 1710.[37]

Moreover, although Delafaye may have lacked the commercial flair of a Fonvive or Steele, he was relatively inexpensive to employ and the secretaries of state in seeking to minimise costs and raise the *Gazette*'s and their own profits would have been content for the editorship be in the hands of a capable man on a modest salary. This was certainly Fonvive's view, who criticised the secretaries of state as short-sighted, arguing that they would

---

[33] Sainty, 'A Huguenot civil servant: the career of Charles Delafaye, 1677-1762', 403.

[34] Described as 'the glory and mirror of news writers ... as his news is good, so his style is excellent'. Cf., John Dunton, *The life and errors of John Dunton, citizen of London* (London: J. Nichols, Son and Bentley, 1818), pp. 428-9; William Bragg Ewald Jr., *Rogues, Royalty and Reporters, The Age of Queen Anne through its Newspapers* (Boston: Houghton Mifflin Company, 1954), pp. 232-3; also *Foundations*, p. 32.

[35] *Journal of the House of Lords: volume 17, 1701-1705* (London: HMSO, 1767-1830), pp. 524-26, 25 March 1704.

[36] Sainty, 'Delafaye, Charles (1677–1762)', *ODNB*.

[37] Cf., Stuart Handley, 'Legge, William, first earl of Dartmouth (1672–1750)', *ODNB*, online edn, Jan 2008.

have generated far greater sales and earned considerably higher profits had the *Gazette* been entrusted to a more commercially-minded operator, in Fonvive's words, 'a gentleman of parts'.[38]

Delafaye's son, Thomas, was born around 1710. An entry in *Alumni Oxonienses* records his matriculation at Merton College on 20 November 1730 aged twenty but there is no date for graduation.[39] Like his father, Delafaye used his position and connections at Whitehall to help secure his son's future.[40] He also aided members of his wife's family, including her brother-in-law, John Wace, for whom he obtained a clerkship in the Northern Department in 1711. Wace was promoted to chief clerk six years later[41] and from 1719[42] became acting under-secretary.[43] He was effective in the role and despite Delafaye's move to the Southern Department as under-secretary to Newcastle, retained his position at the department under Stanhope, Townshend, Harrington and

---

[38]   Fonvive to Harley, 18 July 1705: HMC, Portland MSS (London: HMSO, 1907), vol. viii, pp. 187-8.

[39]   Foster, *Alumni Oxonienses 1715-1886*, vol. 2, p. 360: *Delafaye, Thomas, s. Charles, of Westminster (city) arm. Merton College, matric. 20 Nov. 1730, aged 20*. Theodore Delafaye, the son of James Delafaye, a clergyman from Utrecht, also matriculated at Merton but on 27 August 1724.

[40]   Delafaye settled his position as Clerk of the Signet on Thomas in May 1728 (*Office-Holders in Modern Britain: vol. 2, Officials of the Secretaries of State 1660-1782*); he secured his son the reversionary right to his sinecure as Taster of the Wine at Dublin Castle, an office worth £300 per annum, in 1734 (*Gentleman's Magazine*, 1734, p. 392).

[41]   Cf., *Weekly Journal or British Gazetteer*, 27 April 1717 et al. He was also a Lottery Commissioner: *Weekly Journal or British Gazetteer*, 21 March 1719.

[42]   Cf., for example, *Weekly Packet*, 9 - 16 May 1719.

[43]   Cf., SP 35/9/147, Delafaye to Tilson, 12 September 1717; Delafaye describes Wace as 'our only useful man'.

Carteret until his death in 1745.[44] Wace was succeeded by his son, Francis, who had joined his father in the department as a clerk in 1741.[45]

Having a trusted brother-in-law at the Northern Department was an advantage for Delafaye and the two co-operated, especially in relation to intelligence and security matters.[46] Wace continued to act as a principal point of contact for the Post Office in connection with the issuance of war-

---

[44] *Office-Holders in Modern Britain: vol. 2, Officials of the Secretaries of State 1660-1782*: Wace, John, *Clerk* (Dartmouth) April 1711-Aug. 1713; (Bromley) Aug. 1713-Sept. 1714; (Stanhope) Sept. 1714-April 1717. *Chief Clerk* (Sunderland) April 1717- March 1718; (Stanhope) March 1718-Feb. 1721; (Townshend) Feb. 1721-May 1730; (Harrington) May 1730-Feb. 1742; (Carteret/Granville) Feb. 1742-Nov. 1744; (Harrington) Nov. 1744-19 March 1745. *Deputy Keeper of State Papers* c. 1718-19 March 1745. Notes: appointed as clerk by Dartmouth notified 26 April 1711 (SP 44/110 p. 8); probably continued in office by Bromley; clerk to Stanhope 1716 (Chamberlayne, *Present State* (1716), 528). Appointed chief clerk by Sunderland April 1717 (*Hist. Reg. Chron.* (1717), ii, 20); chief clerk to Stanhope from 6 May to 14 Nov. 1719 (*acting under-secretary*) (T 52/29 p. 403; T 52/30 p. 16), to Townshend from 30 May 1723 to 13 Sept. 1729 (T 52/32 p. 361; T 52/36 p. 403), to Harrington from 10 June 1730 to 20 Oct. 1741 (T 52/37 p. 122; T 52/41 p. 350), to Carteret 1743 (Chamberlayne, *Present State* (1743), pt. ii, 32), to Harrington 1745 (Ibid. (1745), pt. ii, 32). Deputy Keeper of State Papers from 1718 to 1745 (Miège, *Present State* (1718), pt. i, 362; Chamberlayne, *Present State* (1745), pt. ii, 32). Cf., also, *Gentleman's Magazine* (1745), xv, 164; *General Evening Post*, 16 - 19 March 1745 et al; and *Wills Proved at Prerogative Court of Canterbury*, 13 April 1745, LL ref: wills_1740_1749_2531293_571049.

[45] *Office-Holders in Modern Britain: vol. 2, Officials of the Secretaries of State 1660-1782*, pp. 22-58. Also, William A. Shaw (ed), *Calendar of Treasury Books and Papers, volume 4, 1739-1741* (London: HMSO, 1901), pp. 453-61. Francis Wace's appointment as a Gentleman Sewer in 1747 suggests that he may have continued the family's association with intelligence matters.

[46] Wace appears in the Committee of Secrecy's *Report* (1742) in relation to the Secret Department (p. 71), recorded as having receiving £389 10s 3d for expense reimbursement. He was appointed 'Agent of his Majesty's mails belonging to the General Post Office' in 1729: *Universal Spectator and Weekly Journal*, 20 December 1729.

rants authorising mail intercepts after Delafaye's retirement.[47] He was also appointed Deputy Keeper of State Papers (1718), and from 1724 sat on the Westminster bench, a position that underlined the trust placed in him.[48]

The practice of helping family and friends was routine and Delafaye supported other family members including Thomas Coulbourne,[49] his wife's brother, and John Riggs (*d*.1728), another brother-in-law. Riggs was serving in the military in North America and over time Delafaye secured his promotion to a captaincy then colonelcy of a New York regiment.[50] Their correspondence offers a glimpse into eighteenth-century patronage and at the same time illustrates Delafaye's effectiveness.

A letter from Riggs addressed to his 'dear brother [Delafaye] and sister' in November 1716 contains gossip and elements of political intelligence,

---

[47] For example, SP 36/46/249, William Woolley to John Wace requesting the despatch of Harrington's Warrant to the postmaster general; and PP 36/46/260, Barbutt to Wace requesting a new Warrant for the inspection by William Wooley of letters addressed to Lacour.

[48] *Evening Post*, 22 - 25 August 1724 et al.

[49] CUL: Cholmondeley (Houghton) Correspondence, 1, 1193.

[50] John Riggs had served in America from at least 1688-9: *Calendar of State Papers Colonial, America and West Indies, volume 13, 1689-1692* (London: HMSO, 1901); 'Petition of John Riggs to the King. In 1688-1689, I was ensign of a foot-company in New England and was posted at Pojebscot Falls in Maine. On the outbreak of the [Glorious] Revolution I was obliged to quit my garrison and was carried prisoner to Boston, but on being liberated went at once to New York, from whence Colonel Nicholson sent me with despatches to England, and in August 1689, was sent back to New York with despatches, and back once more to England. My expenses for the journeys amount to £80, which I beg may be repaid'. A deposition concerning pay arrears was filed on 7 May 1701: *Calendar of State Papers Colonial, America and West Indies, volume 19, 1701* (London: HMSO, 1910): 'Capt. James Weems, Capt. Peter Mathews, Lieut. John Riggs and Lieut. Charles Ashfield, on behalf of themselves and the rest of the subalterns of H.M. four Foot Companies, to Col. Smith and the rest of the Council of New York. Said officers have laboured under great difficulties for a long time in supporting themselves by credit for want of the greater part of their pay and subsistence'.

including a wry note on the financial status of Robert Hunter,[51] then governor of New York, who 'has made forty thousand pounds' and 'has too sweet a post here to part with'.[52] Another in May 1717 thanked Delafaye for helping Riggs's son, Richard, Delafaye's nephew, and provided an update on his education: 'we keep him close at his school and for his French none here speaks it better, and for his Latin he is pretty forward and in a few years will be able to do his own duty'.[53] Two years on, Riggs, now a captain, asked Delafaye for assistance in obtaining further promotion on his own behalf and for 'your dear Lt. Dick', whom he wished to appoint his deputy.[54] A few months later the commissions were in place and Riggs thanked Delafaye for his intervention;[55] he was now on station at Albany and gave Delafaye brief details of his border command: 'two companies [in] two garrisons on the frontiers, at Schenectady and Fort Hunter in Mohawk country'.

While corresponding with Riggs, Delafaye was simultaneously in communication with Hunter in an exchange that underscores how official and personal matters overlapped. The governor's despatches provided Delafaye with intelligence on Riggs - 'he is happy to his heart's content' - and simultaneously conveyed Hunter's thanks for Delafaye's 'most obliging letters' and support in Whitehall - 'it is no small comfort to me that some men of merit think me

---

[51] Hunter was governor of New York and New Jersey from 1710 until 1720, and governor of Jamaica from 1727 until 1734. Delafaye was Jamaica's London agent between 1728 and 1734.

[52] Riggs to Delafaye, 26 November 1716, New York: *Calendar of State Papers Colonial, America and West Indies, volume 29, 1716-1717* (London: HMSO, 1930).

[53] Riggs to Delafaye, 11 May 1717, New York: *Calendar of State Papers Colonial, America and West Indies, volume 29, 1716-1717.*

[54] Riggs to Delafaye, 2 February 1719, Albany, New York: *Calendar of State Papers Colonial, America and West Indies, volume 31, 1719-1720* (London: HMSO, 1933), p. 21.

[55] Ibid., 15 May 1719, p. 89.

worth room in their remembrance'.[56] Hunter less than subtly acknowledges Delafaye's influence in that regard and with respect to Martin Bladen at the Board of Trade with a request for advice in the disposition of various colonial positions: 'your assistance and interest with your friends and mine to procure commissions for the persons whom I have placed in vacancies according to my standing orders'. The reciprocity of the relationship is self-evident and their willingness to assist one another was repeated during their later careers.

Delafaye continued to be attentive to the Riggs family and in 1725 obtained permission for a one-year leave of absence for his nephew to allow him to 'perfect himself in the knowledge of such arts and sciences as may render him the more capable of doing us service'.[57] Two years later when Riggs complained of Hunter's successor, William Burnet's 'hard usage' and the difficulty of securing a leave of absence for his son,[58] Delafaye responded by writing to Burnet to resolve the issue. Having issued his diktat, Delafaye continued with the comment that he was 'unwilling to make the least doubt of your friendship for me, or your regard for the Office in which I have the honour to serve', and concluded with flattery - 'my Lord Duke of Newcastle approves very well the method in which your Excellency writes to him. You will by the next opportunity receive from his Grace an answer to your last letters. I shall then write more fully than I have time to do at present'. There could not have been a clearer demonstration of his sway in Whitehall; a licence granting Riggs a leave of absence was signed by Newcastle and sent to Burnet by Delafaye the same day.[59]

Letters from the now Colonel and Mrs Riggs continued into the late 1720s, covering the same ground as before. In December 1727, for example,

---

[56] Hunter to Delafaye, 18 May 1719, New York, *Calendar of State Papers Colonial, America and West Indies, volume 31, 1719-1720*; cf., also Hunter to Delafaye, 18 May and 26 May 1719.

[57] Delafaye to Governor Burnet, 30 March 1725, Whitehall: *Calendar of State Papers Colonial, America and West Indies, volume 34, 1724-1725* (London: HMSO, 1936); H.M. Licence of Absence, 30 March, 1725, St James's.

[58] Riggs to Delafaye, 18 December 1727.

[59] Ibid.

Riggs wrote to Delafaye advising that the 'winter has set in very violently, and if Governor Montgomery has sailed, as announced by his letter of 3ʳᵈ Oct., we fear he will be blown off to the West Indies as some of our men-of-war and others of our best ships have been'.[60] Riggs understood the obligation he owed to his brother-in-law and his appreciation 'for all his kindness' was reinforced with modest gifts, including a packet of 'green pickled peppers'.[61]

In early 1729 Delafaye received a letter from New York informing him that Colonel Riggs had contracted pleurisy and died. It advised that Delafaye's nephew, Captain Richard Riggs, had waited upon the governor for a commission to succeed his father,[62] and continued that in the event of him failing to secure promotion, Riggs intended to go to England 'to solicit your favour in having it confirmed for the good of the family'.[63] There would be no need. Governor Montgomery wrote to the Duke of Newcastle the following day confirming that Riggs would succeed to his father's colonelcy: 'Col. Riggs, Capt. of one of the Companies here being dead, I have ordered Richard Riggs, the Capt. Lieut., to be posted in his place'.[64]

Such patronage was commonplace, but Delafaye was unusual to the extent that he took an interest in the well-being of his staff and servants: 'Mr Bleak, a domestic to Charles Delafaye Esq., Under Secretary of State [appointed] Messenger's Servant and Summoner of the Council in the room of

[60] Riggs to Delafaye, 18 December 1727, Albany, New York: *Calendar of State Papers Colonial, America and West Indies, volume 35, 1726-1727* (London: HMSO, 1936).

[61] Ibid.

[62] Paul Richards to Delafaye, 17 December, New York: *Calendar of State Papers, Colonial Series, America and West Indies, volume 36, 1728-1729* (London: HMSO, 1937).

[63] Ibid.

[64] Ibid., Montgomery to Newcastle, 18 December 1728.

Mr Jacob Wall, deceased'.[65] He was also attentive to the interests of friends[66] and masonic colleagues, a potential weakness that Emanuel Bowen,[67] a publisher and engraver arrested and interrogated by Delafaye had hoped to exploit with his request that he might 'interpose in favour of an unfortunate Brother as to have [a set of confiscated prints] restored to me'.[68]

But this was some years in the future. In 1713 following his appointment as Lord Lieutenant of Ireland, the Duke of Shrewsbury asked Delafaye to give up his position in Whitehall to become his private secretary in Dublin.

Born a Catholic, Shrewsbury had converted to Protestantism and was one of the 'immortal seven' who invited William's intervention in 1688.[69] A political survivor, he had served as secretary of state for both the Southern and Northern Departments,[70] and as lord chamberlain. Delafaye had been his junior clerk in Whitehall and chief clerk at the Southern Department when Shrewsbury was ambassador to France.[71]

Delafaye travelled with Shrewsbury for the opening of the Irish parliament and stayed in Dublin until April the following year. He impressed, and Shrewsbury granted Delafaye his first sinecure, that of a Gentleman Sewer. The post was in Shrewsbury's gift in his role as lord chamberlain,

---

[65] *British Journal*, 21 March 1730.

[66] CUL: Cholmondeley (Houghton) Correspondence, 1, 2179, Delafaye to Walpole regarding Richard Meadowcourt, 16 April 1733. There was a masonic link: 'I have been intimately acquainted with him about fifteen years and very often in his company with a little knot of friends'. Delafaye's actions on behalf of John Hammerton are highlighted in chapter two of *Loyalists & Malcontents*.

[67] Emanuel Bowen (1694?–1767), publisher and engraver, esp. maps.

[68] SP 36/27/22 f. 44, 16 June 1732. Emanuel Bowen to Delafaye. My italics. I am grateful to Susan Somers for this reference.

[69] Cf., Stuart Handley, 'Talbot, Charles, duke of Shrewsbury (1660–1718)', *ODNB*, online edn, Jan 2008, accessed 9 Feb 2015. Shrewsbury also held a title in the Irish peerage as Earl of Waterford.

[70] Southern Department 1689-90, 1695-8; Northern Department 1694-5.

[71] He was ambassador at the French court 1712-13.

to which he had been reappointed in 1710.[72] Delafaye was invested in June 1714.[73] The stipend was only modest, £33 6*s* 8*d*, but the post was prestigious. Delafaye passed it to his son in 1728.[74]

Queen Anne's death in August 1714 and George I's coronation in October catalysed changes to the political establishment, including the dismissal of Shrewsbury as Lord Lieutenant. The Earl of Sunderland, his replacement, appointed a new first secretary, Joseph Addison,[75] but Delafaye, known to Sunderland from his time as secretary of state, was retained as second secretary. And when Sunderland was raised to Lord Privy Seal the following year and Ireland placed in the hands of two Lords Justices - the Duke of Grafton and the Earl of Galway - Delafaye was again asked to remain in office.[76]

Delafaye's colleague as first secretary in Dublin under the Lords Justices of Ireland would be Martin Bladen,[77] Galway's former ADC. Bladen had sold his colonelcy in 1710 and given up his army career for politics.[78] He was elected MP for Stockbridge in 1715. He later traded up to represent Maldon,[79] and ultimately obtained the safe Admiralty constituency of Portsmouth. Bladen was a political ally of Walpole and Newcastle, and was later appointed to the Board of Trade and Plantations.[80] He was also a freemason, a member of the

---

[72] Shrewsbury held the post of lord chamberlain for the second time from 1710-15.

[73] *Presence Chamber: Gentlemen Sewers 1660-1782* in *Office-Holders in Modern Britain: volume 11 (Revised), Court Officers, 1660-1837* (London: UL, 2006), pp., 59-63.

[74] Ibid.

[75] He succeeded Sir John Stanley.

[76] *Weekly Journal*, 16 May 1719, et al.

[77] Rory T. Cornish, 'Bladen, Martin (1680–1746)', *ODNB*, online edn, Jan 2008, accessed 20 June 2015.

[78] Bladen had been commissioned into and served in Colonel Fairfax's regiment, later Sir Charles Hotham's regiment, the 5th Regiment of Foot.

[79] He was first elected in 1734.

[80] Bladen was appointed a Commissioner at the Board of Trade & Plantations in 1717 and held the position for almost three decades. He had significant influence with respect to colonial policy and over appointments to office in the American colonies and British Caribbean.

Rummer Tavern at Charing Cross. The lodge had strong links to the military and was close to the army's headquarters at Horse Guards in Whitehall.

It is significant that Grafton and Galway chose to merge the offices of their joint secretaries and that Delafaye and Bladen subsequently shared the fees equally. The immediate consequence was a substantial uplift to Delafaye's compensation. It was customary for each secretary to be paid a proportion of the fees charged by their respective offices and before the merger and when the offices were demerged in May 1717, the first and more senior secretary earned fees from the administration of ecclesiastical and civil business in Leinster and Connaught, and the second a share of that relating to Ulster and Munster. However the first secretary also obtained fees from administering the army's affairs in Ireland while the second participated in those from wool licencing. England's military presence in Ireland was vast and the fees were commensurate. In contrast, wool production was limited by restrictive trade acts and generated only a modest income. In 1758 when the Irish secretaries' fee entitlements were abolished, the first secretary was given an annual allowance of £2,500 from the military budget as payment in lieu; the corresponding payment in respect of wool licencing was a mere £500.[81]

When Grafton and Galway left for London Bladen went with them leaving Delafaye on point in Dublin. His remit included secret service business and with the support of a confidential clerk at Dublin Castle, Delafaye was responsible for the supervision of mail intercepts and scrutinising suspect letters and despatches.

Grafton and Galway returned to Dublin in November 1715 for the new parliamentary session. It would last seven months, a sign of the government's difficulties in pushing through the money supply bills. Faced with growing opposition, the administration sought to add to its support in the Irish Commons. Bladen was given a seat as one of two members for Bandonbridge, Co. Cork, and Delafaye a seat for Belturbet in Co. Cavan.

---

[81] Sainty, 'The Secretariat of the Chief Governors of Ireland, 1690-1800'.

Belturbet was within the plantation of Ulster and part of the fiefdom of the Butler family. They were parliamentary 'undertakers', cross-generational politicians who had undertaken the task of steering Dublin Castle's legislation through the Irish Commons and Lords since the seventeenth century. Delafaye retained his seat for Belturbet through to George II's accession in 1727 when the Irish parliament was dissolved. His fellow MP until 1725 was Brinsley Butler, 2nd Baron Newtown Butler,[82] and thereafter the Hon. Humphrey Butler,[83] who in 1725 was elected deputy grand master of Irish freemasons under Richard Parsons, Earl Rosse, Ireland's first grand master.[84]

But money bills and domestic Anglo Irish opposition were not the only concerns of the Lords Justices. Fears of invasion and Catholic uprising similarly influenced policy and, despite the failure of the 1715 Jacobite Rising, measures were taken to reduce the prospect of a rebellion in Ireland. Delafaye was central to the implementation of the relevant security measures. He issued letters of instruction to magistrates and other officials requiring Catholics to surrender their arms and all 'serviceable horses' in their possession, albeit that the majority of arms had been surrendered in 1714; and ordered reinforcements to the military garrisons at Athlone, Cork, Galway, Kinsale, Limerick and Waterford, positioning them as potential first responders to an insurrection.

The Protestant minority in Ireland might have been staunch in their support for George I and the Hanoverian succession but the majority Catholics took a different view.[85] The Lords Justices' concerns that 'the Papists in this country are very much disposed to rebellion' was communicated to

---

[82]   Later 1st Viscount Lanesborough.

[83]   Cf., *Schism*, pp. 220 & 232.

[84]   Ibid., appendices two and five.

[85]   Archbishop King to Nicolson, 30 July & 15 August 1715, TCD, King Papers, MS 2533, ff. 40-2, 52-4; also King to Delafaye, 6 August 1715, TCD, King Papers, MS 750/4, f. 268. See also, James Kelly, '"Disappointing the boundless ambition of France": Irish Protestants and the fear of invasion, 1661-1815', *Studia Hibernica*, 37 (2011), 27-105.

London, as was intelligence of a possible invasion and accompanying insurgency.[86]   A report from Tralee in south-west Ireland in early 1716 was referred to Whitehall alongside testimony that 'the Papists refused to pay rent because the whisper is that the six thousand Irish abroad are to land this spring in this kingdom … by two or three hundred at a time.'[87]   Other information averred that the exiled Duke of Ormonde was planning to invade.[88]

Although no uprising occurred, the intelligence was not 'frankly unbelievable'.[89]   There may have been opportunism and self-interest in the information provided by Dublin Castle's many informers and agents but there was a genuine risk. The 1715 Rising and the later attempted invasions of Britain suggest that Whitehall's concerns were justified and that it was prudent to give credence to the threat of an insurgency in Ireland.

Townshend was appointed Ireland's Lord Lieutenant in January 1717, albeit that he failed to visit Dublin. Delafaye and Bladen remained in post, with Delafaye at Dublin Castle and Bladen at Whitehall. But the new regime was short lived. Townshend's opposition to government policy led to his dismissal after only three months and when Sunderland was summoned back to the ministry as secretary of state he immediately requested that Delafaye return to London to become his under-secretary.

---

[86]   NA SP 63/373: Lords Justices to Stanhope, 14 November 1715.

[87]   Ibid.

[88]   NA SP 63/374: Lords Justices to Stanhope, 30 January 1716; Delafaye, 30 January 1716.

[89]   Kelly, '"Disappointing the boundless ambition of France": Irish Protestants and the fear of invasion, 1661-1815', p. 54.

CHAPTER TWO

SPYMASTER GENERAL

Deceivers are the most dangerous members of society.
They trifle with the best affections of our nature,
and violate the most sacred obligations.[1]

Bladen had kept Delafaye informed of the goings on in Whitehall during the political upheavals of 1717 and wrote presciently a few days before Sunderland directed him to return to advise that 'I have good reason to believe that My Lord Sunderland will shortly take care of you in England fully to your satisfaction'.[2] He was correct. Back at the centre of government, Delafaye served Sunderland as under-secretary at the Northern Department until March 1718, when Sunderland was replaced as secretary of state by Stanhope. Stanhope's death in February 1721 was followed by Townshend's return to office, a period marked by the South Sea Bubble crisis, a financial crash and a political scandal, with Delafaye tasked with reacting to both civil discontent and the financial fallout from contracting public credit and the self-serving mutual distrust between the South Sea Company and the Bank of England.[3]

---

[1] George Crabbe (1754-1832).

[2] NA SP 63/375, quote from f. 428, 11 April 1717. The position of under-secretary was unsalaried with compensation paid from the allowances and fees that passed through the office. In the eighteenth century the fees of the Southern and Northern Departments were pooled and divided equally between the four under-secretaries, but since the level varied substantially year-on-year it became the practice to grant sinecures to provide the under-secretaries with a base salary and a pension in retirement. Cf., Mark A. Thompson, *The Secretaries of State, 1681-1782* (Oxford: Clarendon Press, 1932), pp. 139-47.

[3] SP 35/23/71, 30 September 1720.

In April 1724, Walpole, first lord of the treasury and *de facto* prime minister, moved Delafaye to the Southern Department to provide support to the Duke of Newcastle, the newly appointed and relatively inexperienced secretary of state.[4] The transfer and more particularly Newcastle's strong political ties to Walpole placed Delafaye even closer to the administration's heart.[5] Fritz suggests that 'Delafaye was one of the most highly trusted members of the English government, especially in all matters involving Jacobites', and a similar conclusion has been reached by other historians including Haffenden, who considers that he 'was the main channel through which much of the pressure directed at Newcastle passed'.[6] Furbank and

---

[4] Newcastle had previously served as lord chamberlain (1717-1724). He would spend twenty-four years as secretary of state for the Southern Department (1724-48) and a further six years at the Northern (1748-54).

[5] Of many examples, cf., Raymond Turner, 'The Excise Scheme of 1733', *English Historical review*, 42.165 (1927), 34-57, esp. 36-7, 40-4.

[6] Paul S. Fritz, 'The Anti-Jacobite Intelligence System of the English Ministers, 1715-1745', *Historical Journal*, 16.2 (1973), 265-89, esp. 276, fn. 78, and 277. Philip Haffenden, 'Colonial Appointments and Patronage under the Duke of Newcastle, 1724-1739', *English Historical Review*, 78.308 (1963), 417-35, esp. 426 and 430-1.

Owens note Delafaye's work within the intelligence sphere, while other historians record his value to the administration, and especially Newcastle.[7]

Delafaye's pivotal role within the intelligence matrix is indicated by his engagement at all levels of national security. His remit extended from the strategic - responding to the threat of a Spanish-backed Jacobite invasion,[8] to ongoing espionage operations,[9] to the apparently mundane - the direc-

---

[7] P.N. Furbank & W.R. Owens, *A Political Biography of Daniel Defoe* (London: Pickering & Chatto, 2006). Also William P. Trent, *Daniel Defoe, how to know him* (Indianapolis, 1916). Patrick McNally, 'Wood's Halfpence, Carteret and the Government of Ireland, 1723-6', *Irish Historical Studies*, 30.119 (1997), 354-76, esp. 359-60, 365-8 & 373-4. Geoffrey Holmes, 'The Sacheverell Riots', *Past and Present*, 72 (1976), 55-85, esp. 59, 66, 75, 3577 and 82. J.A. Downie, 'Swift and Jacobitism', ELH, 64.4 (1997), 887-901, esp. 892. A.C. Wood, 'The English Embassy at Constantinople, 1600-1762', *English Historical Review*, 40.160 (1925), 553-61, esp. 551. D.W. Hayton, 'The Stanhope/Sunderland Ministry and the Repudiation of Irish parliamentary Independence', *English Historical Review*, 113.452 (1998), 610-36, esp. 625 and 631. Jeremy Black, 'Hanover and British Foreign Policy 1714-60', *English Historical Review*, 120.486 (2005), 303-39; 'British Foreign Policy in the Eighteenth Century: A Survey', *Journal of British Studies*, 26.1 (1987), 26-53, esp. 39; 'Fresh Light on the Fall of Townshend', 29.1 (1986), 41-64, esp. 57 and 61-2; 'Interventionism, Structuralism and Contingency in British Foreign Policy in the 1720s', *International History Review*, 26.4 (2004), 734-64, esp. 751, 753 and 755; and 'British Neutrality in the War of the Polish Succession, 1733-1735', *International History Review*, 8.3 (1986), 345-66, esp. 355. There are over 4,000 examples of Delafaye's correspondence, including the BL MS Collection; the National Library of Scotland MS Collection; Domestic, Foreign and Colonial State Papers; the Board of Trade; the Treasury; and the CUL Cholmondeley (Houghton) Papers. Additional material is held elsewhere. Cf., esp., BL MS: Add MSS 28893-900, Add MSS 35585-36139, Add MSS 32686-33607, Add Mss 23782-91; Add MSS 37366-97; NLS MSS 2966-67; CUL Cholmondeley (Houghton) NRA 7114 Walpole.

[8] SP 78/203/61, f. 102: Pelham to Delafaye, Paris, 6 July 1732.

[9] Among many examples, NA SP 78/185/61: Horace Walpole from Paris to Delafaye, 25 April 1727, asks that Delafaye keep a close watch on letters coming to him.

tion and force of the wind at Falmouth. The last was an important factor in calculating the time that would be available for diplomatic and other mail to be opened and copied on the packet boats,[10] a detail that points to another consideration.

A necessary pre-condition for effective intelligence and counter-intelligence is efficient administration, and it was in this arena that Delafaye excelled. His longevity and seniority in Dublin and London was not simply a matter of intelligence, loyalty and discretion, although all were fundamentally important attributes. Delafaye's ability to conduct business effectively had recommended him to both Tory and Whig secretaries of state, and to successive lords lieutenants of Ireland.[11] It was an appreciation of his skillset that explains his transfer to support Newcastle, and that underpinned his appointment as secretary to the Lords Justices on each of the five occasions that they assumed executive authority between 1719 and 1727.

Delafaye's competence as Newcastle's gate-keeper and his effectiveness in exercising influence with respect to both minor and major matters were appreciated by those in the know. When James Brydges, the Duke of Chandos, sought to obtain the release of a convict sentenced to transportation he wrote to Delafaye.[12] When Benjamin Keene, Britain's representative

---

[10]   SP 34/8/18, 14 July 1706. Also SP 89/35/10, 10 February 1728: Arthur Stert to Charles Delafaye. One of the Falmouth packets feared lost in foul weather: 'The packets now on this station are very old and too small, especially for winter service.'

[11]   'Hedges was a Tory and Sunderland a Whig but Delafaye seems to have given equal satisfaction to both.' Cf., Sainty, 'A Huguenot civil servant: the career of Charles Delafaye, 1677–1762', 404. For a parallel view of the importance of administrative efficiency, cf., Jacob Soll, *The Information Master. Jean-Baptiste Colbert's Secret State Intelligence System* (Ann Arbor, MI: University of Michigan Press, 2009).

[12]   Stowe MSS, vols. 25-29: Chandos to Mr. Delafaye, 25 December 1725. Letter books of James Brydges, 1st Duke of Chandos, Stowe Collection, Huntington Library, 1724-27.

in Spain prior to the Treaty of Seville, attempted to reach an accommodation with Newcastle he contacted Delafaye.[13] When the governorship of Bermuda was contested, the post was arranged 'by the help of Charles Delafaye' and awarded to Captain John Pitt, a relative of the governor of Madras.[14] And when Governor Belcher of Massachusetts vied with Bladen at the Board of Trade over whom to choose for various colonial appointments, perhaps unaware of the substance of Delafaye's long-standing relationship with Bladen, he blamed Delafaye for his failure to overcome the Board of Trade, accusing Delafaye of giving the matter 'too little thought'.[15] Haffendon's observation that Delafaye's 'influence upon selection and appointment was inevitably large where the duke was harassed by other demanding duties' is accurate.[16] And Delafaye was admired not only by his superiors[17] but also rivals and colleagues; Haffendon quotes Belcher's[18] observation that Delafaye was 'so influential as to be able to sway Newcastle to almost any decision'.[19]

---

[13]   Richard Lodge, 'The Treaty of Seville (1729)', *Transactions of the Royal Historical Society*, 4th series, 16 (1933), 1-43.

[14]   Haffenden, 'Colonial Appointments and Patronage under the Duke of Newcastle, 1724-1739', quote from 426.

[15]   Ibid., esp. 430.

[16]   Ibid., 431.

[17]   For example, SP 44/121/118: James Craggs to Sunderland.

[18]   Jonathan Belcher (1682-1757), a Massachusetts merchant, businessman and politician was governor of New Hampshire (1729-1741), Massachusetts (1730-1741) and New Jersey (1747-1757). Born into a wealthy Massachusetts mercantile family, Belcher attended Harvard and entered the family business and local politics. He was instrumental in promoting Shute as governor of Massachusetts in 1715 and sat on the colony's royal council but became disenchanted and joined a populist faction. Following the death of Governor Burnet in 1729, Belcher acquired the governorships of Massachusetts and New Hampshire. He had many political enemies and there was an outcry when it transpired that he had permitted his allies to log illegally on crown lands. Belcher was nonetheless rehabilitated and gained appointment as New Jersey's governor in 1747.

[19]   Haffenden, 'Colonial Appointments and Patronage under the Duke of Newcastle, 1724-1739', 431, fn.

Despite writing to Newcastle on one occasion that collating answers to parliamentary questions had forced him to work long hours - 'I am doing what I can that things at the office may be in order against the session and sleep the less that we may not then be taken napping', Delafaye's complaints were infrequent and more whimsical than actual: 'I now write with blood-shot eyes and green spectacles have been in much request'.[20] But his burden was genuine and his workload compounded by his responsibilities as the administration's anti-Jacobite spymaster.

Reliable information was a *sine qua non* of government and Delafaye's remit spanned domestic and foreign intelligence as he monitored and countered the Jacobite threat. He may not have been a Francis Walsingham,[21] but he nonetheless maintained a network of spies across Europe and at home, including double agents, while using the Post Office's Secret Department to source additional information and validate that obtained from the field.

The volume of material passing through Delafaye's office was prodigious, ranging from the routine to the exceptional. A letter from a J. Bell to Delafaye on 8 November 1718 gave information about disaffected persons singing in the streets of London;[22] an intercept in 1722 confirmed the discovery of a cipher in the hand of George Kelly, one of Atterbury's co-conspirators,[23] while another provided Delafaye with details of a plan to seize the Tower of London under the cover of the Duke of Marlborough's funeral.[24] The last led to the

---

[20]   BL Add MSS 32770: Diplomatic Correspondence: Delafaye to Newcastle, 13 December 1730.

[21]   Sir Francis Walsingham (*c.*1532-1590), principal secretary to Queen Elizabeth I and head of her intelligence services. Like Delafaye, Walsingham was a committed Protestant. He went into exile during the reign of Mary and returned only after her death and the accession of Elizabeth, her half-sister.

[22]   SP 35/13/38A.

[23]   SP 35/37/11A: 'we make oath that we evenly believe this paper to be written in the same hand with diverse letters which have been opened at the General Post Office since March last'.

[24]   SP 35/72/70: 13 August 1722.

precautionary despatch of three regiments of Foot from Hounslow Heath to London.[25]

Delafaye's in-tray also included intelligence reports from Daniel Defoe who had secured or been secured the position of editor of the opposition *Weekly Journal or Saturday's Post.* Defoe complained in a letter to Delafaye that he had been 'posted among Papists, Jacobites, and enraged High Tories - a Generation who, I profess, my very Soul abhors; I am obliged to hear traitorous Expressions, and outrageous Words against his Majesty's person and government and his most faithful Servants, and smile at it all as if I approved it.' But Defoe's memorandum was designed less to inform than to put on record his 'sincere attachment to the interest of the present government'.[26] It provided Defoe with insurance against any subsequent accusation of treachery, something essential in the context of the widespread and extensive changes to the composition of the administration following the South Sea Bubble crisis.[27] But what is as significant as the content is that the memorandum was passed to Delafaye. The routing underlines his influence with both past and present secretaries of state and confirms the trust they vested in him and his position at the centre of the intelligence web.

Delafaye's principal national security objectives were to forewarn, forestall and move swiftly against those suspected of Jacobite sympathies,

---

[25] Ibid.

[26] Furbank and Owens argue that Defoe's letters were a hypocritical attempt to rewrite history and that Defoe's founding and editorship of *Mercurius politicus* reveals his true attitude. Cf., P.N. Furbank and W.R. Owens, 'Defoe, the De la Faye letters and *Mercurius politicus*', *British Journal for Eighteenth-century Studies*, 23 (2003), 13-9; also, 'The Myth of Defoe as 'Applebee's Man'', *Review of English Studies*, n.s. 48.190 (1997), 198-204.

[27] SP 35/11, 12, 66 passim. Cf., also, William Lee, *Daniel Defoe: His Life and recently discovered writings* (London: John Camden Hotten, 1869), volume I, p. 461; and William Minto, *Daniel Defoe* (New York, NY: Harper & Brothers, 1887), pp. 115-22.

sedition or treason. It is this that explains his involvement with the Waltham Black Act, described as 'the most severe legislation of the eighteenth century'.[28] Delafaye's concern was not simply that the criminal gangs operating in Hampshire and Berkshire were 'wicked and evil-disposed persons going armed in disguise and doing injuries and violences' who posed a threat to public order.[29] The offences occurred at a time of crisis for the government and there was a need to show that *it* and not the Waltham Blacks controlled the countryside. At the same time, it was equally important for Delafaye to be certain that the disruption was not spearheaded by Jacobite sympathisers seeking to garner support for James Stuart in the countryside.

As the key government official dealing with the matter, Delafaye had responsibility for overseeing the capture and interrogation of the Waltham Blacks.[30] The efficiency with which they were suppressed was down to his efforts - an 'experienced, level-headed and industrious functionary' - rather than Townshend, Walpole or other officials.[31] Delafaye used men he could trust to assist him and among his recruits was Captain William Brereton of the Horse-Grenadiers, a relative of Thomas Brereton, a masonic colleague at the Horn.[32]

The Hampshire and Berkshire disturbances took place at virtually the same time as the Atterbury Plot and Delafaye was occupied simultaneously

---

[28]   Pat Rogers, 'The Waltham Blacks and the Black Act', *Historical Journal*, 17.3 (1974), 465-86. Quotes from 465. The act was passed in 1723.

[29]   Ibid. The offences committed by the Waltham Blacks extended from murder, assault and theft, to blackmail and extortion, and were viewed as a threat to property rights and law and order.

[30]   SP 43/67. Also, SP 44/81/3I2; 4/122/196-7; 44/289/i84-5, 44/289/191-3 et al.

[31]   Rogers, 'The Waltham Blacks and the Black Act', 467-8.

[32]   *Daily Journal*, 7 June 1723. Delafaye engaged both Captain William Brereton and his regimental adjutant. Thomas Brereton (*c*.1680-1756), later MP for Liverpool, was a fellow member of the Horn Tavern and a loyal Walpole supporter. William Brereton was subsequently promoted to major and in 1746 to lieutenant-colonel.

with the surveillance of the Bishop of Rochester, Francis Atterbury, and his collaborators. He would have viewed both through the same politically-aware lens: a direct threat to lawful authority and to the maintenance of the sovereign's peace.

Delafaye was pivotal to the arrest, interrogation and prosecution of Atterbury and his co-conspirators. George Kelly claimed that he had been offered 'his own terms' by Delafaye on condition that he turned King's evidence and act as a witness for the prosecution.[33] Christopher Layer, a second accomplice interrogated by Delafaye, was tried in October 1722 and executed for treason on 17 May 1723,[34] matters discussed in more detail in chapter four.

But while Delafaye's main focus may have been Jacobitism, his responsibility extended into other areas. In November 1723, for example, he assessed intelligence on the impact of the Common Council Bill, gauging the political support for the administration from the City of London.[35] A decade later he collated reports from government agents across the country on the hostility to the proposed Excise Bill.[36] The opposition was considerable and Delafaye advised Newcastle of 'what caballing there has been all over the kingdom to stir up the people against it, there is not a cobbler but is made to believe that he is to pay an Excise before he eats his bread and cheese

---

[33] Philip, Duke of Wharton, *The Life and Writings of Philip, Duke of Wharton* (1732), volume II, p. 678.

[34] C. Layer, *The Whole Proceeding upon the arraignment, trial, conviction and attainder of Christopher Layer* (London: Buckley, 1723).

[35] SP 35/46 56. Delafaye was supplied with information by the gazetteer, Samuel Buckley, whose printing services were also utilised by the government; cf., for example, William A. Shaw (ed), *Calendar of Treasury Books and Papers, volume 2, 1731-1734* (London: HMSO, 1898), 'Warrants for the Payment of Money, 21 June 1733', Order Book XV, p. 310, which discloses a disbursement of £1,228 19s 8d. John Buckley, possibly a relative, was a member of the lodge at the King's Arms, Cateaton Street.

[36] Raymond Turner, 'The Excise Scheme of 1733', *English Historical Review*, 42.165 (1927), 34-57.

and drinks his pot of beer'.[37] Delafaye reiterated his concerns in another memorandum: 'the intended turning the Customs on wine and tobacco, or part of them, into an Excise, is what is likely to give the most occupation this Sessions'. Given the scale of opposition, Delafaye's concluded rightly that the Bill 'will not be attempted without being sure of success'.[38] He was also involved in matters of criminal sentencing. Gerald Howson refers to William Riddlesdon, a thief and forger who in 1720 was condemned to deportation rather than death.[39] Howson's comment is telling: 'why Delafaye should have intervened on behalf of so humble a prisoner is a mystery unless Riddlesdon had rendered the government some service as an informer against Jacobites'.[40]

Delafaye's inter-departmental memoranda in the 1720s and 1730s are significant not only for their content but also their tone. A letter to Waldegrave, a fellow member of the Horn, at the time of writing ambassador to France, is a communication between long-standing friends, despite Delafaye's appreciation of the social gulf between them.

Charles Delafaye to the Earl of Waldegrave
Hampton Court, 16 August 1731

I never read any letter that gave me more pleasure than your Excellency's most private one in your own hand to my lord the duke of Newcastle ... first to see that you had brought the cardinal to explain himself, which

---

[37]   BM, Add. MS. 27732, ff. 93, 94.

[38]   Ibid. Cf., also, Turner, 'The Excise Scheme of 1733'.

[39]   Riddlesdon was deported to Maryland and 'married at Annapolis a woman he had brought with him [and] hiring a house here set up the trade of Tallow Chandler and Soapmaker and pretended to give learned advice in the law': *American Weekly Mercury*, 2 May 1723.

[40]   Gerald Howson, *Thief-Taker General: Jonathan Wild and the Emergence of Crime and Corruption as a Way of Life in Eighteenth-Century England* (Oxford: Transaction Books, 1985), pp. 71-2, 84-6, 135-7.

had been so much recommended to you, and at the same time appeared to me so difficult a talk that I almost despaired of you ever being able to do it; and secondly, that he has told you his grief, which seems to me a plain indication that he is disposed to be well with us. A lady that parleys, your Excellency knows, is not very far from surrendering. I must own I was not a little surprised at the point upon which he puts it. Our engagements with the Emperor for the sake of obliging France to guaranty the pragmatic sanction[41] would have been so monstrous a conduct that I cannot imagine how any man of common sense that is the least acquainted with our constitution could give a moment's attention to so absurd a suggestion…

Now the nation may be brought into a war to keep out the pretender, to do justice to our merchants and preserve and protect our trade, to maintain Gibraltar or any of our other possessions; but it would have been a notable story to have told them that they must raise five millions a year to force France to guaranty the emperor's succession…

I hope your Excellency will be so good as to forgive me if I could have wished you had in your answer to him left out the word 'believe'. You have, I think, seen everything that has passed that is material; you have read our friend Robinson's long dispatches where he sets down every word that is spoke in all his conversations with the Imperial ministers, nay, describes even their looks and gestures, and I am sure I do not remember the least syllable in them that would give one a suspicion that the court of Vienna so much as intimated to us a wish that we would propose to France

---

[41]   In 1713, Charles VI, the Habsburg Emperor, put forward the Pragmatic Sanction to ensure that his territories would pass as a whole to his eldest child. By 1720, it had become obvious that Maria Theresa, his daughter, would be his heiress and the final years of Charles' reign were engaged in obtaining guarantees from the major European powers to ensure her inheritance. Following his death in 1740 France and Spain failed to adhere to their undertakings. The dispute led to the War of the Austrian Succession.

to guaranty their succession. They know we would not undertake it and that it would be to no purpose if we did.[42]

Waldegrave had been an intimate of Delafaye at the Horn for more than a decade and as ambassador at Vienna from 1727/8 and at Paris since 1730 was a key fulcrum on which British diplomacy and espionage turned. Their correspondence, more than six hundred letters,[43] was both professional and familiar, evidence of a personal closeness that extended to exchanging gifts.[44] It also allowed for an uninhibited dialogue, one example being the irreverent note from Delafaye in October 1733 that 'I cannot help wishing the [Holy Roman] Emperor a little mortified for his behaviour in the affairs of Sardinia and Spain'.[45]

Waldegrave's family background, French education, familiarity with Paris society and multiple Jacobite and masonic connections, gave him un-precedented access and a level of understanding of French affairs unavail-able to other ambassadors. His insights and reports were supplemented by a network of spies paid from secret service funds. They included Francois Bussy, codenamed '101', an informant with access to the in-nermost reaches of French government correspondence whose recruit-ment had been approved at the highest level in Whitehall.[46] Waldegrave's

---

[42] William Coxe, *Memoirs of the Life and Administration of Sir Robert Walpole* (London: Cadell & Davies, 1798), volume III, pp. 118-20, also pp. 122-3, 125, 128, 129 & 133.

[43] NRA 28249 Waldegrave, among other sources.

[44] Cf., SP 78/204/20, f. 24: Waldegrave to Delafaye. Covering letter for bags of truffles for Delafaye and Newcastle, 15 February 1733, Paris.

[45] Waldegrave MSS: Delafaye to Waldegrave, 9 Oct. 1733 (o.s.).

[46] Bussy was transcriber to Germain-Louis de Chauvelin (1685-1762), the Keeper of the Seals. At least one other spy was responsible for validating Bussy's reports to Waldegrave. This may have been because he was not entirely trusted by Whitehall or because his intelligence was so valuable that it made corroboration a necessity.

entrée to the French court and to Jacobite circles was thought too convenient by some in London and suspicions were raised within Whitehall
circles as to his loyalty. They were unfounded. Waldegrave was staunch
in his support for the Hanoverian succession and one of Delafaye's most
useful sources.[47]

Delafaye's value to the government was appreciated overtly. He was
granted the office of Wine Taster at Dublin Castle, a position worth £300
per annum granted in 1720, and his wife the position of Housekeeper,[48]
a role that yielded £120 per annum and was later sold for £3,000.[49] The
income from both was tax-exempt.[50] Delafaye was also installed a Clerk
of the Signet under the Lord Privy Seal in 1728.[51] But perhaps the most
poignant example of the regard in which he was held was the award of a
doctorate from the University of Cambridge.[52] The degree was conferred
by George II personally and Delafaye was invested alongside a group of senior peers and politicians including the Dukes of Ancaster, Dorset, Grafton,

---

[47] Philip Woodfine, 'Waldegrave, James, first Earl Waldegrave (1684–1741)',
ODNB, online edn, May 2008, accessed 21 December 2015.

[48] Other sources giving a later date are incorrect.

[49] Toby Barnard, *A New Anatomy of Ireland: the Irish Protestants, 1649-1770* (New
Haven, CN: YUP, 2004), p. 146. The position was sold in 1734.

[50] 'To exempt from the tax of 4s. per £, payable on all salaries, fees, and pensions
there, the following persons ... Charles Delafaye, as Taster of all wines and all
other liquors, and Surveyor of the outports and defects of same, which shall be
imported to any port, haven, or creek of Ireland' in *Calendar of Treasury Books
and Papers, 1729-1730* (London: HMSO, 1897), 26 January 1720; repeated in
subsequent papers, for example, *Calendar of Treasury Books and Papers, 1735-1738*
(London: HMSO, 1900), 15 March 1738 et al.

[51] Cf., for example, *Daily Post*, 9 January 1728 and *London Evening Post*, 16 May 1728.

[52] There were at the time no honorary doctorates *per se*, however the award can
be considered as analogous.

Manchester and Newcastle, and Sir Robert Walpole.[53] It was a telling confirmation of his utility to the administration and to the king.[54]

Acknowledged as an exceptional and effective public servant, Delafaye's letters and memoranda demonstrate that he was not simply engaged in executing policy but also determined it. An exchange of letters with Bladen and Newcastle concerning French encroachment on Britain's West Indian colonies in 1729 and 1730 is insightful.[55] The papers they exchanged created the strategy that was presented to the Commons and reflected both his and Bladen's input. (Bladen had by this time acquired a direct interest in the Caribbean following a second marriage which had endowed him with plantations in Nevis.[56]) It was nonetheless Delafaye who selected the necessary papers for Newcastle to pass to the relevant ministers - the Lord Privy Seal, Lord Chancellor and the Secretary at War – which set the basis on which the policy was agreed.[57]

Delafaye was also at the centre of the deliberations that preceded The War of Jenkins' Ear. He had taken Captain Jenkins' deposition in June 1731 and while circulating it commented to Keene, the minister plenipotentiary at Madrid, of the need for political rather than military action: 'in short, my

---

[53] Cf., for example, *London Evening Post*, 18 May 1728.

[54] There were many lesser testaments, including an invitation to his wife to act as godmother to the daughter of George Chamberlayne, Whig MP for Buckingham. Cf., *London Journal*, 21 April 1733.

[55] Cornish in his *ODNB* entry describes Bladen as 'possibly the most influential and best-informed official regarding the American colonies between the retirement of William Blathwayt (1649-1717) in 1710 and the appointment in 1748 of George, 2nd Earl of Halifax, as President of the Board'.

[56] Cf., Cornish, *ODNB*. Also, Sedgwick, *The History of Parliament: the House of Commons, 1715-1745.*

[57] *Calendar of State Papers Colonial, America and West Indies, volume 37, 1730* (London: HMSO, 1937).

dear friend, unless we do something to stop the clamours of people, all we have done will be of little service here at home'.[58]

His influence is similarly underscored by the willingness of Francis Nicholson,[59] the royal governor of South Carolina,[60] to intercede on behalf of John Hammerton, Delafaye's job-hunting masonic colleague at the Horn. Nicholson agreed to 'attend at the Duke of Newcastle's office [to present] a memorial'[61] to assist Hammerton to secure the positions of secretary and register in the South Carolina colony. The rapport between the three men is evident in their correspondence,[62] and it is unlikely to have been a coincidence that Nicholson acted as Delafaye's sponsor in his election as FRS the same year.[63]

But perhaps the clearest indication of Delafaye's standing as the most trusted and effective crown servant was his appointment as secretary to the Lords Justices, a role for which he was selected on every occasion the Lords Justices held the regency in George I's absence.[64] He received an additional

---

[58] Delafaye to Keene, 1 October 1731: SP Foreign, Spain, 109. Quoted in Harold W.V. Temperley, 'The Causes of the War of Jenkins' Ear, 1739', *Transactions of the Royal Historical Society*, 3rd Series, 3 (1909), 197-236.

[59] Kevin R. Hardwick, 'Nicholson, Sir Francis (1655–1728)', *ODNB*.

[60] Francis Nicholson took office in May 1721 but returned to England four years later. He was not replaced formally until Robert Johnson succeeded him as governor in 1729. Arthur Middleton served as acting governor between May 1725 and December 1730.

[61] Headlam, *Calendar of State Papers Colonial, America and West Indies* (London: IHR, 1936), vol. 35, 7 January 1726.

[62] Cf., for example, Nicholson to Delafaye, 5 May and 16 October 1722, and 4 December 1723: *Calendar of State Papers Colonial, America and West Indies, volume 33, 1722-1723* (London: HMSO, 1934).

[63] The Sackler Archives of the Royal Society. Cf., also, *Foundations*, p. 79.

[64] Although the Prince of Wales had been regent on the first occasion George I travelled to Hanover, relations between the two deteriorated to the point where the king declined to reappoint him.

£500 on each occasion that he served, a fee that almost doubled his salary as an under-secretary.

Delafaye was throughout this period a senior magistrate, a position he had held for more than two decades. Unsurprisingly he was one of the government's most favoured justices of the peace, especially in political matters.[65] Although it was common for under-secretaries to be nominated to the bench in order to allow their examination of potential witnesses and defendants under oath, and facilitate involvement with sensitive matters including intelligence, Delafaye was appointed a magistrate several years before he became an under-secretary. He took depositions in connection with the Sacheverell Riots in 1710,[66] and appears in press reports from 1714 and 1715.[67]

In the course of twenty-five years on the Middlesex and Westminster benches, Delafaye's cases included examining and sentencing a Jacobite sympathiser 'for publicly affirming in St James's Park that the Pretender was the only rightful and lawful King',[68] and a printer suspected of 'printing the libels dispersed in Westminster Hall'.[69] He also investigated numerous alleged plots against the crown, including a prosecution of 'persons who were talking of some misfortune that should happen to the King tomorrow as his Majesty should pass over Sandy End Bridge on his way to London'.[70] There

---

[65] Cf., among many reported examples, *Country Journal or The Craftsman*, 17 November 1733.

[66] Blenheim MSS, box vii, 18.

[67] LMA, Middlesex Sessions, Sessions Papers, Justices' Working Papers, April 1715: LMA: MJ/SP *1715*. He also adjudicated cases in the Cities of London and Westminster.

[68] *Original Weekly Journal*, 31 August 1717.

[69] *Old Whig or The Consistent Protestant*, 29 July 1736.

[70] LMA: Middlesex Sessions Papers, Justices' Working Documents, 27 October 1731: *Information of William Steele of St Clements Danes in the County of Middlesex, tobacconist*.

is no doubt that his judicial decisions were political. One of the more obvious examples is the trial and execution for treason of the nineteen-year old John Matthews in 1719. Delafaye's judgment was not principally to punish Matthews for printing the satirical Jacobite pamphlet *Ex Ore Tuo Te Judico. Vox Populi, Vox Dei* so much as to discourage other printers and publishers from following in his footsteps.[71]

Delafaye also participated in the Quarter Sessions, determining cases that could not be tried by a single magistrate sitting alone. In 1722 for example he adjudicated alongside eleven other justices of which at least seven and possibly nine were also freemasons.[72] Five were members of his own lodge;[73] four members of other London lodges.[74] And whereas provincial Quarter Sessions were unable to judge trials involving sentences of execution or life imprisonment, those that sat in Westminster and Middlesex had that authority and could determine the most serious cases, including treason.[75]

---

[71]   R.J. Goulden, 'Vox Populi, Vox Dei: Charles Delafaye's Paperchase', *Book Collector*, 28 (1979), 368-90. Also, Monod, *Jacobitism and the English People*, p. 40; and Paula McDowel, *The Women of Grub Street: Press, Politics and Gender in the London Literary Marketplace* (Oxford: Clarendon Press, 1998), p. 74.

[72]   LMA: Middlesex Sessions, 6 December 1722. The twelve were Sir Thomas Jones, Sir John Gonson [Johnson], Charles Delafaye, William Wickam, Gwyn Vaughan, Richard Newton, Nathaniel Blackerby, William Cowper, Joseph Hayne, Francis Sorrel, Alexander Hardine and Matthew Hewitt.

[73]   The Horn Tavern: Nathaniel Blackerby, William Cowper, Charles Delafaye, Alexander Hardine and Francis Sorrel.

[74]   Jones was a member of Martin Folkes's lodge at the Bedford's Head; Johnson a possible member of the Swan Tavern in Fish Street Hill; Vaughan a possible member of the Rummer, the lodge attended by Martin Bladen; and Haynes a member of the Royal Vine Yard in St James's. Cf., *Foundations*, esp. chapters three and four.

[75]   Norma Landau, 'Indictment for Fun and Profit', *Law and History Review*, 17.3 (1999), 507-36; and Robert B. Shoemaker, 'The London Mob in the Early Eighteenth Century', *Journal of British Studies*, 26.3 (1987), 273-304.

The importance of the magistracy in cementing order in the eighteenth century should not be undervalued. The justice of the peace 'occupied a pivotal position' in society,[76] and the bench was concerned not simply with 'the preservation of the king's peace and justice' but also determined the legal status of offences brought before it and thus the severity of the sentence handed down.[77]

Delafaye's prominence on the bench reflected the 'might of party' as well as his value to the government.[78] The new ministry that accompanied George I's accession had been followed by substantive changes to the composition of the magistracy that were designed to reinforce the Whigs' political ascendancy. Although there were notable exceptions, it became a matter of course for Whig lord chancellors to appoint political allies and remove opposition Tories and those suspected of Jacobite sympathies. This was the case above all in the sensitive areas of Middlesex, Westminster and the City of London, where the bench was moulded to give an explicitly pro-government bias.[79] After 1714, to be appointed a London magistrate was a public statement of 'fidelity to the Hanoverians'.[80]

William Cowper, a fellow member of the Horn, grand secretary and later deputy grand master of Grand Lodge, chairman of the Westminster and

---

[76] P.B. Munsche, 'Review: The Justice of the Peace, 1679-1760', *Eighteenth Century Studies*, 20.3 (1987), 385-7.

[77] Landau, 'Indictment for Fun and Profit'; and Shoemaker, 'The London Mob in the Early Eighteenth Century'. The magistracy also had responsibility for several fundamental administrative issues, including licencing, local tax assessment and the implementation of the parish poor laws.

[78] Norma Landau, *Justices of the Peace 1679-1760* (Berkeley, CA, 1984), esp. pp. 69-95, 96-145 and 146-73.

[79] The government's influence over the provincial magistrates' benches was relatively modest when compared to London. Cf., Norma Landau, 'Country Matters: The Growth of Political Stability a Quarter Century On', Albion, 25.2 (1993), 261-74.

[80] Landau, *Justices of the Peace 1679-1760*, p. 88.

Middlesex benches for much of the 1720s, is a leading example.[81] His *Charge* to the Grand Jury of Middlesex on 9 January 1723 epitomises Whig loyalism: 'It ought always to be a matter of particular distinction … that Justices would be vigilant to detect and produce to punishment all those who … attempt the subversion of the great basis upon which stands all that is or can be dear to England and Protestants … our Religion, our Liberty and our Property'.[82]

An exhortation to his fellow magistrates in 1730 was in the same vein: 'the magistrate … is trusted to uphold the honour, the dignity and the majesty of the state, to see that order is observed, that equal right be done according to known and approved law … and ever to bear in mind the high nature and vast importance of this trust, and whoever assumes … such powers upon any other principle is and should be treated as a subverter of peace, order and good government of the world and an Enemy to human society'.[83]

The parallel with the new *Charges* in the 1723 *Constitutions* is obvious. Not only was a freemason 'a peaceable Subject to the Civil Powers … never to be concerned in Plots and Conspiracies against the Peace and Welfare of the Nation', but each was obliged to agree specifically 'to be a good man and true … to be a peaceable subject, and cheerfully to conform to the laws of the country in which [he] resides … not to be concerned in plots and conspiracies against government [and to] submit to the decisions of the supreme legislature [and] the civil magistrate'.

Nathaniel Blackerby, another member of the Horn and the grand treasurer at Grand Lodge, was elected chair of the Westminster bench in 1738[84] shortly after having been appointed Deputy Lord Lieutenant for

---

[81]   Cowper was Clerk of the Parliaments, that is, the senior administrative official or chief executive for the House of Lords and House of Commons. He was a member of the Horn Tavern lodge, grand secretary of Grand Lodge from 1723-7 and deputy grand master in 1726.

[82]   *Pasquin*, 17 January 1723.

[83]   William Cowper, *The Charge delivered …* (London, 1730), pp. 5-6.

[84]   *Daily Gazetteer,* 6 April 1738.

Middlesex.[85] Blackerby's address, like Cowper's, reminded his colleagues that duty, liberty and property rights were the foundation stones of society: 'the cause you are engaged in is the cause of your God, your King and your Country ... consider the duty you owe as subjects to your King, under whose mild government and wise administration every man enjoys the fruits of his labour, his liberty, his property'.[86]

Blackerby's loyalty to the government was also expressed in freemasonry, not least on 28 August 1730 when sitting as deputy grand master he 'proposed several Rules to the Grand Lodge to be observed in their respective Lodges for their Security against all open and Secret enemies to the Craft', a resolution that had everything to do with anti-Jacobitism.[87]

The prominence of freemasons within the magistracy underscored the government's acceptance of the organisation as pro-Hanoverian.[88] At least three members of the Horn chaired the Westminster and Middlesex benches in the 1720s and 1730s,[89] as did members of other lodges.[90]

George II succeeded in 1727 and Delafaye stepped down as MP for Belturbet, replaced in the new Irish parliament by Thomas Butler.[91] With a new monarch on the throne there was no immediate requirement for the Lords Justices to act as regent and it is possible that the reduction in Delafaye's prospective income may explain why he 'developed an interest in

---

[85] John Chamberlayne, *Magnae Britanniae* (1736), p. 160.

[86] Nathaniel Blackerby, *The Speech of Nathanial Blackerby* (London, 1738), p. 18.

[87] Grand Lodge *Minutes I*, p. 128.

[88] *Foundations*, esp. pp. 70-97.

[89] The third was Leonard Streate, Steward of the Borough Court in Southwark and a barrister in the Middle Temple; he chaired the bench in 1725 and 1727.

[90] For example, John Rotherham, a member of the Anchor, Duchy Lane; and Sir John Johnson.

[91] Cf., SP 63/389/1309, W. Conolly at Dublin to Delafaye, 20 June 1727, regarding *inter alia* Delafaye's possible candidature for Irish Parliament following the king's death.

colonial affairs' and in 1728 became Jamaica's political agent in London, a post he held until 1734 and his retirement.[92]

Delafaye's nomination may have been initiated by Robert Hunter, Jamaica's governor. Hunter had been a staunch Walpole supporter and had benefited from a professional and personal relationship with Delafaye that dated back over two decades. Hunter's links to Bladen traced back nearly as far to 1717, when Bladen was appointed to the Board of Trade and Plantations.[93] The position of governor of Jamaica was one of the most lucrative in the colonies and considered as, and was, a reward for loyal service. Hunter held the job from 1727 until his death in 1734.[94]

Given his influence as an under-secretary in the department responsible for colonial affairs and his personal relationship with Bladen, there can be little doubt of Delafaye's involvement in Hunter's move to Jamaica. But although Delafaye's selection as the island's parliamentary agent might appear to be an act of reciprocity, other factors were at work.

Delafaye was appointed by Jamaica's House of Assembly, not by Hunter or London, and was confirmed only afterwards by the royal council and governor. The position was in any event unofficial from 1728 until 1732, when Jamaica was allowed to pass an Agency Act, and only then were Delafaye and John Gregory named formally as joint London agents.

That the Agency Act received the consent of Jamaica's assembly and the council, and had Hunter's support, was a function of Delafaye and Gregory's reputation. Indeed, Whitehall held Gregory in sufficient esteem to appoint him president of Jamaica's royal council just three years later when John

---

[92] Sainty, 'A Huguenot civil servant: the career of Charles Delafaye, 1677–1762', p. 408.

[93] Mary Lou Lustig, 'Hunter, Robert (1666–1734)', *ODNB*, online edn, Jan 2008, accessed 13 June 2015.

[94] Hunter had exchanged his position as governor of New York and New Jersey for the well-remunerated office of Comptroller of Customs in London. The previous incumbent, William Burnet, received Hunter's governorship in America.

Ayscough, the former president, succeeded as governor.[95]   Previous attempts by Jamaica to secure representation in London via an Agency Act had failed - vetoed by London - and no formal arrangements had been in place since 1704. But with Delafaye and Gregory in the frame, Whitehall had its own men acting on behalf of the Caribbean's economic powerhouse.[96]

A senior civil servant in the department of state responsible for the administrative oversight of Jamaica acting simultaneously as its parliamentary agent or lobbyist may be a splendid example of eighteenth-century dysfunction. But it is also an indication of Jamaica's ability to exercise influence. Delafaye's remuneration as the island's man in London is not known but is likely to have been significant; as Ian Steele notes, the work of a colonial agent was not designed to be a sinecure.[97] And there is evidence that Delafaye did not treat the appointment as such but engaged fully to represent the colony.[98] At the same time Delafaye was mindful of his obligation to Hunter and used his influence to protect the governor, on one occasion writing to Walpole in defence of Hunter against a serious accusation that he

---

[95]   Gregory was president of Jamaica's royal council (1735, 1736-8).   Cf., Frederick G. Spurdle, *Early West Indian Government: Showing the Progress of Government in Barbados, Jamaica and the Leeward Islands, 1660-1783* (London: Forgotten Books, 2013), pp. 206-9. Originally published privately.

[96]   Spurdle, *Early West Indian Government*, pp. 206-9.

[97]   Ian K. Steele, *The English Atlantic, 1675-1740: An Exploration of Communication and Community* (Oxford: OUP, 1986), p. 246.

[98]   For example, Delafaye's attendance before the Board of Trade on 6 August 1728, 17 July and 20 July 1731; 3 August 1731; and 19, 26 and 27 July 1732. There are many other examples. Cf., *Journals of the Board of Trade and Plantations, volume 5, January 1723 - December 1728* and *volume 6, January 1729 - December 1734*. Also, SP 36/27/20, f. 41, Alfred Popple, to Delafaye, 18 June 1731, 'the Commissioners for Trade intend to take into further consideration matters relating to Jamaica the next day'; SP 36/25/45, f. 45, W. Smith to Delafaye, 5 November 1731, 'enc. letters showing the harmful practices of Guarda Costa Patrols'.

had flouted government policy having 'called his Assembly out of course on purpose … contrary to an instruction from the King'.[99]

Alongside his more routine departmental work Delafaye continued to be engaged with intelligence issues both administratively and operationally. A notable instance was his association with John 'Orator' Henley,[100] whom Delafaye arrested and interrogated in 1728 and persuaded to become a paid government agent.[101] The context was his press management brief which included taking direct action against papers that gave offence and using government advertising and other payments for the benefit of newspapers that toed the government line.[102] Delafaye was clear on the rationale: 'I must own that to those who do not thoroughly understand our constitution, and have no notion of the excess to which the liberty of the press may be carried here, the weekly insults upon the king and his ministry carried on with impunity may give an opinion of the administration being very weak'.[103]

In the light of Henley's new Whig loyalties it was no coincidence that he was made a member of Prince William Lodge, Charing Cross, on 11 June 1730, his initiation announced in the press and supported by 'noblemen and gentlemen',[104] nor that government funds were invested in his paper, the

---

[99]   CUL: Cholmondeley (Houghton) Correspondence, 1, 1899, 26 August 1732.

[100]   John 'Orator' Henley (1692-1756). Cf., Graham Midgley, *ODNB*, online edn, September 2010, accessed 14 April 2015.

[101]   NA SP 36/5/93-4. Cf., also SP 36/5/100: Cracherode to Delafaye: 'Approval of bail proposed for Mr. J. Henley viz. Joseph Booth and Simon Henley for £100 apiece, 9 February 1728'.

[102]   Among many sources, Paula McDowell, *The Women of Grub Street: Press, Politics, and Gender in the London Literary Marketplace 1678-1730*, pp. 61, 66, 75-7, 80-6, 92-4, 101-3. Also Jeremy Black, *Parliament and Foreign Policy in the Eighteenth Century* (Cambridge: CUP, 2004), pp. 152-3, and Black, *The English Press in the Eighteenth Century* (Abingdon: Routledge Revivals, 2010).

[103]   BL Althorp MS, E3, Delafaye to Poyntz, 14 January 1729.

[104]   *British Journal*, 13 June 1730. But cf. W.B. Hextall, *AQC*, 29, pp. 368-71, where this is disputed.

Hyp Doctor, set up as a counterpoint to the Tory *Craftsman* and the *Grub Street Journal*.[105]

Two days after his initiation Henley advertised that he would give a 'Eulogium on Masonry ... to dispute Gormogonism'.[106] And a few months later in November his association with freemasonry was reconfirmed in the dedication of *A New Model for the Rebuilding of Masonry on a Stronger Basis*.[107] To cap his conversion, on 9 June 1732 Henley was appointed grand chaplain of the Grand Lodge of England.[108]

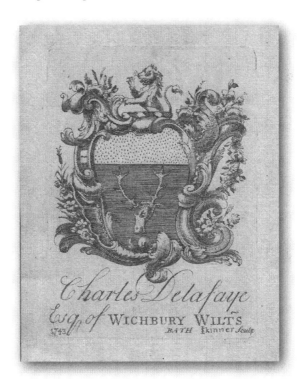

Charles Delafaye – Armorial Plate, 1743

[105] Midgley, 'Henley, John (1692–1756)', *ODNB*.

[106] Hextall, *AQC*, 29, pp. 368-9.

[107] *Daily Journal*, 18 November 1730.

[108] *Read's Weekly Journal*, 9 June 1733; *St James's Evening Post*, 7 - 9 June 1733.

Delafaye had held senior office at the Southern Department for a decade when he stepped down in July 1734 due to ill health.[109] He was fifty-seven. His resignation was noted in the *Gentleman's Magazine* that month and in the press more widely.[110] Delafaye nonetheless continued to act informally[111] and remained in contact with Newcastle[112] and retained his connections with Whitehall into the 1740s.[113] He also continued as a magistrate[114] and retained several less arduous roles.[115]

---

[109] Sainty, *Office-Holders in Modern Britain, volume 2: Officials of the Secretaries of State 1660-1782*, pp. 63-85. Delafaye had suffered recurrent gout since the 1720s. His poor health is the subject of four letters with Robinson: SP 78/185/6 & 19, 29 January and 21 February 1727; and SP 78/196/123 & 126, 20 March and 6 April 1729. Pelham and Waldegrave were equally solicitous: respectively, SP 78/192/2, 13 January 1731; and SP 78/199/15, 17 January 1731.

[110] *Weekly Miscellany*, 3 August 1734; *London Evening Post*, 25 - 27 July 1734. It had been flagged for some years: *Grub Street Journal*, 26 March 1730: 'Charles Delafaye … is dangerously ill [and] attended by several physicians.'

[111] Cf. for example, *Read's Weekly Journal Or British Gazetteer*, 21 April 1739, also *London Evening Post*, 19 April 1739. There was no secretary of state for Scotland at this time and the description of Delafaye as the deputy secretary of state for Scotland may refer to his intelligence oversight.

[112] For example, SP 36/38/74, Delafaye to Newcastle, 16 January 1736, offering to take the place of Couraud, who (ironically) also suffered from gout; SP 36/80/1/17, Delafaye to Newcastle, 1 January 1746, offering congratulations for 'the peace lately concluded'; SP 36/80/3/111, 8 February 1738, suggesting that Delafaye provide a character reference; SP 36/44/77, 10 December 1737, thanking Newcastle for his friendship and presenting his respects; and SP 36/80/3/111, H. Duncombe to Newcastle, 19 January 1746, suggesting Delafaye act as a referee.

[113] 'Letters to Lord George Sackville': Derbyshire Record Office: D3155/C1015, 24 June 1749; D3155/C1568-1571, 15 May 1754 and D3155/C1577-1578, 25 July 1754.

[114] *Old Whig or The Consistent Protestant*, 29 July 1736.

[115] *London Evening Post*, 17 - 19 April 1739. *Read's Weekly Journal Or British Gazetteer*, 21 April 1739 et al.

Delafaye retired to Wichbury near Salisbury in Wiltshire in 1735, leasing a property from Anthony Ashley-Cooper, the 4th Earl of Shaftesbury, one of the former proprietors of the Carolina colony and a Georgia Trustee.[116] The address features on the armorial plates of his library books,[117] many of which record him as an original subscriber.[118] He died in 1762 at the age of 86.[119] His wife had predeceased him in 1742, his daughter in 1722[120] and his son in 1746. Delafaye's closest living relatives prior to his death were his brother's daughter and his nephew, Richard Riggs, who with Delafaye's probable support had been appointed by Grand Lodge as provincial grand master of New York.[121]

---

[116] SP 36/36/61 f. 61. Delafaye, from Wichbury, to Newcastle, 27 September 1735. Offers his thanks for all his favours and speaks of himself as a 'poor invalide'.

[117] *A catalogue of the valuable libraries of the following gentlemen, lately deceased. Charles Delafaye … which will be sold on August 23 1763* (London, 1763). Cf., also, *London Chronicle*, 2 - 4 August 1763 et al.

[118] For example, John Senex, *A New General Atlas* (London: Senex, 1721); Joseph Addison *The Works of the Rt. Hon Joseph Addison* (London: Tonson, 1721); Gilbert Burnet, *Bishops Burnet's History of His Own Time* (London: Ward, 1724); Ercole Bentivoglio, *Les Fantomes et le Jaloux Comedies Italiennes traduites en francois* (Oxford, 1731); *A Catalogue of the Rarities to be seen at Don Saltero's Coffee House* (London, unknown); Roger Bacon, *Ordinus Minorum* (London, 1733); Charles King, *The British Merchant Preserved* (London: Darby, 1721); and J. Morgan, *A Complete History of Algiers* (London: Morgan, 1728/9). Delafaye's library was sold at auction by the leading Fleet Street booksellers and publishers, John Whiston and Benjamin White, in August 1763.

[119] *Lloyd's Evening Post and British Chronicle*, 10 - 13 December 1762 et al. His life had been assured by the Amicable Society of which a number of fellow freemasons, including Fotherley Baker, deputy grand master 1747-52, had been directors. Cf., *Schism*, pp. 133-44.

[120] Nicholson to Delafaye, 16 October 1722, *Calendar of State Papers Colonial, America and West Indies, 1722-1723*, pp. 154-5.

[121] The Grand Lodge of England appointed Captain Richard Riggs provincial grand master of New York in 1737; but cf. Joseph Balestier, *Historical Sketches of Holland Lodge* (New York, NY: Holland Lodge, 1862), p. 12: 'Riggs did nothing to establish Masonry here'.

Delafaye's will was proved at Canterbury on 5 February 1763. Under its terms his personal correspondence was delivered to the Collector of State Papers, the majority of which are now held in collections at the British Library,[122] the Cholmondeley (Houghton) collection at Cambridge University Library,[123] the National Library of Scotland[124] and the Waldegrave family papers.[125] Delafaye left his house to Richard Riggs and a legacy to the descendants of the daughter of his deceased brother, Captain Lewis Delafaye. Among several charitable legacies he bequeathed £200 in Old South Sea Annuities to establish Delafaye's Charity, a foundation in Wichbury 'for the sick and industrious poor'.

---

[122] BL, Add MSS 28893-900, Add MSS 35585-36139, Add MSS 23782-91, Add MSS 32686-33067 passim and Add MSS 37366-97 passim.

[123] CUL (Houghton), NRA 7114 Walpole

[124] National Library of Scotland, MSS 2966-67.

[125] NRA 28249 Waldegrave.

Chapter Three

The Secret Department of the Post Office

Intelligence ... is the soul of Government and directs
all its actions properly ... without it you consult in the
dark and execute blindfold you know not what to act,
what to fear, where to attack or where to defend.[1]

An espionage organization is a collector:
it collects raw information ... [that] gets
processed by a machinery in the system.[2]

The Secret Department of the Post Office, the precursor to Britain's GCHQ[3] and America's NSA,[4] was one of the administration's principal intelligence sources. The department was a core part of the government's espionage network and staffed by those deemed intellectually able and politically loyal. Its existence was revealed and reconfirmed in three parliamentary reports produced almost a century apart. The first in 1742 was a politically motivated enquiry into Robert Walpole's conduct during the last decade of his ministry and a fishing exercise searching for evidence of cor-

---

[1] Daniel Defoe, *A Dialogue Betwixt Whig and Tory, alias Williamite and Jacobite* (London, 1693), pp. xi-xii.

[2] Aldrich Ames (1941-), former Central Intelligence Agency counter-intelligence officer imprisoned in 1994 for espionage against the United States: http://nsarchive.gwu.edu/coldwar/interviews/episode-21/aldrich3.html.

[3] Government Communications Headquarters, Cheltenham, Gloucestershire.

[4] National Security Agency, Maryland; part of the US Department of Defence. An internal paper from the Central Intelligence Agency: *Counterintelligence in 1814 – A Historical Damage Assessment*, provides a useful perspective. Cf., https://www.cia.gov/library/readingroom/docs/DOC_0006183748.pdf, approved for release on 2 September 2014, accessed 30 October 2015.

ruption.[5] The second in 1844[6] was commissioned in the wake of the Mazzini scandal.[7] It focused on the legality of Post Office operations, on 'the state of the Law in respect to the detaining and opening of letters at the General Post Office and into the mode under which the authority given for such detaining and opening has been exercised', and covered the same ground as its predecessor. The third was undertaken in 1957 by the Privy Council and examined the basis on which the secretary of state could authorise the interception of private communications.

Each reached an identical set of conclusions: that the detention and opening of letters and parcels was permissible if under the warrant of the secretary of state; that the power to issue such warrants was itself legal; and that the legislation passed in the late seventeenth and early eighteenth centuries served to formalise pre-existing practice.[8]

It is a statement of the obvious that governments have always sought to intercept the communications of those considered a potential threat. The process evolved over time as interception, opening, and decoding and decryption techniques became more sophisticated. In Britain the process was handled by the Secret Department of the Post Office and managed by a head of section known as the 'Secret Man' or the 'Foreign Secretary of the Post

---

[5] *A Report from the Committee of Secrecy* (1742). At the time of the enquiry Walpole had been elevated to Earl of Orford.

[6] *Report from the Secret Committee on the Post Office* (London: House of Commons, 1844).

[7] Giuseppe Mazzini, the founder of the Young Italy movement which sought to unify Italy and end Austrian occupation, was living in exile in London. The Austrians requested that Mazzini be monitored and a warrant was issued by the secretary of state permitting the interception and opening of his mail. Mazzini suspected the intercept and test letters proved it. When a question in Parliament from Thomas Duncombe was answered with the response that 'it was not for the public good to pry or inquire' into the issue, the response led to uproar and committees of inquiry were established by the Lords and Commons respectively.

[8] *Report of the Committee of Privy Councillors appointed to inquire into the interception of communications*, (London: HMSO, 1957), esp. part 1, (9) and (39).

Office'. The intelligence supplemented and confirmed that obtained from diplomats and domestic and overseas agents, and on occasion supplanted it.

Established in the second half of the seventeenth century, the Secret Department was located within the warren of buildings that comprised the headquarters of the General Post Office on Lombard Street, close to the centre of the City of London. The division initially occupied three rooms, access to which was via a private entrance in Abchurch Lane guarded by a well-paid door keeper.[9] It was financed off-the-books from secret service monies controlled by the secretaries of state and excised from the *Declared Accounts of the Post Office*.[10] The agency was expanded over the first half of the eighteenth century in line with the demand for its output, and in the 1740s and 1750s the interception, opening, copying and decryption of correspondence was undertaken on an almost industrial scale.

Although based in the City of London and occupied mainly with London's postal services and those routed through the capital, the department also sourced intercepts via a network of postal clerks based across England, Wales, Scotland and Ireland. Other information was gathered through paid and informal agents overseas and at home. Sources included port officials who reported *inter alia* on ship movements and troop deployments, paid and informal agents, and post office staff across continental Europe who received regular bribes.[11]

Sensitive political and commercial material was often encoded or encrypted and a team of 'decipherers', experts in decoding and decryption, complemented the department's operation. Simple cyphers had been in use since at least the fourteenth century but were enhanced in the fifteenth

---

[9]   Kenneth Ellis, *The Post Office in the Eighteenth Century* (Oxford: OUP, 1958), p. 65.

[10]   Although several officials appeared in contemporary directories as Post Office employees their declared pay was a fraction of what they actually received and their job titles were designed to mislead.

[11]   In particular staff at the post offices at Celle and Nienburg who intercepted post between France and the Nordic countries.

by Leon Batista Alberti, 'the father of Western Cryptography'.[12] Alberti's methodology became widely known and by the following century was being applied across much of Europe. England was no exception and Francis Walsingham, Elizabeth I's spymaster, schooled his recruits in encryption and decryption. It was the interception and decoding of correspondence to and from Mary, Queen of Scots that would lead directly to her later execution.[13]

Building on Walsingham's foundations, England's intelligence capabilities advanced further in the seventeenth century as a function of the self-taught cryptanalysis of John Wallis, a Cambridge-educated natural scientist and mathematician.[14] Obliged to resign as a Fellow of Queens Cambridge following his marriage, Wallis was appointed to the Savilian chair of geometry at Oxford in 1649. He acted as a codebreaker on the parliamentary side in the English civil war and was the first of a series of Oxbridge-educated mathematicians and natural philosophers to hold what became a permanent government position: 'chief decipherer'.[15] Wallis's abilities made him indispensable and despite having served Cromwell he subsequently worked for each administration through to Queen Anne.[16] Wallis received in return a quarterly stipend of £25 and additional rewards by way of ecclesiastical and other offices. He was appointed secretary to the Westminster Assembly in 1644 and made rector of St Gabriel's Church in Fenchurch Street from

---

[12] He invented the polyalphabetic cipher. Cf., David Kahn, *The Codebreakers* (New York, NY: Macmillan, 1967).

[13] This was the Babington Plot in which Mary was deemed to have 'sanctioned' a conspiracy to assassinate Queen Elizabeth.

[14] Cf., Domenico Bertoloni Meli, 'Wallis, John (1616-1703)', *ODNB*, online edn, May 2007, accessed 11 March 2015.

[15] Cf., http://wallis.clp.ox.ac.uk/about_wallis, accessed 1 August 2016. He was also a founder member of the Royal Society, contributing more than sixty papers

[16] A collection of letters deciphered by Wallis was published by John Davys in *Essay on the Art of Decyphering* (London, 1737).

1645 until 1647, afterwards receiving the more remunerative living of St Martin's Church in Ironmonger Lane.[17]

Information from decoded mail intercepts supplemented the regular communications between the offices of the secretaries of state and Britain's ambassadors and envoys stationed abroad whose correspondence almost always included intelligence material. This was arguably their principal role: 'all Sovereign Princes & States ought like Cunning Gamesters to use all Endeavours ... to know what Cards are in their neighbours hands, that so they may play their own to the best advantage'.[18] Other reports, sometimes accurate but more often exaggerated or fabricated, were supplied by informers and paid agents. Propaganda and counter-intelligence, including articles in the *London Gazette*, were deployed by the government alongside. The basic foundations of the secret state were in place by the end of the seventeenth century, many laid by Sir Joseph Williamson, secretary of state for the Northern Department from 1674-79.[19]

Other countries operated on a similar basis. In France, decryption and encoding relied on a series of talented mathematicians from François Viète[20] in the sixteenth century to Antoine Rossignol[21] and his son and grandson, Bonaventure Rossignol and Antoine-Bonaventure Rossignol, in the eighteenth. The Rossignol family developed the concept of the *Cabinet Noir* or Black Chamber, which became a synonym for intercepting and reading and

---

[17] Wallis educated his grandson, William Blencowe, in cryptography, and Blencowe succeeded Wallis as chief decipherer in 1703.

[18] BL Add. Mss 47133, ff. 8-13.

[19] Joseph Williamson (1633-1701). Cf., Alan Marshall, *Intelligence and Espionage in the Reign of Charles II, 1660-1685* (Cambridge: CUP, 1994), and Marshall, 'Williamson, Sir Joseph (1633-1701)', *ODNB* (Oxford: OUP, 2004; online edn, Jan 2008).

[20] François Viète (1540-1603).

[21] Antoine Rossignol (1600-1682). The Rossignols created the virtually unbreakable 'Great Cipher' which used 578 numbers to encode syllables. It included blank numbers as traps for those seeking to decrypt the code.

decoding targeted correspondence. The Low Countries' Black Chamber concentrated predominantly on French and Bavarian mail.[22] That in Hanover also focused on the French, often in co-operation with the Dutch and British.[23] And Black Chambers in Spain[24] and Austria[25] had been active since the sixteenth century.

The riots that followed the coronation of George I and the abortive Jacobite Rising of 1715 raised a justifiable fear within government of further insurrection and led almost inexorably to an increase in demand for a better and broader intelligence product. Mail intercepts were expanded, specialist letter-openers recruited, and what had been a relatively limited decoding and decryption capability was replaced within a decade by several decryption experts and their assistants. They became known collectively as the Deciphering Branch of the Secret Department.

Like the Secret Department, the Deciphering Branch was funded by the secretaries of state from crown monies, in this case derived notionally from Post Office revenues.[26] An annual grant of £6,000 was increased to more than £8,000 and supplemented by one-off payments linked to specific projects. The circuitous funding arrangements were not published in the public accounts which had the advantage of allowing the department to operate outside of parliamentary and foreign scrutiny. Its activities were hidden until 1722, and then disclosed only obliquely when its senior members were

---

[22] Karl Maria Michael de Leeuw, Jan Bergstra (eds), *The History of Information Security* (Amsterdam, NL: Elsevier, 2007), pp. 361-4.

[23] Ibid., pp. 12, 12, 343, 371-2.

[24] Ibid., p. 308.

[25] Ibid., pp. 328-32.

[26] NA HD 3/17 Papers Concerning the Secret Office. Also NA PRO 30/8/83, Chatham Papers, Part 1: Miscellaneous papers - Parliamentary, Legal, Post Office.

called to give evidence before the House of Lords and House of Commons in connection with the Jacobite conspiracy involving Francis Atterbury.[27]

The procedures, codes and regulations that covered mail interception and detention had been laid out in the 1710 Post Office (Revenues) Act.[28] This stated that 'no person or persons shall presume wittingly, willingly, or knowingly, to open, detain or delay, or cause, procure, permit or suffer to be opened, detained or delayed, any letter or letters, packet or packets, after the same is or shall be delivered in the General or other Post Office'. There was however an exception to this over-riding obligation where a warrant under the hand of one of the secretaries of state had been issued.[29] It was an exemption that gave the administration a virtual carte blanche.

Warrants to authorise mail intercepts dated back to 1660, the year the Post Office had been established by Charles II. They were considered one of the 'best means to discover and prevent any dangerous and wicked designs',[30] but although there was a legal requirement for a warrant to be issued, they could be and were issued *ex post*, especially where mail had raised the suspicions of Post Office staff. Podhurst cites several examples, including that of John Barbutt, then secretary of the Post Office, writing proactively to John Wace, Delafaye's brother-in-law,[31] requesting 'a new warrant for certain

---

[27] For example, 1 May 1723. Cf., *Journal of the House of Lords: volume 22, 1722-1726* (London: HMSO, 1767-1830), p. 173.

[28] The Post Office (Revenues) Act 1710: 9 Anne c 11. The Act was implemented the following year.

[29] Ibid, clause XLI.

[30] *Report of the Committee of Privy Councillors appointed to inquire into the interception of communications*, part 1, (15).

[31] As noted, Delafaye had secured Wace an entry level position in the Northern Department in 1711. Wace was promoted to chief clerk in 1717 and later served as acting under-secretary.

assignees'.[32] Fritz references similar cases,[33] including warrants issued by the secretary of state following specific requests by the Secret Department, most frequently by its head, the Foreign Secretary, John Lefebure.

JOHN LEFEBURE

John Lefebure (*d*.1752), an anglicisation of the French 'Jean Le Fevre', joined the Post Office as a clerk in 1715; he was promoted to succeed William Brocket as head of the Secret Department three years later.[34] Lefebure's nominal position in the Post Office administration was known. He appears in Chamberlayne's *Magnae Britaniae Notia*[35] and Miège's *The Present State of Great Britain*, each of which give his title as 'foreign secretary' and record a salary of £50 per annum.[36] But the designation, suggestive of a mid-level clerical role, and the publicly-stated pay grade which would substantiate

---

[32] Suzanne Joy Podhurst, *The Scriblerians Uncensored: libel, encryption and the making of copyright in eighteenth-century Britain and Ireland* (PhD Dissertation: Princeton University, 2012), p. 117, fn. 87.

[33] Paul S. Fritz, 'The Anti-Jacobite Intelligence System of the English Ministers, 1715-1745', *Historical Journal*, 16.2 (1973), 265-89; also Fritz, *The English Ministers and Jacobitism between the Rebellions of 1715 and 1745* (Toronto: University of Toronto Press, 1975), p. 52.

[34] Ellis, *The Post Office in the Eighteenth Century*, pp. 66-7. Brocket had himself succeeded Sir Samuel Morland (1625-1695), the inventor, diplomat and sometime tutor to Samuel Pepys. Cf., Alan Marshall, 'Morland, Sir Samuel, first baronet (1625-1695)', *ODNB*, online edn, Jan 2008, accessed 14 April 2016.

[35] John Chamberlayne, *Magnae Britaniae Notitia Or the Present State of Great Britain* (London, 1725): 'A General List or Catalogue of all the Offices and Officers employed in the several branches of his Majesty's Government'.

[36] Guy Miege, *The Present State of Great Britain and Ireland in Three Parts* (London: Bettesworth et al, 1731), part I, p. 131; John Mottley, *A survey of the cities of London and Westminster, borough of Southwark, and parts adjacent* (London: J. Read, 1733-5), book 2, p. 430.

such a pedestrian position, were designed to understate the importance of his office.

Evidence to the Committee of Secrecy published in 1742 indicates that Lefebure's actual remuneration was around £800 per annum, sixteen times higher than that given by Chamberlayne and Miège. It placed Lefebure at the same level as a senior under-secretary and well within the upper decile of London Society. It is thus unsurprising that his name appears in the lists of those insured by the *Amicable Contributor for Insuring Houses against loss by Fire* (1714),[37] a preserve of the affluent, and that he was one of the many upper middling subscribers to the (later failed) Charitable Corporation.[38] Lefebure also features in the Westminster Rate Books, where his houses in St Anne's parish in King Street and then Wardour Street had a deemed rateable value of over £20.[39]

In common with Delafaye to whom he reported, Lefebure was a Huguenot and a freemason. He is recorded as 'Le Favre' in the member-ship list of the King's Head lodge in Pall Mall alongside other Huguenots including Edward Lambert, John Regnier, Henry Recin, John Milxan and Messrs Richard and Guidon.[40] The same names appear in the congregations of the nearby churches of Le Carré and St James's,[41] and at Glass House

---

[37] *A list of the names of the members of the Amicable Contributor for insuring houses against loss by fire, at Angel-Court on Snow-Hill, September 29, 1714* (Andover: Gale ECCO, 2010), reprint.

[38] *London Evening Post*, 23 - 26 October 1731.

[39] Westminster Ratebooks: Property Values of Westminster Electors, 1634-1900; Wardour Street, £21, 1 January - 31 December 1749.

[40] Cf., William J. Songhurst (ed.), *Minutes of the Grand Lodge of Freemasons of England, 1723-1739* (London: Quatuor Coronati Lodge, No. 2076, 1913), p. 34; published as *QCA, Masonic Reprints, Vol. X*.

[41] William & Susan Minet (eds.), *Registres des Eglises de la Chapelle Royale de Saint James, 1700-1756, et de Swallow Street, 1690-1756* (London: Huguenot Society, 1924), p. 6.

Street and Leicester Fields,[42] where the church register chronicles Charlotte Lefebure's wedding to Jean Yve. One of the two 'témoin' or witnesses was Isaac Coustos, the father of John Coustos, a member of the French Lodge in nearby St Albans Street and another government spy.[43] He was not alone; other members of that lodge also acted formally or informally as agents, including Vincent La Chapelle and John Laroche.

Lefebure remained a central figure in the Secret Department for more than three decades. An émigré whose family had found sanctuary in England, he was supportive of the Hanoverian *status quo*, unstinting in outing potential Jacobites and proactive in requesting warrants to detain and open suspect letters.[44] It was on Lefebure's watch that the 1717 and 1719 invasion plans were uncovered, as was the Atterbury Plot.

Monod[45] and Cruickshanks[46] have argued that Lefebure was less a Hanoverian loyalist than, in Monod's words, a 'highly placed Stuart agent'. Monod references *English Ministers and Jacobitism* and 'The Anti-Jacobite Intelligence System of the English Ministers, 1715-1745',[47] although in neither does Fritz claim that Lefebure was a Jacobite or Stuart spy. However Monod also points to *Political Untouchables*, where Lefebure is pictured as 'a secret Jacobite … whose "zeal, fidelity and services" were said to be well known to James and Charles Edward'.

---

[42]   William & Susan Minet (eds.), *Registers of the Churches of The Tabernacle Glasshouse Street and Leicester Fields, London 1688-1783* (London: Huguenot Society, 1926).

[43]   William & Susan Minet (eds.), *Registers of the Churches of The Tabernacle Glasshouse Street and Leicester Fields*, p. 129, *1 March 1723*.

[44]   Cf., 'Fritz, 'The Anti-Jacobite Intelligence System of the English Ministers, 1715-1745'.

[45]   Paul Monod, *Jacobitism and the English People, 1688-1788*, p. 102.

[46]   Eveline Cruickshanks, *Political Untouchables: The Tories and the '45* (New York, NY: Holmes and Meier, 1979). Cf., also the review of Hugh Douglas' *Jacobite Spy Wars: Moles, Rogues and Treachery* by Eveline Cruickshanks in *Albion*, 32.4 (2000), 648-9.

[47]   Ibid., fn. 8.

Cruickshanks argues cogently that Lefebure's letters to Sempill,[48] a Jacobite agent, prove that Lefebure deliberately suppressed damaging letters, disclosed which correspondence was being opened, and acted as a conduit for Jacobite despatches from the 1740s onward.[49] Several examples are cited including an apparently conclusive proof: a letter from Lefebure to Sempill that gives details of the disposition of regular English troops at home, in Ireland and in Flanders.[50]

Cruickshanks' evidence is garnered principally from the French Foreign Office archives and the Stuart manuscript collection at Windsor, and is compelling. But it can be challenged. The most obvious ground is that the material relates to the 1740s and Lefebure's prior conduct, together with the absence of any earlier incriminating material, suggests that regardless of what is alleged to have occurred after 1740, it is improbable that Lefebure was either a closet Tory or a Jacobite sympathiser during the first twenty-five years of his service within the Secret Department. But regardless of this, if Lefebure had experienced a political epiphany and become a 'secret Jacobite', there are at least three possible explanations.

First, Lefebure's political stance may have changed. If so, it would have mirrored the growing and increasingly successful opposition to Walpole in Parliament and in the country more broadly that would see him leave office and become the subject of a political witch hunt. Second, it is feasible that in the 1740s Lefebure considered that a Jacobite invasion would

---

[48] Francis Sempill (*d.*1748), a Jacobite agent. His father, Robert, had been created a Jacobite peer in 1712 by the exiled James Stuart.

[49] Cruickshanks, *Political Untouchables*, p. 47. The same sentiment is expressed in Romney Sedgwick, *The House of Commons 1715-1754* (London, HMSO, 1970), preface, p. ix. But cf., for example, Linda Colley, *In Defiance of Oligarchy: the Tory Party 1714-1760* (Cambridge: CUP, 1982) and Andrew Hanham, '"So Few Facts": Jacobites, Tories and the Pretender', *Parliamentary History*, 19 (2000), 233-57, for opposing views.

[50] Cruickshanks, *Political Untouchables*, p. 54: French Foreign Office List AEM & D. Ang. 86f. 340. Also p. 82, quoting Stuart MSS 268/5; 269/109.

be successful and may have wished to protect his position in government. This option potentially has substance: he was exceptionally well-placed to assess the relevant military and political facts.[51] Third, despite the apparent evidence, Lefebure's political loyalties were unaltered and rather than a convert to Jacobitism he was instead engaged in counter-intelligence. In short, Lefebure's communications with his Jacobite handlers were those of a double agent.[52]

Cruickshanks unknowingly validates the last argument with her observation that Lefebure in writing to France and warning that Jacobite correspondence was subject to interception and decryption, advised the Pretender's agents in England to cease communications. The consequent absence of reliable intelligence - 'not knowing what was happening in England', caused severe delays to the implementation of Jacobite plans[53] and is acknowledged to have had 'bad consequences'.[54] In the same vein, Cruickshanks's comment that 'official sources in England show that a government spy reported that Lefebure had been seeing Jacobites, *but this was not followed up by Newcastle*',[55] can be read as an indication that officials at the Northern Department, including Newcastle, were aware of the ruse.[56]

Monod has suggested privately a fourth option: that Lefebure was not a Jacobite agent *per se* nor had his political views necessarily altered, but he may have been concerned at the decline in Walpole's authority and

---

[51] Bernard Porter, *Plots and Paranoia: A History of Political Espionage in Britain 1790-1988* (Abingdon: Rourtledge, 2016), pp. 20-1.

[52] Langford accuses Lefebure of acting with 'impartial, patriotic cynicism'. Cf., Paul Langford, *A Polite and Commercial People: England, 1727-1783* (Oxford: OUP, 1998), p. 408.

[53] Ibid., p. 62. Quotes French Foreign Office List AEM & D. Ang. 77ff. 129-31, 140-1, 194; 83ff. 176-7, 179-80; Ang. 86f. 115.

[54] Ibid., p. 76.

[55] My italics.

[56] Ibid., p. 91. My italics. Key officials at the Northern Department included John Couraud and Andrew Stone, both acolytes of Delafaye.

approaching the Jacobites would have gained him friends and allies among those who were seeking to harry Walpole from office. By doing so, Lefebure would have been seeking to pre-empt any threat to his position and retain financial and political security.

Lefebure's support for successive Whig administrations and his working relationship with Delafaye and Wace, among other colleagues, also militates against him having been a Jacobite agent. He was part of a Huguenot community that had dedicated itself to supporting the Hanoverian succession for decades and his membership of a French lodge in London can be regarded as the mark of a loyalist. But perhaps one of the strongest arguments against Lefebure being a Jacobite is that had he been so the nature of his position was such that history might well have played out differently. Lefebure was at the core of Britain's secret service for four decades. Anecdotally at least, the failure of Jacobite intrigue to restore the Stuarts to the throne despite years of conspiracy might be regarded as the ultimate proof of Lefebure's loyalty to the administration and to the Hanoverians.

Janetta Guite's unpublished research corroborates the use of counter-intelligence by the Post Office.[57] Guite quotes a 1732 report from Daniel O'Brien, a Jacobite agent in Paris, which discloses that a key source of his intelligence was 'a secretary in the Post Office who is in all the secrets of the government and who writes to him about Waldegrave's dispatches'.[58] But the 'faithful and disinterested' source described by O'Brien was not a political fellow traveller. O'Brien later acknowledged that he had been duped and that 'if anyone shall think fit to charge [his source] with working for Walpole I shall not take it upon me to defend him'.[59] O'Brien's informant was a British double agent who 'had begun by producing genuine information about the secret negotiation at Vienna, so they might now hope to be

---

[57] Janetta Inglis Keith Guite, 'The Jacobite Cause, 1730-1740: The International Dimension', PhD thesis (Hamilton, Ont.: McMaster University, 1987).

[58] Ibid., p. 162.

[59] Ibid., pp. 163-4, 183, fns. 116-20.

believed when it suited them to pass off as ascertained fact a palpable misinterpretation of British policy'.[60]

This is a classic example of disinformation and O'Brien's assessment was probably accurate. Only a handful of people were involved in the Secret Department and Deciphering Branch and those with access to its product usually numbered less than thirty. It is reasonable to consider that a sustained leak would have been detectable with relative ease. O'Brien's comment that his source 'thinks to prevail upon my wants by offering me advantages from the benefit he might make of some material intelligence in the stocks, which you are sensible he has often proposed to me' is also significant.[61] The Secret Department had access to commercially-sensitive material[62] as well as political and military data, and exploitation of insider information for personal gain may have been viewed as a perk of the job. Such a perspective would fit comfortably within an eighteenth-century moral mould;[63] indeed, insider trading was only declared illegal in Britain the late twentieth century.

JOHN BARBUTT

Lefebure's colleagues at the Post Office included several other freemasons, perhaps most notably John Barbutt and John Jesse. John David Barbutt (1709-17..?), served as secretary to the Post Office and the postmasters general from 1738 to 1742. He had been born in Königsberg, Prussia,[64] was

---

[60] Ibid., p. 169.

[61] Ibid., p. 163.

[62] Cf., John Harris, *Industrial Espionage and Technological Transfer: Britain and France in the Eighteenth Century* (Aldershot: Ashgate, 1997).

[63] Cf., *Foundations*, pp. 54-5.

[64] Margrit Schulte Beerbühl, *Deutsche Kaufleute in London: Welthandel und Einbürgerung (1660-1818)* (London: German Historical Institute, 2007), p. 425: '1753, 17. April - BARBUTT, John David, Esq. - b. Konigsberg'.

admitted as a scholar to Merchant Taylors' school[65] and studied law at the Middle Temple.[66] He appears in the membership list of the Prince Eugene's Head Coffeehouse in 1732, when he would have been twenty-three,[67] and is listed in the register of the French church of Savoye de Spring Gardens et des Grecs.

From the mid-1730s Barbutt held office as a government 'examiner', ascertaining the value of securities placed in escrow to cover debts owed to the government.[68] He may also have been the Barbutt to whom Horatio Walpole gifted 'a place worth about £400 per annum … as Cofferer [a treasurer] to his Majesty' in October 1732.[69] Were this to have been so, Delafaye is likely to have been involved.

Barbutt was appointed secretary to the Post Office in or around September 1738[70] and it is from this date that his name appears at the foot of newspaper announcements 'on behalf of the Postmaster General'.[71] His replacement as 'examiner' was announced two months later: 'Owen McSwiny, examiner of the sufficiency of officers' securities … *loco* John David Barbutt, to be superseded'.[72] Confirmation of Barbutt's value to the administration

---

[65] Charles John Robinson, *A Register of the Scholars Admitted Into Merchant Taylor's School London* (London, 1883).

[66] Cf., Herbert Arthur Charlie Sturgess, *Register of Admissions to the Honourable Society of the Middle Temple, from the Fifteenth Century to the Year 1944* (London, 1949), p. 327.

[67] Written as 'Barby'.

[68] William A. Shaw (ed), *Calendar of Treasury Books and Papers, volume 3, 1735-1738* (London: HMSO, 1900), pp. 282-91, *1 July 1736*.

[69] *London Evening Post*, 28 - 31 October 1732. Also *Daily Journal*, 30 October 1732 and elsewhere.

[70] The signatory on a Post Office communication in October 1738 is given as 'W. Barbutt', but this is a misprint.

[71] For example, *London Daily Post and General Advertiser*, 21 September 1738.

[72] William A. Shaw (ed), *Calendar of Treasury Books and Papers, volume 3, 1735-1738* (London: HMSO, 1900), pp. 623-34, 4 November 1738.

is suggested by his preferment in 1741 to become Deputy Lieutenant at the Tower of London.[73]

Barbutt's testimony the following year before the secret committee investigating the Post Office demonstrates his knowledge of the Secret Department and its operations, and of the 'very troublesome' position held by Lefebure, the foreign secretary.[74] As secretary, Barbutt was responsible for the disposition of the departmental overheads, including the payment of salaries and expenses. Following Walpole's fall from political grace and in the absence of evidence that would hold him to account, Barbutt was made a scapegoat, giving the committee and Parliament a stand-in victim:

> It farther appears to your Committee that, besides the sum of £1,453,400 6s 3d already mentioned, there has been paid, in the 10 years ... the sum of £45,675, without account, to the Society or the Post-office for the time being ... by virtue of a warrant from the Treasury; and this for a service formerly inconsiderable. Your Committee find, by papers laid before them, that the first payment of this kind was in the year 1718, and amounted to £446 2s, and the succeeding payments for some years were about £750 per annum; from whence it has gradually increased to £4,700, the present annual allowance ... the present secretary, John David Barbutt, Esq., being examined as to this allowance, said 'that the greatest part of this money is for defraying the expense of ... inspecting foreign correspondence; that he cannot say as to the first establishment of this office, having been but three years and a half in the Post-office; but he apprehends there was always an office of this kind, and that it was defrayed formerly by the Secretaries of State.'

Barbutt suffered considerably as a result of the committee's report. He was criticised for receiving and using funds without a warrant and removed as

---

[73] John Chamberlayne, *Magnae Britanniae Notitia* (1741).

[74] *A Further Report from the Committee of Secrecy* (1742), p. 132.

secretary in July 1742 when the committee's findings were completed. To add to his discomfort, he was lampooned in the press, most notably in the anti-masonic *Epistle from Dick Poney*,[75] where he appears as 'Colonel Ding-Dong of the P[os]t O[ffic]e'. Unemployed and out of favour, Barbutt was forced into bankruptcy. A memorandum from the Treasury dated 15 July notes a letter 'written to the Postmasters for a state of Mr Barbutt's accounts and how far his misfortunes may affect the revenue';[76] and on 27 July the Treasury recorded 'a report read from the Postmasters General of the 23rd instant, relating to the failure of Mr. Barbutt'.[77]

Barbutt was nonetheless protected (in part) by his former patrons. A letter to Andrew Stone, Delafaye's successor as Newcastle's under-secretary and Keeper of the State Papers, enclosed documents 'on which he [Barbutt] hopes Newcastle's support may be subscribed before he proceeds to apply to other ministers and officers of state'.[78] Barbutt and Stone knew each other and had corresponded officially when Barbutt had been secretary. Barbutt's status recovered. His address in the 1749 Poll Books in Carteret Street, Westminster, south of St James's Park near Queen Anne's Gate, was relatively exclusive.[79] But a better indication of his return to favour is the Bill to confirm his naturalisation which was introduced in the House of Lords on March 1753 and passed within a week. Naturalisation by private act of Parliament was expensive, especially where progress was so rapid.

> The Earl of Warwick likewise reported from the Lords Committees to whom the Bill, entitled, "An Act for naturalizing of John David Barbutt

---

[75] *An Epistle from Dick Poney, esq: Grand-master of the Right Black-guard Society of Scald-miserable-masons* (London, 1742).

[76] William A. Shaw (ed), *Calendar of Treasury Books and Papers, volume 5, 1742-1745* (London: HMSO, 1900), pp. 51-62.

[77] Ibid.

[78] SP 36/72/192.

[79] *Westminster Pollbooks: Votes in Westminster Elections, 1749-1820, 1 January - 31 December 1749.*

and Fortunatus Planta," was committed: "That they had considered the said Bill, and examined the Allegations thereof, which were found to be true; and that the Committee had gone through the Bill, and directed him to report the same to the House, without any Amendment."[80]

One of Barbutt's fellow lodge members was his brother-in-law, John Coustos, whose release from prison in Lisbon, to which he had been sentenced by the Portuguese Inquisition, Barbutt helped to secure in 1744.[81] Members of the lodge included several who were or had been members of the Rainbow Coffee House, York Buildings:[82] Lewis Mercy, the master of the lodge;[83] Thomas Lance and Noel Protin, the wardens;[84] and Vincent La Chapelle, John Coustos and William St. Jean. Wonnacott has suggested that another member, 'Mr Delahaye', was Francis Delahaye, also from the Rainbow Coffee House.[85] This may be correct, but there is evidence that points to the possibility that 'Delahaye' was 'Delafaye'.

Not only is Delafaye's name occasionally misspelled in government records, one example of which refers to 'Delahaye' as Jamaica's London

---

[80] *Journal of the House of Lords volume 28, 1753-1756* (London: HMSO, 1767-1830), pp. 56-70, 30 March 1753.

[81] John Coustos, *The Sufferings of John Coustos ... in the Inquisition at Lisbon* (London: Coustos, 1746), pp. 69-70.

[82] The lodge at the Rainbow Coffee House (subsequently named 'Britannic Lodge') was constituted in 1730 and remained at the Rainbow Coffee House until 1739.

[83] Lewis Mercy (*c*.1695-*c*.1750), a highly-regarded musician and composer.

[84] Thomas Lanse [also 'Lance' or 'Launce'] may have been the 'Frère de Lansa' who translated *The Entered Apprentice's Song* and *The Master's Song* into French for inclusion in Louis-François de La Tierce's *Histoire des Francs Maçons* (1742). Lanse also published a collection of masonic songs in French: *Chansons Originaires de Francs Macons* (The Hague, 1747). Noel Protin, the junior warden, was a peruke (wig) maker.

[85] W. Wonnacott, 'The Rite of Seven Degrees in London', *AQC*, 39 (1928), 64-7.

agent,[86] but the misspelling was commonplace elsewhere, even within the same correspondence:

> Mr *Delafaye* at Sheerness has complained [that] Mr Wigmore of Chatham has obtained certificates from the Captains of several Guardships, lately or yet to be paid off, for the time they lay within his Ordinary and also for the time they were at Sheerness within Mr *Delahaye's* Ordinary.[87]

Delafaye knew Mercy, 'a celebrated performer on the flûte à bec[88] and an excellent composer for that instrument', whose solos were 'ranked among the best compositions for that instrument extant';[89] he had penned a musical score to accompany Delafaye's *Fellow-Craft's Song*. A copy was written on the fly-leaf of the 1723 *Constitutions* presented to Mercy by James Anderson and inscribed *Viro Generoso Ludovico Mercy hunc Librum dicat Eiusdem Author Jacobus Anderson*.[90] Mercy's patrons also included the Duke of Chandos,[91] whose scientific factotum was Desaguliers.

---

[86]   Cecil Headlam and Arthur Percival Newton (eds), *Calendar of State Papers Colonial, America and West Indies, volume 36, 1728-1729* (London: HMSO, 1937), pp. 605-7. Cf., also Derbyshire Record Office, D3155/C406: Whitehall. Ch. Delahaye [to Mr Secretary Cary], encloses letter from the Lords Commissioners of the Admiralty to the Duke of Newcastle.

[87]   National Maritime Museum: The Caird Library, Manuscripts Section: ADM 354/154/128. My italics. Thomas Delafaye was Chaplain to the ships in Ordinary. He died at Canterbury on 25 July 1772.

[88]   A small recorder, literally, a 'beaked flute'.

[89]   John Hawkins, *General History of the Science and Practice of Music* (London: Payne, 1776), p. 364-5. Cf. also *Newsletter of The American Handel Society*, XXVIII.3 (2013), 2.

[90]   UGLE, Library & Museum of Freemasonry: BE 94 GRA, item ID L2409. The inscription is on the half-title page. The score referred to in Wonnacott 'The Rite of Seven Degrees in London' is no longer extant.

[91]   Cf., Susan Jenkins, *The Patronage and Collecting of James Brydges, 1st Duke of Chandos (1674-1744)* (Farnham: Ashgate Publishing, 2007). Chandos was associated with a number of leading artists, architects, scientists, poets and composers including Jean Theophilus Desaguliers, Godfrey Kneller, William Talman, Sir John Vanbrugh, Sir James Thornhill, John Gay and George Frederick Handel.

John La Roche [also Laroche] (*c.*1700-1752), a Whig MP and trustee of the Georgia colony, can also be linked to Delafaye.[92] La Roche had studied at Queens Cambridge, matriculating in 1717. He was afterwards admitted to the Middle Temple and became legal adviser and steward to the Robartes family, the Earls of Radnor,[93] who owned large estates near Bodmin in Cornwall. The connection explains how La Roche became MP for Bodmin in 1727. He sat for twenty-five years and although he spoke on no more than a handful of occasions, La Roche voted as a loyal Whig until his death.[94]

Sedgwick describes La Roche as a merchant rather than a lawyer (he founded a trading business in Bristol),[95] but regardless of the source of his wealth it was sufficient to permit the purchase of a townhouse in King Street, St James's,[96] and a country estate in Surrey at Englefield Green, east of Windsor Great Park.[97] La Roche was at the core of the Whig establishment: an 'exempt' or captain in the Yeoman of the Guard;[98] a trustee for Georgia; and a senior magistrate alongside other prominent freemasons

[92] Cf., Sedgwick, *The History of Parliament: the House of Commons 1715-1754.*

[93] Henry Robartes, the 3rd Earl of Radnor, a bachelor, bequeathed La Roche £1,000 in 1741; and John Robartes, the 4th Earl, Henry Robartes' cousin, left an estate in Cornwall to La Roche's children.

[94] Sedgwick (ed), *The History of Parliament: the House of Commons 1715-1754.*

[95] Geraldine Meroney, 'The London Entrepôt Merchants and the Georgia Colony', *William and Mary Quarterly*, 25.2 (1968), 230-44, esp. 235.

[96] Westminster Pollbooks: Votes in Westminster Elections, 1749-1820, 1 January - 31 December 1749.

[97] Sedgwick, *The History of Parliament.*

[98] *Weekly Journal or British Gazetteer*, 10 July 1725.

including George Carpenter,[99] to whom he was also connected through his wife. La Roche's mother-in-law, Eleanor Garnier, was the sister of 1ˢᵗ Baron Carpenter of Killaghy, Carpenter's father.[100]

Margaret Jacob notes that 'M. Laroche, a French Huguenot and member of the lodge at Prince Eugene's Head coffee house in St Alban's Street [sic] spied on the Jacobites in Paris and reported back directly to Walpole'.[101] The statement is probably correct but the relevant correspondence at Cambridge is more equivocal.[102] The letters are signed 'Laroche' with no indication of forename.[103]

---

[99] La Roche was in addition one of several worthies who oversaw the construction of the New Westminster Bridge from 1738 until 1750, and the reconstruction of Brentford Bridge from 1740 to 1742. Charles Labelye, Desaguliers' protégé and a member of Solomon's Temple, among other lodges, was chief engineer to both projects. La Roche was also a member of the Court of Assistants of the Royal African Company, where James Oglethorpe was among his co-directors, and of the Board of the Chelsea Waterworks Company. Cf., *Read's Weekly Journal Or British Gazetteer*, 3 April 1736; *Order concerning the rebuilding of Brentford Bridge & receiving proposals for the same and appointing a Committee for the Bridges*: General Orders of the Court, Middlesex Quarter Sessions, 13 September 1739; *London Evening Post*, 20 - 22 January 1732 et al; and *Fog's Weekly Journal*, 8 April 1732.

[100] Arthur Edmund Garnier, *The Chronicle of the Garniers of Hampshire, 1530-1900* (Norwich & London: Jarrold & Sons, 1900). George, 1ˢᵗ Baron Killaghy (1657-1732), had been appointed to command British forces in northern England against the Jacobites in 1715. He was made commander-in-chief in Scotland in 1716 and elected MP for Whitchurch (1715-22) and then Westminster (1722-27). He may have influenced Garnier's appointment as Apothecary to the Army.

[101] Margaret Jacobs, *The Radical Enlightenment*, p. 101.

[102] CUL: Cholmondeley (Houghton) Correspondence, 1, 1178, 29 October 1724; 1371, 19 October 1726; 1454, 26 July 1727; 1864, 4 June 1731.

[103] A third but more remote possibility is that Walpole's agent 'Laroche' was another person entirely or a nom de plume. Laroche was certainly not the M. Laroche who was steward to the Duke of Newcastle - *The Weekly Journal or British Gazetteer* reported his death on 8 April 1721. It is also improbable that he was the man of that name who served as valet to Madame de Luxembourg.

EXPANSION

The Secret Department expanded in the early 1720s with the recruitment of Peter Thouvois[104] and Robert Clarke, each of whom reported to Lefebure. Both men appear in the parliamentary journals in 1722 and 1723 when they gave individual and joint depositions with Lefebure in connection with George Kelly's prosecution.[105] Described as 'gentlemen ... employed to copy certain letters ... opened at the General Post Office' which are 'transmitted to the Secretaries of State', their formal depositions were given before Delafaye. Thouvois and Clarke are recorded as 'clerks', but this understates their standing. Each received an annual salary of £300, vastly higher than the £50 earned by those with analogous titles in other government departments.

The number of senior staff in the Secret Department rose to five in the 1730s with additional recruits joining in the 1740s. John Ernest Bode, the most senior of the new entrants, had previously been employed by the Hanoverian secret service as chief clerk.[106] He worked alongside Peter Hemett, a member of the lodge at the Bedford Head in Covent Garden.[107]

---

[104] Peter Thouvois [also Thouveis] (*d.*1759), 'a gentleman of Highgate, Middlesex'. His Will was proved at Canterbury 23 March 1759.

[105] 'An Act to inflict Pains and Penalties on George Kelly, alias Johnson', 1 May 1723. For example, 24 August 1722 and 1 January 1723. Cf., *Reports from Committees of the House of Commons Miscellaneous Subjects 1715-1735* (London: HMSO, 1803), vol. 1, pp. 271 & 304. Cf., also, *Journal of the House of Lords: volume 22, 1722-1726* (London: HMSO, 1767-1830), 22 April 1723, 1 May 1723, and 28 January 1725.

[106] 6 November, Whitehall, Treasury Chambers: 'Mr. Chancellor of the Exchequer, Sir Geo. Oxenden, Mr. Clayton, Sir Wm. Yonge. The £4,000 per annum payable to the hands of the secretary to the postmaster general by the Receivers General of that revenue is to be enlarged £300 per annum more from Michaelmas, 1732, in favour of J. Ernest Bode.' From *Calendar of Treasury Books and Papers, volume 2, 1731-1734* (London: HMSO, 1898). Bode joined in 1732.

[107] Grand Lodge *Minutes*, p. 27. A Peter Hemett had been naturalised in 1704. Cf., *Journals of the House of Commons* (London, 1803), volume 14, p. 519.

Both were experts in opening and resealing letters without detection and each received a base salary of £300.[108] Bode subsequently recruited four family members to assist him: two brothers and two sons. Their training, termed 'educating his sons to the business', was part-financed by Newcastle who provided an annual grant of £100 for the purpose.[109]

Aside from the native Hanoverians, the Secret Department's Huguenot connections are obvious. 'Thouvois' and 'Hemet' feature in the registers of several of London's French churches: Hemet at St Martin Orgars, Rider Court and the Savoy; and Thouvois at the Artillery, Spitalfields.[110] The aggregate number of Huguenots working in the offices of the secretaries of state and the foreign service was considerable.[111] In addition to Lefebure, Thouvois and Hemet, examples include Lord Carteret's agent, John Anthony Balaguier, later deputy secretary of St Christopher and then secretary of Jamaica;[112] Anthony Corbière, a senior decipherer; and John Couraud, a senior clerk at the Southern Department and Delafaye's replacement in the pivotal position of secretary to the Lords Justices.[113] One rung beneath were

---

[108] BL Add MSS 32731, ff. 7-11.

[109] NA HD 3/17: Papers Concerning the Secret Office; and NA PRO 30/8/83, Chatham Papers Part 1. Also see Fritz, *The English Ministers and Jacobitism between the Rebellions of 1715 and 1745*, p. 110.

[110] Susan & William Minet, *Register of the Church of Rider Court, London, 1700-1738* (London, 1927); *Register of the Church of St Martin Orgars with its History and that of Swallow Street,* (London, 1935); and *Registres des Eglises de la Savoye de Spring Gardens et des Grecs 1684-1900* (London, 1922). All published by the Huguenot Society.

[111] Sainty, 'A Huguenot civil servant: the career of Charles Delafaye, 1677-1762', pp. 398-9.

[112] *Calendar of State Papers Colonial, America and West Indies, volume 35, 1726-1727*; *Calendar of State Papers Colonial, America and West Indies, volume 36, 1728-1729*; *Calendar of State Papers Colonial, America and West Indies, volume 39, 1732*; *Calendar of State Papers Colonial, America and West Indies, volume 42, 1735-1736*; *Journals of the Board of Trade and Plantations, volume 10, 1754-1758* et al; all London: HMSO.

[113] Sainty, *Office-Holders in Modern Britain, volume 2*, pp. 59-62. Also, *London Evening Post*, 17 - 19 April 1739; and *London Gazette*, 24 - 27 May 1740.

John Larpent, chief clerk at the Northern Department;[114] Daniel Prevereau, clerk, later chief clerk, under Delafaye at the Southern Department;[115] and James Payzant, another clerk at the Southern Department.[116]

Employing Huguenots was considered advantageous until at least the mid-eighteenth century. Linguistic proficiency was an obvious benefit, especially since French remained the language of diplomacy. But the greater benefits were political loyalty, probity and diligence, all deemed to be a direct function of their French Protestant faith. Another attraction was their supposed (and probably actual) ability to use the Huguenot diaspora as an informal intelligence network.

Aside from any moral imperatives, the advantages obtained by Huguenot employees were a combination of financial gain and enhanced social status. This is epitomised in newspaper reports of the marriage of Daniel Prevereau's eldest daughter, a 'young lady of merit, beauty and fortune', to Major Francis Naizon of the Royal Regiment of Horse Guards. The event, reported widely in the press, was marked by a 'splendid entertainment' and 'fine ball' at Prevereau's residence in Craven Street.[117] This was a recent 1730s development east of Charing Cross that ran down from the Strand to the Thames. It was redolent of upper middling affluence: parallel rows of aspirational three-storey residences with wrought iron balconies, basements and stabling to the rear.[118] Other lessees included Thomas Thynne, 2nd Viscount Weymouth at No. 31, then 33; and Benjamin Franklin at No. 36.[119]

---

[114] Ibid.

[115] Ibid.

[116] Ibid.

[117] *General Evening Post*, 25 - 27 December 1739. Also *London Evening Post*, 25 - 27 December 1739 et al.

[118] 'Craven Street and Hungerford Lane', in G.H. Gater & E.P. Wheeler (eds.), *Survey of London* (London: London County Council, 1937), vol. 18, pp. 27-39.

[119] Ibid.

Lefebure was succeeded at his death by Anthony Todd. He had joined the Post Office at the age of 14[120] and worked initially for Charles Westgarth, the Clerk of the West Road.[121] Todd was promoted to the Secret Department in 1738 and apprenticed to Charles's brother, John, one of the department's six clerks.[122] Todd was promoted again in 1747 to become second clerk to George Shelvocke, the secretary to the Post Office. Five years later he was chosen to take over from Lefebure. Todd had overall charge of mail intercepts and copying, the transfer of encrypted correspondence to the Deciphering Branch, and liaising with the offices of the secretaries of state and first lord of the Treasury. His salary was some £850, of which around £650 was paid from secret service funds. He retained his position until his resignation thirty-five years later, prior to which he appointed his nephew, John Maddison, to succeed him.[123]

Todd expanded staff numbers and recruited additional translators, letter openers and code breakers. He also moved the training and employment of forgers from Hanover to London to avoid the delay caused by the casting and engraving of seals overseas. The move expedited the flow of intelligence and allowed duplicate – forged - seals to be produced and replaced far more rapidly.[124] The innovation was appreciated and Todd received a bonus of £500.

Todd retired or transferred many of the incumbent clerks in the department and appointed his own dependents to fill the vacancies. His relationship

---

[120]   Anthony Todd (*c.*1717-1798).   Cf., Patrick Woodland, 'Todd, Anthony (*bap.*1718, *d.*1798)', *ODNB*, online edn, January 2008), accessed 11 October 2016.

[121]   Charles Westgarth (*d.*1733). There were six Clerks of the Roads, viz. Chester Road, North Road, West Road, Bristol Road, Yarmouth Road, Kent Road. A seventh was responsible for the Kent Road by night.

[122]   The Westgarths had the patronage of a close neighbour, Ferdinand Craggs, the brother of James Craggs, the postmaster general 1715-20. Cf., Woodland, 'Todd, Anthony'.

[123]   John Maddison (1741-1808).

[124]   Cf., also, NA PRO, FO 83, f .5; HO 33, ff. 1-4; 42, ff. 206-14; 79, ff. 1-4.

with the secretaries of state and the Post Office Board nonetheless remained excellent and Todd was in addition appointed secretary to the Post Office in 1762, a combination of roles that gave him unprecedented control over both the secret and visible arms of the organisation. The promotion also augmented his income, which reportedly increased to above £4,000 per annum, around half of which was derived from a commission on packet expenditures. The value of his estate at death exceeded £80,000. The majority was placed in trust for his daughter, Eleanor, who had married exceptionally well to James, Viscount Maitland, the heir to the 7th Earl of Lauderdale, one of Scotland's sixteen representative peers. In answer to the hypothetical question 'what attracted Viscount Maitland to the daughter of a Post Office official', the receipt of a £30,000 dowry cleared his family debts.[125]

---

[125]   Roland Thorne, 'Maitland, James, eighth earl of Lauderdale (1759-1839)', *ODNB*, online edn, Jan 2008, accessed 2 January 2016.

CHAPTER FOUR

THE DECIPHERING BRANCH

I hope you become comfortable with the use of logic
without being deceived into concluding that logic will
inevitably lead you to the correct conclusion.[1]

EDWARD WILLES — CLERIC, CODEBREAKER

Until the second decade of the eighteenth century the decryption of mail was almost a cottage industry. Intercepted packets were opened at Abchurch Lane and encrypted or encoded despatches taken by special messenger to the government decipherer, usually at his Oxbridge college. For his efforts, the decipherer received a modest quarterly retainer supplemented by results-based success fees. Between 1713 until 1716, the principal decipherer was John Keill, a Scottish mathematician and Desaguliers' former lecturer at Oxford.[2] He had been appointed with the patronage of Sir Isaac Newton and Robert Harley, later Earl of Oxford,[3] but his relative incompetence and Tory leanings led to his removal from what was now a pivotal position.

His replacement was Edward Willes,[4] and it was under Willes's aegis that decryption would be developed over the following decades. Willes,

---

[1] Neil Armstrong (1930-).

[2] John Henry Keill (1671-1721); cf., *ODNB*, online edn, Sept 2010, accessed 5 March 2015; also *Foundations*, esp. pp. 43-4, 48; William A. Shaw (ed.), *Calendar of Treasury Books* (London, 1958), vol. 30, *11 June 1716* and *26 November 1716*; and Wiltshire & Swindon Archives: 161/130, *1716-1823*.

[3] Sainty, *Office-Holders in Modern Britain, volume 2: Officials of the Secretaries of State 1660-1782*.

[4] Cf., William Marshall, 'Willes, Edward (1694-1773)', *ODNB* (Oxford: OUP, 2004), accessed 5 March 2016; also William Gibson, *British Journal for Eighteenth-Century Studies*, 12 (1989), 69-76.

an Oxford mathematician and the younger brother of the future Chief Justice, Sir John Willes,[5] was reputedly fluent in French, Latin, Spanish and Swedish. He was aided initially by a single colleague but later added numerous subordinates, including three of his sons and several nephews.[6] As with John Ernest Bode, this was not entirely nepotistic. Restricting confidential knowledge to close family relations was thought prudent in order to maintain secrecy. It was also believed that the relevant skills could be passed from one family member to another.[7]

Willes had studied at Oriel and learned his deciphering skills not from Keill but from William Blencowe, formerly the government's chief decipherer.[8] Blencowe, a Fellow of All Souls until his suicide in 1712, had studied under and succeeded his maternal grandfather, John Wallis.[9] Both were affiliated to the Southern Department when Delafaye was editor of the *London Gazette* and his father responsible for the *French Gazette*.

Willes's loyalist Whig political credentials had been demonstrated at Oxford where he was an ordained Low Church Protestant and member of the Constitution Club. He had also clashed publicly with Oxford's many Tories. Willes's allegiance to the Hanoverians and cryptographic training, combined with his mathematical and linguistic skills, made him an obvious

---

[5] Sir John Willes (1685-1761), one of the longest serving chief justices of the Court of Common Pleas (1737-*d*). Willes was an MP from 1724 until 1737, representing Launceston, Weymouth and West Looe, respectively.

[6] Willes had five sons and four daughters from his marriage to Jane White in 1718. The three sons involved in the department were Edward Jr. (*bap.*1721), William (*bap.*1732) and Francis (*bap.*1735).

[7] As an aside, between 1716 and the mid-nineteenth century, when the Deciphering Branch was notionally abolished, there was never less than one Willes family member employed within the department.

[8] Cf., T.F. Henderson, 'Blencowe, William (1683–1712)', rev. Philip Carter, *ODNB*, online edn, Oct 2005, accessed 5 March 2016.

[9] Cf., Domenico Bertoloni Meli, 'Wallis, John (1616–1703)', *ODNB*, online edn, May 2007, accessed 6 March 2016.

choice to replace Keill when the latter was ousted in 1716, and the government's eagerness to secure him is indicated by the decision to raise the annual retainer to £200, double that received by Keill. Five years later it was increased again to £250, and by 1740 it stood at £1,000, albeit that a fifth - £200 - was given to his son and later successor, Edward Jr.

Willes also earned success fees. These principally took the form of ecclesiastical appointments. His first, the living of Barton-in-the-Clay in Bedfordshire, was granted in 1718 and retained until 1730. But following the decryption of Atterbury's correspondence and the bishop's conviction and banishment, Willes was granted the more valuable canonry of Westminster (1724-43) and the deanery at Lincoln (1730-43), alongside the prebends of Weston Paynshall (1730–37) and Milton Ecclesia (1737–44). Willes's work for the government in the 1734 Bedfordshire election resulted in two other church benefices: Bonsall in Derbyshire and the more recently created St John's, Westminster.

The total financial value of Willes's ecclesiastical positions was considerable and with regard to Westminster, Gibson comments that in a year in which Willes undertook only limited duties he might expect fees of around £200, but additional work could more than double that figure. And regular church fees were often topped-up with one-off gratuities, for example, the two gold wedges that Willes received in 1727 for attending the coronation of George II.[10]

Despite his affluence and rising status within the Church of England, Willes remained dedicated to cryptanalysis and to his responsibilities within the Deciphering Branch. He refused additional preferment until 1742, arguing that he wished to wait until his eldest son was sufficiently skilled in decoding and decryption before taking another office. However once Edward Jr. had received a patent in his own right, Willes was offered and accepted

---

[10]   William Gibson, 'An eighteenth-century paradox: the career of the Decipherer-Bishop, Edward Willes', *Journal for Eighteenth-Century Studies*, 12.1 (1989) 69-76.

the bishopric of St David's and the following year was promoted to what would be his last position, that of Bishop of Bath & Wells.

Willes continued to be engaged in deciphering and remained titular head of the department until his death in November 1773. He died at his London home close to Berkeley Square and was buried on 1 December in the north ambulatory of Westminster Abbey.[11] It was then, as now, one of Britain's most significant honours. His wife, Jane, and two sons, Edward Jr. and Sir Francis, were later interred alongside him.[12]

During Willes's tenure the operations and cost of the Deciphering Branch expanded in parallel with the workload, a product of the demands of an increasingly anxious government. Until 1721 part of the expense was borne by the Treasury, but from 1722 the entire cost was covered by secret service funds disbursed by the secretaries of state though the relevant under-secretaries.

ANTHONY CORBIÈRE

Four other senior code breakers joined the deciphering team in the two decades that followed George I's accession. The first, in 1715, pre-dating Willes by a year, was Anthony Corbière, a Fellow of Trinity College Cambridge.[13] The second, Frederick Ashfield, was recruited in 1723[14] and

---

[11]   Marshall, 'Willes, Edward', *ODNB*.

[12]   www.westminster-abbey.org/our-history/famous-people?collection=wma-people&query=willes+family, accessed 8 November 2016.

[13]   Gibson, 'An eighteenth-century paradox: the career of the decipherer-Bishop, Edward Willes'.

[14]   Frederick Ashfield (*d*.1729). Little is known of Ashfield but newspaper advertisements for the auction of his estate, for example, *Daily Post*, 18 & 22 February 1729, suggest some affluence. The contents of his house in Richmond, west of London, included 'fine silks and furniture, a chamber organ, and a horse drawn chariot and harnesses'. His library was extensive and the subject of its own auction.

succeeded by John Lampe in 1729.[15] And the fourth, Philip Zollman, the foreign secretary of the Royal Society, joined in 1735.[16]

Anthony [Antoine] Corbière (1687-1743),[17] was the most senior of the four. The Corbière family had migrated to England shortly after the Revocation of the Edict of Nantes and James Corbière, Anthony's father, established a shoe and boot-making business in London. His customers included the army, something with both positive and negative repercussions:

A Petition of *James Corbier*, Shoemaker, was presented to the House, and read, setting forth that the Petitioner served the regiment commanded by Brigadier *Belcastle* with 800 Pair of Shoes; and that *Janson de Tudebeuf*, Agent of that Regiment, had received the Money for them, but refused to pay the Petitioner, who is threatened to be laid in Gaol by his Creditors for those Goods.[18]

---

[15] Ashfield had been ill for some time. He died while travelling to Italy to recuperate. Cf., *London Evening Post*, 31 December 1728 - 2 January 1729.

[16] Philip Heinrich [Henry] Zollman (*d*.1748); employed by the Royal Society from 1723; elected FRS, 1727. He was fluent in French, Dutch, German and Italian, as well as Latin. Cf., Derek Massarella, 'Philip Henry Zollman, the Royal Society's First Assistant Secretary for Foreign Correspondence', *Notes and Records of the Royal Society of London*, 46.2 (1992), 219-34.

[17] Cf., *Weekly Journal or Saturday's Post*, 25 August 1724 et al.

[18] 11 December 1696, *Journal of the House of Commons: volume 11, 1693-1697* (London: HMSO, 1803), pp. 622-3. Also Petition 6 November 1699 'James Corbier for himself *et al* for payment of 25*l* due to them for boots for Lord Arran's Regiment in 1694', *Calendar of Treasury Books, volume 15, 1699-1700* (London: HMSO, 1933). Cf., also *23 February 1720*: 'Mr. Secretary Craggs to the Governor of the Leeward Islands. Anthony Corbiere, heir to his father, James, having debts due to him from Peter Soulegre now settled in St Christophers, you are to procure him speedy justice he having complained that he has been some years without so much as hearing from said Soulegre': *Calendar of State Papers Colonial, America and West Indies, volume 31, 1719-1720* (London: HMSO, 1933), pp. 362-3.

Following their arrival in London, the family became members of the congregation of the French Church in Glasshouse Street and Leicester Fields. Anthony Corbière's abjuration and reconnaissance is recorded in the church register 1702.[19] He was educated at St Paul's School in London and admitted to Trinity College in 1703 at the age of 16.[20] Awarded a scholarship the following year, he graduated in 1706/7 and was granted a fellowship in 1709, a year before he received his MA.[21]

Corbière's government service had begun a year earlier, shortly after his graduation, with an appointment as secretary to the naval officer and diplomat, Captain George Delaval,[22] Britain's Extraordinary Envoy to Morocco.[23] Corbière accompanied Delaval on his missions to Portugal between 1710 and 1714, and reported back to Whitehall.[24]

Corbière had been known to Delafaye since at least 1710,[25] not least because the two were on the same circulation list for Portuguese diplomat-

---

[19]   Minet (eds.), *Registers of the Churches of The Tabernacle Glasshouse Street and Leicester Fields, London 1688-1783*, p. 185.

[20]   http://venn.lib.cam.ac.uk/Documents/acad/2016/search-2016.html, accessed 6 October 2016.

[21]   Ibid.

[22]   George Delaval (1667-1723), also written as de la Val, negotiated a treaty with the Emperor of Morocco for the redemption of English captives. Cf. William Shaw (ed.), *Calendar of Treasury Books, volume 15, 1699-1700* (London: HMSO, 1933), pp. 411-28. Delaval was promoted to Rear Admiral in 1718 and to Admiral in 1722. He was Whig MP for West Looe from 1715-23.

[23]   *London Gazette*, 5 - 8 January 1708. Cf., BL Add MS 61542, Vol. CCCCXLII (ff. 215). (10) Morocco, 1706-1710; including ff. 1-117, papers by and relating to Jezreel Jones, mainly as translator and interpreter to the Moroccan ambassadors, Ahmad ibn Ahmad Cárdenas and Dr Joseph Diaz, 1706-10; also Add MS 61603.

[24]   Sedgwick, *History of Parliament: the House of Commons*.

[25]   The majority of Corbière's correspondence at this time was with Erasmus Lewis, under-secretary of state to William Legge, 2nd Lord Dartmouth, and his successor, William Bromley. Lewis's principal patron was Robert Harley, Lord Oxford. Cf., SP 89/21 and esp. 22.

ic intelligence.[26] The following year he was writing directly to Delafaye[27] with personal observations.[28] It would not have been a coincidence that Corbière secured the position of translator and decipherer only a few years later in 1715, earning the same quarterly retainer of £25 as by Keill.[29] His employment, pre-dating that of Willes, suggests that he had been engaged to supplement and perhaps supplant Keill's deciphering work.[30] It may also indicate that Keill was not wholly trusted.

Corbière was effective.[31] His retainer was doubled to £200 in 1716 and doubled again in 1721. The annual payment of £400 was £150 more than that received by Willes. It was increased to £500 in 1722 and two decades later had plateaued at £800.[32] The successive rises place him *pari passu* with Willes financially, and although he is often referred to as Willes's assistant they are more properly regarded as professional equals and colleagues.[33]

Corbière was sufficiently secure in his position to press his interests freely, and in a letter to Townshend argued the case for either a salary rise or

---

[26] SP 89/21/13, f. 25, Consul John Milner to Charles Delafaye, 17 January 1711, Lisbon.

[27] SP 36/17/111, f. 111, 112.

[28] SP 89/21/71, f. 152.

[29] BL Add MS 45518, vol. I, 1706-bef. 1766: Anthony Corbière, under-secretary of state: Correspondence rel. to ciphers: 1706, 1726.ff. 4-7b. Also cf., for example, *Calendar of Treasury Books, volume 30, 1716* (London: HMSO, 1958), p. 497: money warrant dated 29 September 1716.

[30] *Calendar of Treasury Papers, volume 5, 1714-1719* (London: HMSO, 1883), 27 February 1716; see also 29 July 1717.

[31] Cf., for example, SP 89/21/86 f. 191, Anthony Corbière to Erasmus Lewis; and SP 94/88, Colonel William Stanhope, Anthony Corbière and Earl Stanhope. Cf., also, *Reports on the manuscripts of the Earl of Eglinton et al* (London: HMSO, 1885).

[32] Sainty, *Office-Holders in Modern Britain, volume 2: Officials of the Secretaries of State 1660-1782*, pp. 22-58.

[33] Gibson, 'An eighteenth-century paradox: the career of the decipherer-Bishop, Edward Willes'.

a sinecure to the same effect.[34] He was also honest when faced with cryptographic challenges. A letter to Newcastle through Delafaye records his response to a complex cipher introduced by the Prussian embassy:

> What I have been fearing for some time is now come to pass; the letter
> from [Count] Degenfeld to his master, which your Grace was pleased to
> send me this morning, is in a cypher entirely new ... even more difficult
> than the former and consists of at least two thousand different characters.
> I beg ... that for some time to come, I may be allowed to peruse the whole
> correspondence, as well out of as in cyphers, to and from that minister ...
> for they will certainly afford me helps and lights.[35]

Corbière and Willes's workload varied month-on-month, ranging from deciphering a handful of letters to decoding a torrent of correspondence at times of crisis. Gibson records that the two men deconstructed over three hundred pages of despatches in a week in 1717 when a Jacobite invasion loomed.[36] The attention given to Atterbury's papers four years later was similarly intense. The correspondence was supposedly deciphered independently by Willes and Corbière, a detail that gave their subsequent testimony to the House of Lords considerable weight: 'several letters written in this cypher had been deciphered by them separately, one being many miles distant in the country and the other in town, and yet their deciphering agreed'.[37]

---

[34] SP 36/18/142, 19 April 1730.

[35] SP 36/22/53, 27 January 1731.

[36] Gibson, 'An eighteenth-century paradox: the career of the decipherer-Bishop, Edward Willes', 70.

[37] *Journal of the House of Lords: volume 22, 1722-1726* (London: HMSO, 1767-1830), 23 April 1723. Cf., also, Jeremy Black, *British Politics and Foreign Policy, 1727-44* (Abingdon: Routledge, 2016), pp. 97, 126; and Black, *British Diplomats and Diplomacy, 1688-1800* (Exeter: University of Exeter Press, 2001), pp. 134-5.

Willes and Corbière's testimony before the Lords opened their work to scrutiny although for obvious reasons the minutiae of their decryption methodology was not disclosed:

> The Lords' Committee, observing that some paragraphs of the letters referred to them were writ originally in Cypher, thought it proper to call the Decipherers before them, in order to their being satisfied of the truth of the deciphering. The account they received from those persons was, 'that they have long been versed in this science, and are ready to produce witnesses of undoubted reputation, who have framed letters in cypher on purpose to put them to a trial; and have constantly found their deciphering to agree with the original keys which had been concealed from them.' It was likewise confirmed to the Committee, that letters deciphered by one or other of them in *England* had exactly agreed with the deciphering of the same letters performed by persons in foreign parts, with whom they could have no communication; and that, in some instances, after they had deciphered letters for the government, the keys of those cyphers had been seized and, upon comparing them, had agreed exactly with their deciphering.
>
> With respect to the intercepted letters in question, they alleged, 'that, in the cypher used by *George Kelly*, they find the words ranged in an alphabetical order, answering the progressive order of the figures by which they are expressed; so that the farther the initial letter of any word is removed from the letter A, the higher the number is by which such word is denoted; that the same word will be found to be constantly denoted by one and the same figure, except in the case of particles, or words of very frequent use, which have two or three Figures assigned to them, but those always following one the other, in a progressive order.' They likewise set forth, 'that, in the cypher above mentioned, a certain order is constantly observed as to the placing of the words made use of, that under each letter of the alphabet, the first cyphers are allotted to

the proper names of places, the next to the proper names or titles of persons, the next to whole words in common use, and the last to denote single letters.'

As to the truth of the deciphering, they alleged, 'that several letters written in this cypher had been deciphered by them separately, one being many miles distant in the country and the other in town, and yet their deciphering agreed; that facts unknown to them and the government at the time of their deciphering had been verified in every circumstance by subsequent discoveries as, particularly, that of *H*—'s Ship coming in ballast to fetch *O*— to *England*, which had been so deciphered by them two months before the government had the least notice of *Halstead's* having left *England*; that a supplement of this cypher, having been found among *Dennis Kelly's* papers the latter end of *July* agreed with the key they had formed of that cypher the *April* before; that the deciphering of the letters signed *Jones Illington* and 1378, being afterwards applied by them to others written in the same cypher, did immediately make pertinent sense, and such as had an evident connection and coherence with the parts of those letters that were out of cypher, though the words in cypher were repeated in different paragraphs and differently combined.' And they insist, 'that these several particulars, duly weighed, amount to a demonstration of the truth of their deciphering'.[38]

Given the volume of correspondence and complexity of the ciphers - and the pressure brought to bear by Walpole and Delafaye - it is reasonable to believe that the decoding was not independent and that Willes and Corbière colluded to arrive at a common analysis that would support the government's desired verdict. Although the reality of Atterbury's participation in the plot was known, the administration lacked the hard proof necessary to

---

[38] *Journal of the House of Lords: volume 22, 1722-1726* (London: HMSO, 1767-1830), 23 April 1723.

achieve a judicial conviction for treason and the decrypted letters plugged the evidential gap.

Cruickshanks goes further, arguing that the Atterbury correspondence was wholly forged and the decryption exercise therefore specious. Although there is no proof that this is accurate, the possibility should not be disregarded. Fabricated documents and deceits were common currency, including the disinformation later propagated by London regarding the Earl of Mar that was designed to split the Jacobite camp.[39]

Regardless of the truth or otherwise of the Atterbury disclosures, Corbière's service was recognised at the most senor levels of government and rewarded with money warrants, government favours and an appointment as Naval Officer for Jamaica in 1721, a sinecure he held *in absentia*.[40]

> *Duke of Newcastle to Governor, the Duke of Portland.*
>
> I trouble your Grace with this letter in behalf of Mr Corbiere, a gentleman who is very usefully employed in H.M. service in the Secretary's Office. His brother-in-law, Mr Moses Montel[41] is going to Jamaica to

---

[39] Cf., Eveline Cruickshanks & Howard Erskine Hill, *The Atterbury Plot* (London: Palgrave Macmillan, 2004.)

[40] Warrant appointing Anthony Corbiere Naval Officer in Jamaica: Ceceil Headlam (ed), *Calendar of State Papers Colonial, America and West Indies, volume 32, 1720-1721* (London: HMSO, 1933), 4 February 1721. Also cf., among many examples, '50l. to Anthony Corbiere for 1717 Lady day quarter on his allowance for extraordinary service performed in the Treasury', 'Money warrant for 50l. to Anthony Corbiere, gent., for 1717 June 24 quarter on his allowance for extraordinary service performed in the Treasury' in William A. Shaw and F.H. Slingsby (eds), *Calendar of Treasury Books, volume 31, 1717* (London: HMSO, 1960), 26 March and 27 June 1717.

[41] The name is French Huguenot. 'Montel' appears in the church registers of Le Carre Berwick Street and elsewhere. His son was christened in Jamaica later the same year: Jamaica, Church of England Parish Register Transcripts, 1664-1880, entry for Anthony Montel, 18 September 1725, Christening; citing p. 7, Kingston, Jamaica, Registrar General's Department, Spanish Town; FHL microfilm 1,291,763.

officiate there as his deputy in the place of Naval Officer of that island. I beg leave to recommend him to your favour and protection, which I shall acknowledge as a particular obligation.

Holles Newcastle[42]

Corbière was appointed to the Middlesex bench in August 1724.[43] Coincidentally or otherwise, Wace, Delafaye's brother-in-law, was sworn a magistrate on the same day. Other positions followed. In 1728 Corbière was selected as a commissioner to oversee the building of a wooden bridge across the Thames between Fulham and Putney,[44] and in 1730 he received a sinecure as one of five national commissioners for wine licences, a lucrative post worth at least £300 annually.[45] Corbière would have been among men that he knew. The Wine Licence Office was dominated by Whig loyalists, many of whom were engaged in composing and disseminating government propaganda.[46]

Corbière married in 1722. His wife, Jane, was the daughter of Sir Peter Vandeput, a wealthy Huguenot merchant originally from Antwerp, and

---

[42] Cecil Headlam and Arthur Percival Newton (eds), *Calendar of State Papers Colonial, America and West Indies, volume 34, 1724-1725* (London: HMSO, 1936), pp. 367-81, 5 May 1725.

[43] *Evening Post*, 22 - 24 August 1724; *Weekly Journal or Saturday's Post*, 22 August 1724.

[44] Constructed by John Phillips (*c.*1705-1775), probably a member of the lodge at The Sun, south of St Paul's Cathedral.

[45] *London Evening Post*, 11 - 13 June 1728; *Calendar of Treasury Books and Papers, volume 4, 1739-1741* (London: HMSO, 1901), 11 March 1740. Also *Monthly Chronicle*, October, 1730; *London Evening Post*, 20 - 22 October 1730, et al; *London Gazette*, 15 - 18 March 1740; *General Evening Post*, 18 - 20 March 1740 et al; and *London Gazette*, 11 - 14 June 1743.

[46] Cf., Tone Sundt-Urstad, *Sir Robert Walpole's Poets: The Use of Literature as Pro-government Propaganda, 1721-1742* (Delaware: University of Delaware Press, 1999), pp. 89-90.

Margaret, the daughter of Sir John Buckworth, a City grandee.[47] The marriage, a large second house in London - a leasehold property – *Black Lands* – on Chelsea Common, myriad book subscriptions, and his charitable and other donations, not least £30 given to Trinity to improve the college chapel, attest to Corbière's standing and wealth.[48] And although there are no extant records that prove that Corbière was a freemason, there is a strong probability given that so many of his colleagues on the bench, at the Post Office, in government, and even within the vestry at St George's Church, Hanover Square, were members of the fraternity.[49] Corbière died in 1743 at his town house in St George Street.[50] He had worked as a government decipherer for 28 years, fully one half of his life.

COLLEAGUES AND SUCCESSORS

Corbière was succeeded by 'Mr Scholing', who was active from 1743 until 1748 but about whom nothing is known, and thereafter by the Neubourg brothers: P.F. Neubourg (active 1750-53) and G.W. (George) Neubourg (active 1753-60). The Neubourgs, like John Bode, were recruited from

---

[47] In addition to his merchant trading activities, Vandeput owned leasehold properties in Long Acre; houses and property lots in Tower Street; leasehold properties in Gracechurch Street and St James's; property and land in Lambeth; and shares in the New River Company. His will was proved at Canterbury on 30 April 1708. LL ref: wills_1700_1709_2531055_720038.

[48] *Daily Advertiser*, 2 June 1743; James Henry Monk, *The Life of Richard Bentley, D.D., Master of Trinity College* (London: J.G. & F. Rivington, 1833), vol. I, p. 208.

[49] Cf., *Foundations*, p. 85.

[50] He had owned property in the area since *c.*1725, the date that his name appears on a 'list of persons to compose [the] vestry of St George'. Cf., M.H. Port (ed), *The Commissions For Building Fifty New Churches the Minute Books, 1711-27, A Calendar* (London: London Record Society, 1986), p. 335. Jane Corbière died some five years later at Brook Green, Hammersmith: *London Evening Post*, 19 - 21 July 1748.

Hanover where they had been engaged in similar work. Each received a basic annual salary of £300, the same as Scholing.[51]

John Frederick Lampe worked alongside Corbière from 1729 until the latter's death fourteen years later. A native of Saxony, Lampe had migrated to London in around 1725 and was fluent in several European languages.[52] He was a musician and composer, a vocation that would have been made secure by a salary that had reached £500 per annum by 1740. As with Delafaye, Lefebure and Hemet, there is evidence that Lampe was a freemason. His setting of the *Apprentice's Song* was published in 1739 by Benjamin Cole, as was his score to accompany Delafaye's *Fellowcraft's Song*.[53] But although he is noted as a member of the Black Bear lodge in Hanover, the date stated in *AQC* 110 is too late and incorrect.[54]

Philip Zollman, a linguist, mathematician and natural scientist, worked as foreign secretary or 'secretary for foreign languages' at the Royal Society with responsibility for overseas correspondence.[55] He joined the department

---

[51] A Treasury Warrant of 19 March 1745 authorised 'the sum of £4,700 issued to the Secretary of the Post Office' to clear payments due to, amongst others, 'the Bishop of Bath and Wells and his son, 1,000l. per an., and two others, named, all decipherers; six of the Secret Office; Edward Hill, porter and messenger of the secret service; and five others, officers or pensioners, viz., Scholing, Bode, Zollman, Edward Willes and William Willes'. Cf., William A. Shaw (ed), *Calendar of Treasury Books and Papers, volume 5, 1742-1745* (London: HMSO, 1903), pp. 672-9.

[52] John Frederick [Johann Friedrich] Lampe (*c.*1703-1751). Cf., Suzanne Aspden, 'Lampe, John Frederick (1702/3-1751)', *ODNB*; also, *Daily Post*, 15 November 1732; *St James's Evening Post*, 1 - 3 February 1733; et al.

[53] J.F. Lampe & B. Cole, *British Melody or the Musical Magazine* (London: B. Cole, 1739).

[54] *AQC*, 110, p. 191. The date is given as 1774.

[55] Cf., *Daily Journal*, 2 April 1731 et al; also Albertus Seba, 'The Anatomical Preparation of Vegetables', *Philosophical Transactions of the Royal Society* (1729), 441-44, 'translated from the German by Mr Zollman, FRS'; and 'Proposals for the Improvement of the History of Russia', *Philosophical Transactions of the Royal Society* (1735), 136, 'translated from the German by Mr Zollman'; and *Daily Journal*, 2 April 1731: 'translated into English [from Latin] by Mr Zollman'.

in 1735 at an initial salary of £200 which had increased to £300 by 1742.[56] Schuchard has suggested that Zollman's correspondence with Sweden was to gain intelligence on Swedish Jacobites and insight into Swedish thinking. This may be correct but many of his letters were to intellectuals and other contacts dating from his time at the British embassy in Stockholm.[57]

Zollman was well-connected to senior figures within the Walpole administration having been secretary to Horace Walpole when the latter was ambassador in Paris, and thereafter to Poyntz in Sweden.[58] Poyntz subsequently advanced his name to the Royal Society as a prospective hire. Zollman also impressed Townshend, who recruited him to accompany George I on his third visit to Hanover.

Zollman's connections to the Huguenot *qua* masonic community in London can be traced through Pierre des Maizeaux,[59] a stalwart of the lodge at the Rainbow Coffee House in York Buildings.[60] Des Maizeaux has been described as a father confessor to Zollman,[61] and the two had known each other since 1716.[62]

---

[56] Sainty, *Office-Holders in Modern Britain, volume 2: Officials of the Secretaries of State 1660-1782*, pp. 22-58. Also, Fritz, *The English Ministers and Jacobitism between the Rebellions of 1715 and 1745*, p. 110.

[57] Private conversation, 6 June 2016. But cf. Massarella, 'Philip Henry Zollman, the Royal Society's First Assistant Secretary for Foreign Correspondence'; also Sackler Archives: EL/Z/9-13.

[58] *London Gazette*, 28 March – 1 April 1727. Stephen Poyntz was later the British chargé d'affaires in Paris. Cf., Philip Woodfine, 'Poyntz, Stephen (*bap.*1685, *d.*1750)', *ODNB*.

[59] Pierre [Peter] des Maizeaux (*c.*1672-1745), elected FRS 1720. He was naturalized in 1707: House of Lords, PO/JO/10/6/131.

[60] And by inference, possibly also of the lodge at the Prince Eugene's Head Coffee House.

[61] Massarella, 'Philip Henry Zollman, the Royal Society's First Assistant Secretary for Foreign Correspondence'. Massarella errs in characterising Zollman's position at the Secret Department as a sinecure. It was not.

[62] BL Add MS 4289.

Among the department's later decipherers were James Rivers, who succeeded Scholing and became 'Interpreter of Southern Languages' at an annual salary of £200; James Wallace, who succeeded Zollman; William Fraser, a German language specialist; and a Mr Boelstring, originally from Hanover. With such hires the number of foreign countries whose despatches could be decrypted expanded to cover the majority of Europe.[63]

DEPARTMENTAL METHODOLOGY

Warrants authorising the interception and detention of mail were either specific, with named recipients, or general, for example, 'all mail to and from Flanders'. Few records remain extant. Political warrants addressed to the postmaster general were frequently burned by the foreign secretary with no particulars maintained;[64] other sensitive requests were informal and given verbally. Moreover, when warrants were issued they could be and were back-dated. In short, the department's operations made the idea of auditable compliance with the Post Office (Revenues) Act impossible.

There was no public accountability and information on staff numbers and pay was undisclosed until 1742 following *A Further Report from the Committee of Secrecy appointed to Enquire into the Conduct of Robert, Earl of Orford*:

> The annual expenses of this office are as follows: to the chief decipherer, Mr Willes, for himself and his son, £1,000; second decipherer, Mr Corbière, £800; third decipherer, Mr Lampe, £500; to the fourth decipherer, Mr Zolmon [sic], £200; to the chief clerk, Mr Le Fevre, £650; to the four other clerks, Messieurs Bode, Thouveis, Clark, Hemmitt, £300 each; to

---

[63] The countries whose despatches are known to have been intercepted include Austria, Denmark, France, the German states, Greece, the Italian states, the Low Countries, Poland, Portugal, Russia, Spain and Sweden.

[64] *Report from the Secret Committee on the Post-Office, together with the appendix; Ordered, by the House of Commons, to be printed, 5 August 1844* (London, 1844).

the comptroller of the foreign office, Mr Day, £60; to the doorkeeper, £40 or £50, but this examinant believes £50.

There are besides accidental [incidental] charges for seals etc. an account of which is brought in by one of the Clerks, which may amount to £100, and to Mr Lavalade, formerly alphabet keeper but now superannuated, £40 ... When these sum were discharged, the over plus, which may amount to £90, is divided between the two Post Masters and the Secretary.

Mr Le Fevre, besides his abovementioned salary, is paid something out of incidents so that his whole salary may amount to, as he believes, £800 per annum ... His is a very troublesome post, it being necessary he should always be present at the going out and coming in of mail.[65]

The day-to-day operations and practices of the Secret Department had become a matter of routine by the 1720s and designated mail and that raising the suspicions of local Post Office agents would be passed to the department for scrutiny. But although straightforward in-principle there were in practice numerous hurdles, especially the time required to open, copy and reseal letters, with complex diplomatic and other seals taking several hours or more to process.

Various means were used to obscure such delays to give the impression of a normally functioning mail. One technique was to hold back entire batches of letters rather than a single despatch. Staff would also work through the night to process the intercepted mail before postal deliveries began the following day. Diplomatic and other letters to and from overseas destinations faced potentially fewer time-related problems but although they could be opened and copied in transit, specialist re-sealing was required to avoid the risk of detection.

Although testimony before Parliament had revealed the existence of the Secret Department and Deciphering Branch, the scale of their activities was

---

[65] *A Further Report from the Committee of Secrecy* (Dublin: 1742), pp. 131-2.

underestimated, something evident in the extent to which mail of all sorts continued to be sent through the ordinary post rather than via special messenger or informal channels, including merchant and traders. Many may have suspected that their letters had been read, but they could not be certain that this was the case. And if seals were unbroken and mail delivered on schedule, correspondence was generally thought to be secure. But precautions were nonetheless taken. Complex cyphers and increasingly detailed seals were barriers to disclosure, and counter-measures included the addition of hidden marks to a letter and, most commonly, monitoring posting and delivery times.[66]

Only a few insiders were aware of the comprehensive technical skills that allowed letters to be opened and resealed expertly with forged seals indistinguishable from the originals. And there were few if any leaks. Those privy to the intelligence that flowed from the department were limited to the most senior levels of the administration.

The resulting intelligence product was vast. The records held in the National Archives alone exceed one hundred volumes in the four decades from 1726 to 1766, and to these can be added an array of additional letters and reports in the British Library and elsewhere. The collection is not comprehensive; as noted, at least some confidential material was destroyed intentionally.

It should be no surprise that the Post Office was viewed by government not as a neutral means by which mail could be collected and distributed but rather as a key intelligence resource. And in the first half of the eighteenth century the Secret Department and its Deciphering Branch had many objectives. They were a means to combat the putative Stuart threat; access the policies and plans of overseas governments, allies included; and obtain insights into the intentions of domestic opponents, parliamentary and otherwise. The benefits of such information were tangible and led to the thwarting of three successive Jacobite Plots in 1717, 1719 and 1721/2.

---

[66] Marsha Keith Schuchard, *Emanuel Swedenborg, Secret Agent on Earth and in Heaven* (Leiden, NL: Koninklijke Brill, 2012), p. 612.

THE JACOBITE PLOTS OF 1717 AND 1719

The Anglo-French accord that followed the Treaty of Utrecht reduced the extent of French support for the Jacobites and their sympathisers turned their sights elsewhere. Sweden and Spain were approached for financial and military backing and alerted by agents on the continent and at home, the Post Office was tasked with monitoring the communications between Georg Heinrch von Görtz, Sweden's minister plenipotentiary in Europe, and Carl Gyllenborg, the Swedish ambassador in London.[67]

Although written in Swedish diplomatic code, a cypher based on mathematics, French and Swedish, Willes and Corbière succeeded in decrypting the correspondence. Its content gave the government such unease that regardless of international law and that it would be an assault on diplomatic immunity, Gyllenborg was arrested on 29 January 1717. His ambassadorial residence in London was searched and his papers seized. Unfortunately, Gyllenborg, forewarned, had destroyed any incriminating letters and his key to the cipher.

Sweden responded to Gyllenborg's arrest with manufactured and probably genuine fury at what was seen as an egregious breach of protocol and retaliated by arresting the British ambassador in Stockholm, Robert Jackson. Britain in turn went public to justify its actions. Gyllenborg's intercepted diplomatic correspondence was published[68] and the government initiated and encouraged an anti-Swedish propaganda campaign co-ordinated by Delafaye and led by Daniel Defoe.[69] A selection of Gyllenborg's letters were reproduced in the press accompanied by editorials outlining British grievances against Sweden - political, maritime and commercial. Defoe's

---

[67] Georg Heinrch von Görtz (1668-1719); Carl Gyllenborg (1679-1746).

[68] *Letters which passed between Count Gyllenborg and Barons Gortz, Sparre, and others* (London, 1717).

[69] In addition to his writing and business interests, Defoe was a government spy and double agent. Cf., Paula R. Backscheider, 'Defoe, Daniel (1660?–1731)', *ODNB*, online edn, Jan 2008, accessed 12 March 2015.

contribution, *An Account of the Swedish and Jacobite Plot*,[70] vilified Sweden more broadly and attacked their apologists in Britain.

AN

ACCOUNT

OF THE

Swedish and *Jacobite*

PLOT.

WITH

A VINDICATION of our Government from the horrid Aspersions of its Enemies.

AND

A POSTSCRIPT, relating to the *Post-Boy* of Saturday, *Feb.* 23.

In a Letter to a Person of Quality, occasion'd by the Publishing of Count Gyllemborg's *Letters.*

LONDON;

Printed for *S. Popping* at the Black Raven in *Pater-noster-Row*, *J. Harrison* at the *Royal-Exchange*, and *A. Dodd* at the Peacock without *Temple-Bar*. M. DCC. XVII. (Price Six-Pence.)

An Account of the Swedish and Jacobite Plot
Frontispiece, 1717

---

[70] Cf., Daniel Defoe, *An Account of the Swedish and Jacobite plot* (London, 1717) but also see *A Short View of the conduct of the King of Sweden* (London, 1717).

Nonetheless, as a Protestant monarchy and former ally, Charles XII's Sweden had its defenders and a large minority in Parliament viewed the contretemps as a function of Hanoverian foreign policy interests rather than those of Britain. George I's policy towards Sweden, and Hanover's occupation of the ex-Swedish duchies of Bremen and Verden, split the Whigs. And when George I put pressure on Parliament to suspend trade with Sweden many MPs took a contrary position.

Britain and Sweden eventually stepped back from the brink and released their respective hostages. But Gyllenborg's experience of arrest and public denigration reinforced his enmity towards Hanover and the British government. Notwithstanding that the planned invasion was abandoned, on their return to Sweden Gyllenborg and von Görtz, arrested in the United Provinces at Britain's request but later released, moved to establish a second plan to reinstate James Stuart and cut the Hanoverian line from the British throne.

The scheme would be put into execution two years later when Sweden backed a Jacobite uprising in conjunction with a Spanish military and naval invasion. Spanish agreement had been secured through Cardinal Giulio Alberoni, a favourite of Philip V. But Alberoni's mail had been intercepted and the information it revealed was substantiated by other sources, including letters intercepted at Nienburg in Lower Saxony by post office staff in Whitehall's pay.[71]

Notwithstanding only limited funding from Jacobite sympathisers at home and abroad, an invasion force was put together in Spain and some twenty-seven vessels carrying an estimated 5,000 Spanish troops set sail

---

[71] Nicholas Rescer, *Leibnitz and Cryptography* (Pittsburg, PA: University of Pittsburg, 2012), p. 28: 'The Hanoverians ran an elaborate and efficient cryptographic service in which the Brunswick dukedoms of Callenberg and Celle functioned as one. Several postal interception stations were in operation. That at Nienburg intercepted post between France and the Nordic countries. That at Gifhorn processed north-south post between Wolffenbüttel and Braunschweig on the one side and Hamburg and the north on the other. The Thurn and Taxis station at Sulingen also provided material.'

from Cádiz in March 1719 with the intention of making landfall in south-west England.[72] The force was commanded by James Butler, 2nd Duke of Ormonde, who had previously served as Captain General of the British Army. His invasion was to be preceded by a diversionary attack in Scotland by a contingent of Spanish troops under the command of the exiled George Keith, 10th Earl Marischal.

Marischal had sailed from Spain in advance of the main invasion. The intention was to tie-down British troops in Scotland and with the backing of the pro-Jacobite Highland clans, march south to join ranks with Ormonde's forces. In the event, a storm in the English Channel dictated that the invasion would fail. The main Spanish fleet was dispersed by heavy seas and the ships that survived were instructed to return to port. Unable to communicate with Ormonde, Earl Marischal was unaware of the disaster and continued to Scotland.

Marischal's diversionary attack began with his two frigates landing three hundred troops at Loch Duich where they met little resistance and captured the garrison at the mediaeval castle at Eilean Donan. There was however only limited support from the Scottish clans and a British reconnaissance force landed from three frigates recaptured the castle within the month. Marischal's forces, including those who had rallied to James Stuart's colours, numbered barely more than a thousand and after a few weeks of skirmishing the rebel army was defeated on 10 June at Glen Shiel by a small loyalist force. The Jacobite rebels fled and the Spanish troops surrendered.

---

[72] Some sources give twenty-nine vessels. 'Five thousand men, of which four thousand are to be foot, a thousand troopers, of which three hundred with their horses, the rest with their arms and accoutrements, and two month's pay for them, ten field pieces, and a thousand barrels of powder and fifteen thousand arms for foot, with everything necessary to convey them.' Alberoni to Ormonde, quoted in David Sharp, *The Battle of Glen Shiel 1719*: www.thesonsofscotland. co.uk/thebattleofglenshiel1719, accessed 10 December 2015.

THE ATTERBURY PLOT

The unmasking of the Atterbury Plot in 1721/22 was one of the Deciphering Branch's most celebrated achievements. Francis Atterbury, the Bishop of Rochester, had been a King's Scholar at Westminster School from where he went up to Christ Church, Oxford. He graduated in 1684 and taught at the university for three years before being ordained into the Church of England. Atterbury had been a brilliant scholar and an effective speaker, and in 1691 he obtained his first ecclesiastical appointment as lecturer at St Bride's Church, Fleet Street, recommended by the Bishop of London, Henry Compton. Atterbury's oratory brought him to the attention of other patrons and within two years he had become minister of the City of London's Bridewell and Bethlem hospitals, and chaplain-in-ordinary to William & Mary. With his personal finances and social position now secure, Atterbury resigned his teaching position at Christ Church and moved to London; he married in 1695.

Atterbury's High Church orthodoxy gained him a public following and his self-publicity brought national attention, but his views were considered extreme by many in the Church of England hierarchy and his sermons and pamphlets, including *Letter to a Convocation Man*,[73] set him against the political establishment. Atterbury responded not by toning down but by aligning himself with a group of rising High Church Tory politicians led by Robert Harley, later Earl of Oxford, Henry St John, later 1st Viscount Bolingbroke, and Simon Harcourt, later 1st Viscount Harcourt.

With the support of his patrons, Atterbury gained additional preferment in 1711, albeit at a second tier level as dean of Christ Church. However he continued to alienate many who might have been supportive and his hope of rapid ecclesiastical advance was frustrated.[74] It was a further two years before Atterbury obtained promotion to a bishopric, and this was only that

---

[73] Francis Atterbury, *Letter to a Convocation Man* (1697).

[74] D.W. Hayton, 'Atterbury, Francis (1663–1732)', *ODNB*.

of Rochester, albeit that it also brought the more financially important and prestigious role of dean of Westminster.

Atterbury took his seat in the House of Lords in July 1713, just over a year before Queen Anne's death. But notwithstanding that he was part of the committee that drafted the congratulatory address from the Lords to George I the following year, he was suspected of Stuart loyalties and as one of the Tory leaders in the Lords had been identified as opposed to Whig interests. The post-coronation Whig hegemony removed Atterbury from influence and he was relegated to the ecclesiastical side lines as Low Church Anglicanism became ascendant within the establishment.

Atterbury's dislike of the Whig's political and religious policies became tangible. He excoriated the administration in two anonymous pamphlets, the first of which also contained a personal attack on George I. And although Atterbury was not proven to be the author his role was suspected.[75] Self-interest allied to a despondency that only the Tories would be able to restore High Church Anglicanism to the centre of English society allowed Atterbury to be persuaded to support the Pretender with the aim of disrupting the Hanoverian succession, reinstating a Tory government and restoring himself to influence and power.

During the public outcry and parliamentary unrest that followed the collapse of the South Sea Company's share price amid widespread evidence of fraud, Atterbury began a correspondence with Jacobite agents and developed plans for insurrection.[76] Various proposals were debated but the strategy finally selected centred on an invasion force of Jacobite regiments in the

---

[75] Anonymous [Francis Atterbury], *English Advice to the Freeholders of England* (1715) and *An argument to prove the affections of the people of England to be the best security of government* (1715).

[76] The conspirators included John Erskine, 6th Earl of Mar (1675-1732); Sir Henry Goring, 4th Bt. (1679-1731); William North, 6th Baron North and 2nd Baron Grey (1678-1734); Charles Boyle, 4th Earl of Orrery, (1674-1731); Thomas Wentworth, 1st Earl of Strafford (1672-1739); and Christopher Layer (1683-1723), who was later prosecuted, found guilty, and hanged, drawn and quartered.

service of the French and Spanish armies which would provide a catalyst for a general uprising led by Jacobite sympathisers within the Tory aristocracy. Key buildings in London - the Bank of England, the Tower of London and the adjacent Royal Mint – would thereafter be assaulted and captured. And although Atterbury became impatient at the glacial speed of execution and frustrated that funding failed to materialise, he nonetheless remained a central figure in the plot and its planning.

Atterbury's correspondence and that of his co-conspirators was monitored throughout the period by the Secret Department and the Deciphering Branch. With the secretaries of state and Walpole aware of their actions and identities, and fearful of what was being planned by Atterbury and his associates, the government moved pre-emptively to arrest and interrogate those deemed to be at the core of the conspiracy. That the discovery of the Plot also distracted the public and press from the South Sea crisis was an additional bonus.

The main protagonists, including Atterbury, had been guarded and their letters offered few grounds for a formal prosecution. Given the real risk that a court case would be challenged and dismissed for lack of evidence, the administration was unwilling to begin formal legal proceedings.[77] Instead, Atterbury, George Kelly and John Plunket, another associate, were subjected to 'Pains and Penalties' Bills in Parliament with the objective, in Atterbury's case, of depriving him of his ecclesiastical position, proscribing communication and sending him into exile.[78] He had limited support – albeit Wharton was one ally - and the Bills were approved by the Commons and Lords in

---

[77] Of the very few co-conspirators tried in court, only Layer was found guilty of treason and executed. The execution took place in May, the month before the Pains & Penalties Bills were debated.

[78] A bill of pains and penalties was a legislative act without a judicial trial for high crimes, such as treason. In so doing, Parliament was acting as the highest court of justice.

mid-June. Atterbury was exiled and Kelly and Plunkett sentenced to life imprisonment.[79]

The parliamentary vote hinged on the evidence of the conspirators' intercepted and now decoded letters, many of which were examined at length:

> *Robert Franklyn*, second mate of the Ship *Revolution*, deposes, that letters, directed to *John* or *James Jacobs*, at *Genoa*, were taken up at the posthouse by *Gallwey*. The Committee observe that *Jones*, in his Letter to *Chivers*, mentions his having communicated the copies of *Manfield's* and *Jacobs'* letters. And *Glascock*, in his letter to *George Kelly* of the 1st of *May* says he hopes money is sent to pay for the barrels which *Jacobs* has at his disposal, in both which places, it is probable that *Jacobs* means *Gallwey* and that barrels mean stands of arms; [this] is confirmed by a letter of *Morgan's* in which, speaking of that very ship that brought the arms abovementioned from *Gottenburg* and *Hamburgh* to *Cadiz*, he says she had received orders for taking in nineteen barrels with everything necessary to make use of them, which last words seem to refer to the bayonets, flints and powder.
>
> The intelligence sent by Mr *Crawfurd* on the 27th of *May* that *Gordon* of *Boulogne* was to have a ship ready to transport some of the chiefs of the conspiracy to *England* is confirmed by the deposition of *Roger Garth* ... who declares that the said *Gordon* (whom he had good reason to believe to be an agent of the Pretender's) did some time last summer endeavour to engage him to ply off of that station with his sloop, in order to carry over such persons as he the said *Gordon* should recommend to him; promising him that he should have Employment enough.
>
> The Lords Committees conceive that the several particulars above related will appear to the House very much to corroborate the accounts received from abroad of ships provided for transporting the late Duke of *Ormonde* to *England* with arms and officers the beginning of last Summer,

---

[79] Cf., Cruickshanks and Erskine-Hill, *The Atterbury Plot*.

and that they also confirm the deciphering of the letters and explication of the names, contained in the Report of the Committee of the House of Commons.[80]

The decision of the House of Lords to summon the decipherers to give evidence and their 'satisfaction' as to the accuracy of the decryption was a turning point in the debate. But at the same time, the extent to which the burden of proof relied on decryption emphasised the paucity of corroborating evidence, an absence highlighted by another development.

Charles Spencer, Lord Sunderland, the former First Lord of the Treasury who had been obliged to resign following the South Sea scandal, had died in April 1722 in the middle of the Atterbury Crisis.[81] Despite having been a Whig, he had been suspected of - and had been - intriguing with Atterbury and Jacobite and opposition Tories in an attempt to restore his influence following his departure from office. He was also known to have written to the exiled Lord Bolingbroke.[82]

Walpole and Townshend reacted swiftly on being informed of his death, seizing personal papers and searching for incriminating material. They were probably correct to do so. While Sunderland's papers were being taken apart, a despatch arrived from Paris containing a memorandum from Philippe II, Duc d'Orléans, the French Regent,[83] confirming that the Jacobites had requested French military assistance. Adding to the government's concerns, the Secret Department intercepted a letter dated 20 April

---

[80] *Cobbett's Parliamentary Debates* (London: Hansard, 1811), volume VIII, 222.

[81] Charles Spencer, 3rd Earl of Sunderland (1675-1722). Lord Lieutenant of Ireland (1714-17), Lord Privy Seal (1715-16), Lord President of the Council (1717-19) and First Lord of the Treasury (1718-21).

[82] Bolingbroke had by this time broken with the Jacobites. He hoped to receive a pardon and offered to bring Jacobites dissenters back into allegiance to George I and the Hanoverian succession. Sunderland believed that their support, with that of other allies, might be used to displace Walpole.

[83] Philippe II, Duke of Orléans (1674-1723), Regent from 1715 to 1723.

from Atterbury – designated 'T. Jones' – to a 'Mr Chivers' with a postscript stating that 'nothing of importance should be trusted to the post, and am resolved myself not to send that way'; the letter concluded that 'the death of Lord Sunderland makes such a caution more indispensably necessary'.[84]

The Privy Council was convened on 23 April. In addition to Walpole and Townshend, the attendees included their closest political allies: Duke of Devonshire; the Duke of Newcastle, then lord chamberlain; Lord Carleton, the lord president of the council; Lord Carteret, secretary of state for the Southern Department; and Lord Macclesfield, teller of the exchequer. A flurry of instructions followed, including a warrant to the Post Office 'to Authorize & Empower you to Open & Detain all letters & pacquets that shall come to your Office in the French & Flanders Mails from time to time until you receive Orders to the contrary, and to cause such of them to be copied wherein you shall find anything contained which may be for His Majesty's Service'.[85]

Government agents were ordered to the French coast to report on troop movements and Charles Churchill, a trusted intimate of Walpole and MP for Castle Rising, sent to Paris to obtain further intelligence. Concerned that a rebellion might be imminent, George I was persuaded to delay his journey to Hanover and the military placed on high alert. Troops were recalled from Ireland. Regiments of Foot Guards ordered to encamp in Hyde Park. And regiments of Horse and Foot repositioned south from Scotland. They were billeted on Salisbury Plain from where they could be despatched anywhere within southern England, and at Hounslow Heath, a short distance to the west of London.

With the military in place to put down any putative rebellion, the government revealed to the press on 8 May the 'traitorous design to over-throw our excellent constitution both in Church and State and to subject

---

[84] *Reports from Committees of the House of Commons, 9 June 1715 - 2 May 1735* (London: House of Commons, 1715-1735), vol. 1, pp. 247-8.

[85] SP George I, XXXI, 23 April 1722.

a Protestant free people to tyranny and superstition'.[86] The establishment closed ranks and the following day the Lord Mayor and Aldermen of the City of London issued a loyal address that was published immediately. It railed against 'those vile and detestable persons who shall again conspire and attempt to bring a free and happy people under the yoke and tyranny of superstition and to involve this nation in a state of blood, misery and the utmost confusion'.[87]

The 'design to raise an insurrection in this kingdom in favour of the Pretender'[88] was lambasted elsewhere, not least by the Middlesex and Westminster Justices who used a loyal address to condemn the Jacobites' 'wicked and traitorous designs' and protest their 'zeal and affection' for the king and the royal family.[89]

Alongside these denunciations and loyal protestations the government sought to maintain public calm. Newspaper articles were planted by Delafaye to offer reassurance to middling Britain: 'we hear that in His Majesty's German dominions above 21,000 men, all regular troops, are kept in readiness'; a 'report of the Pretender's being arrived in France is too ridiculous to be credited';[90] and regardless of the furore, 'the Pretender … seems too inconsiderable to alarm us'.[91]

The administration nonetheless remained concerned privately and Horatio Walpole, Walpole's younger brother,[92] a diplomat and politician in his own right, was despatched to The Hague. The press reported slavishly that 'we are assured that Mr Walpole, who receives many expresses from England, hath demanded the auxiliary troops of this state to be in

---

[86] *London Gazette*, 8 - 12 May 1722.

[87] *Evening Post*, 8 - 10 May 1722 et al.

[88] *Freeholder's Journal*, 16 May 1722.

[89] *London Gazette*, 12 - 15 May 1722.

[90] *Weekly Journal or British Gazetteer*, 12 May 1722.

[91] *Freeholder's Journal*, 16 May 1722.

[92] Horatio Walpole, later 1st Baron Walpole (1678-1757).

readiness',[93] and that he had yesterday 'presented a memorial to the States General desiring them to hold in readiness 6,000 men of their troops to be sent to England'.[94]

With the country roused and the government wary of any secret gathering, Grand Lodge was reported to be concerned that the upcoming Quarterly Communication could be misconstrued and supposedly sent a deputation to Townshend to obtain his consent for their forthcoming meeting. The *London Journal* of 16 June 1722 gives an account:

> A select body of the Society of Freemasons waited on the Rt. Hon. the Lord Viscount Townshend, one of his Principal Secretaries of State, to signify to his Lordship, that being obliged by their Constitutions to hold a General Meeting now at Midsummer, according to ancient custom, they hoped the Administration would take no umbrage at their convention as they were all zealously affected to His Majesty's Person and Government.

It has been argued elsewhere that the purpose of the press report was not to seek formal permission to hold the Quarterly Communication but rather to put on record the political loyalty of freemasonry to the Whig administration, something necessary with the mercurial Duke of Wharton having wrested the position of grand master from the Whiggist Duke of Montagu.[95]

Townshend's consent for the General Meeting was forthcoming. Indeed, a refusal would have been improbable. His eldest son, Charles, MP for Great Yarmouth, was himself a freemason, a member of the lodge at the Old Devil Tavern in Temple Bar, and more importantly so was Delafaye, Townshend's under-secretary of state and the government's anti-Jacobite spymaster. In the unlikely event that Grand Lodge had succumbed to

---

[93] *Post Boy*, 19 - 22 May 1722.

[94] *Daily Post*, 22 May 1722.

[95] *Foundations*, pp. 138-43.

Jacobite influence, Delafaye would have been ideally placed to identify and pluck out the conspirators.

The government's reliance on deciphered mail intercepts to convict Atterbury and his co-accused came under attack from the Tory opposition and its press sympathisers, criticism that reached an apotheosis in Swift's *Gulliver's Travels*:

> … in the kingdom of Tribnia [Britain] by the natives called Langdon [England] where I had sojourned some time in my travels, the bulk of the people consist in a manner wholly of discoverers, witnesses, informers, accusers, prosecutors, evidences, swearers, together with their several subservient and subaltern instruments, all under the colours, the conduct and the pay of ministers of state and their deputies…
>
> It is first agreed and settled among them, what suspected persons shall be accused of a plot, then effectual care is taken to secure all their letters and papers and put the owners in chains. These papers are delivered to a set of artists, very dexterous in finding out the mysterious meanings of words, syllables, and letters, for instance, they can discover a close stool to signify a privy council; a flock of geese, a senate; a lame dog, an invader; the plague, a standing army; a buzzard, a prime minister; the gout, a high priest; a gibbet, a secretary of state; a chamber pot, a committee of grandees; a sieve, a court lady; a broom, a revolution; a mouse-trap, an employment; a bottomless pit, a treasury; a sink, a court; a cap and bells, a favourite; a broken reed, a court of justice; an empty tun, a general; a running sore, the administration.
>
> When this method fails, they have two others more effectual, which the learned among them call acrostics and anagrams. First, they can decipher all initial letters into political meanings. Thus 'N', shall signify a plot; 'B', a regiment of horse; 'L', a fleet at sea; or, secondly, by transposing the letters of the alphabet in any suspected paper, they can lay open the deepest designs of a discontented party. So, for example, if I should say, in a letter to a friend, 'Our brother Tom has just got the piles', a

skilful decipherer would discover that the same letters which compose that sentence may be analysed into the following words: 'Resist ---, a plot is brought home--The tour.' And this is the anagrammatic method.[96]

A postscript to a letter from William King to Swift's cousin, Martha Whiteway, was equally satirical:

> *To the gentleman of the Post Office who intercepted my last letter addressed to Mrs Whiteway at her house in Abbey Street, together with a letter enclosed to the dean of St Patrick's* [i.e. Swift].
>
> Sir, when you have sufficiently perused this letter, I beg favour of you to send it to the lady to whom it is directed. I shall not take it ill though you should not give yourself the trouble to seal it again. If I have said any-thing against the copper halfpence and excise should offend you, blot it out. I shall think myself much obliged to you if, at the same time, you will be pleased to send Mrs Whiteway those letters that are now in your hands with such alteration and amendments as you think proper...[97]

Lampoons were also directed at freemasonry itself, perhaps recognising the role played by freemasons, including Delafaye, in the excising of Atterbury. *The Daily Post*'s *The Freemasons: An Hudibrastick Poem* mocked freemasonry for its supposed links with whores and sodomites, and for its coded conversa-tions and deemed deciphering skills:

> And to these Signs I' here to add,
> What may be deem'd almost as bad,
> Their messages, and Scraps of Paper,

---

[96] Jonathan Swift, *Travels into several Remote nations of the world by Lemuel Gulliver* (London: Charles Bathurst, 1742), 4th edition, corrected, pp. 216-8.

[97] William King to Martha Whiteway, 24 June 1737 in John Nichols (ed.), *The Works of the Rev. Jonathan Swift* (London, 1801), vol. 13, pp. 353-4. King was a Jacobite sympathiser.

Which are not seal'd with Wax or Wafer,

Nor writ upon, and yet make known

The greatest Secrets of the Town...

A Mason, when he needs must drink,

Sends Letter, with Pen and Ink,

Unto some Brother, who's at hand,

And does the Message understand;

'The Paper's of the Shape that's square,

Thrice folded with the nicest Care;

For it 'tis round (which is ne'er it ought)

It will not then be worth a Groat,

Have any Force or Meaning good,

By which it may be understood;

And in it there must never be

Least Writing which the Eye may see,

For it may prove as empty ever,

And are their Pates under the beaver,

Or is it not Purpose fit,

Or consonant with Mason's wit ...

And he that can interpret these

Unwritten Scrolls and messages,

It is alone is welcome Guest,

And fit to be a Mason's Feast.[98]

This was not simply carping. Disapproval of what was seen as encroachment on civil liberties was as intense in the eighteenth century as it is today. And the impact of such opposition was as limited and ineffective then as it is now. The Secret Department and Deciphering Branch had become integral to the

---

[98] *Daily Post*, 15 February 1723.

collection and interpretation of intelligence and a central part of the weaponry deployed by Walpole and his ministers against their enemies and allies. Indeed, the material was so important that in 1730 Newcastle, through Delafaye, issued a warrant to the postmasters general instructing that *all* letters addressed to a list of 112 individuals, including many of Europe's monarchs and leading politicians, should from that date be intercepted and copied.[99]

The Department was at the same time put to work by other government offices and allied organisations, targeting suspected criminals and rooting out tax fraud and commercial espionage. Examples include warrants authorising the interception of mail 'addressed to two persons believed to be carrying on correspondence with someone who had fled from England with jewels so that his whereabouts might be ascertained', and 'all letters for John Peele, merchant, [to] be detained' and thereafter passed to the Customs Commissioners. The Bank of England also tabled requests,[100] including the detention of mail to and from Amsterdam.[101]

One warrant issued to the Post Office in April 1735 instructed the Secret Department to open all letters from and to Britain's envoy to Portugal, together with packages and correspondence 'wherein you shall suspect the said Envoy's letters to be enclosed ... as there is reason to believe that this Minister's correspondence will partly be carried on by the means of some merchants under whose cover his letters may be conveyed whose names not being known they cannot be particularly described'.

The instruction was delivered at almost exactly the same time that a request was made by the Grand Lodge of England to George Gordon, one of Desaguliers' acolytes, to convey a masonic warrant to Lisbon following a

---

[99] SP George II, XIX, 31 July 1730.

[100] Raymond Turner, 'The Secrecy of the Post', *English Historical Review*, 33.131 (1918), 320-7.

[101] SP 36/23/241: Governor of the Bank of England to Delafaye or Tilson, 16 July 1716. Cf., also, SP 36/23/239 16 July 1731: Rouse to Delafaye or Tilson, 'The warrant for stopping letters to Mordecai Jacobs de Vries may be signed as desired by the Governor of the Bank of England'.

petition from the city that a 'deputation might be granted ... for constituting
... a regular lodge'.[102] This was probably the lodge founded by British merchants and traders and recorded by the Portuguese Inquisition as the 'Lodge
of Heretical Merchants'.[103]

Merchant houses played a significant role in international espionage
and were used by all sides to bypass normal postal channels and transmit
confidential intelligence. Frederick of Prussia, for example, entrusted his
London envoy's diplomatic dispatches to David Splitberger, a merchant, although the 'subterfuge ... does not seem to have given the Secret Office any
trouble'.[104] Merchants also offered a conduit for private money transfers
and were used for that purpose by all sides. All governments were aware
that mail could be subject to interception, as did the Jacobites, and all sides
used couriers and smugglers to reduce the risk.

Gordon's success in establishing the lodge was reported widely; the reference to the presence of the English fleet, a symbol of projected naval and
military power and by inference British political protection, is of particular
significance:

> They write from Lisbon, that by Authority of the Right Hon The Earl
> of Weymouth, the then Grand Master of all Mason Lodges, Mr George
> Gordon, Mathematician, has constituted a Lodge of free and accepted
> Masons in that City; and that a great many Merchants of the factory, and
> other people of distinction, have been received and regularly made Free
> Masons; that Lord George Graham,[105] Lord Forrester,[106] and a great many

---

[102] Grand Lodge *Minutes*, p. 254.

[103] Cf., Vatcher, 'A Lodge of Irishmen at Lisbon, 1738', *AQC*, 84 (1971), 75-115.

[104] Philip Woodfine, *Britannia's Glories: The Walpole Ministry and the 1739 War with
Spain* (London: Royal Historical Society, 1998), p. 33.

[105] Lord George Graham was appointed a Grand Steward in 1734 but declined
or was unable to attend, possibly because of his naval duties. He was appointed a
grand warden in 1737.

[106] The pro-Hanoverian George Forrester, 6th Lord Forrester.

other gentlemen belonging to the English Fleet, being Brethren, were present at constituting the lodge; and 'tis expected that in a short time it will be one of the greatest abroad.[107]

On his return to England, Gordon was granted a sinecure as Page of the Backstairs to the Princess of Wales.[108] Although conjecture, such an appointment was unlikely to have been granted if unconnected with government business and it is probable that Gordon's journey was directly concerned with facilitating the flow of intelligence from Lisbon.

POSTSCRIPT: THE SECRETARIES TO THE POST OFFICE

Although the Secret Department reported via the foreign secretary of the Post Office to the secretaries of state, the administrative head of the Post Office, the secretary to the Post Office,[109] was the formal conduit for the receipt of warrants from the secretaries of state. The secretary was also responsible for the disbursement of secret service funds to cover the costs and expenses of the Secret Department. And from the 1730s and possibly earlier, he provided an additional channel for the transmission of intelligence reports.

The first office holder was John Avent at an annual salary of £100.[110] He was replaced by Benjamin Waterhouse in 1700 who was succeeded in 1714 by Henry Weston.[111] Weston was followed by Joseph Godman, who

---

[107] *London Evening Post,* 1 June 1736.

[108] *Daily Journal,* 18 October 1736.

[109] The office was created in June 1694 via Treasury Warrant.

[110] 'Secretaries to the Post Office': the Royal Mail Archive, Postal Heritage Trust Information Sheet, July 2010.

[111] Cf., *Declared Accounts: Post Office* in William A. Shaw and F.H. Slingsby (eds), *Calendar of Treasury Books, volume 29, 1714-1715* (London: HMSO, 1957); Treasury Warrants, *9 April 1718*; Joseph Redington (ed) *Calendar of Treasury Papers, volume 5, 1714-1719* (London: HMSO, 1883), pp. 372-98, 3 May 1718, et al. If the same man, Wills Proved at Prerogative Court of Canterbury, 2 October 1714.

was replaced by William Rouse in 1729.[112] Thomas Robinson, the solicitor to the Post Office, became secretary in 1737, John Barbutt held the office from 1738 until 1742,[113] and George Shelvocke from 1742 to 1760.[114] The number of support staff rose over time and the secretary's office contained at least three clerks by the 1740s, at which point he had become the *de facto* chief executive of the organisation. The transformation was complete by 1760, when it was the secretary who would convene Board meetings with the postmasters general ratifying decisions already taken.

Many were freemasons. Barbutt's membership of the Prince Eugene's Head lodge has been discussed. Rouse, with whom Delafaye corresponded directly,[115] was a probable member of the Bear and Harrow lodge which included many senior figures in London freemasonry, not least the grand master, Viscount Montagu, and the deputy grand master, Thomas Batson, alongside other grand officers.[116] Thomas Robinson may have been the master of the lodge at the Ship on Fish Street Hill, although there were many 'Thomas Robinsons' in London.

John Jesse (*d.*1753), who succeeded Barbutt, was a past master of the Queen's Head and St Paul's Head lodges and in 1735 a grand steward. He

---

[112] Wills Proved at Prerogative Court of Canterbury, 14 June 1729. Cf., also, for example, 'Warrants for the Payment of Money: 1733, October-December' in William A. Shaw (ed), *Calendar of Treasury Books and Papers, volume 2, 1731-1734* (London: HMSO, 1898), pp. 503-15, *15 November 1733*. An Edward Parsons is also named as secretary to the Post Office between 1721 and 1723: cf., for example, Joseph Redington (ed), *Calendar of Treasury Papers, volume 6, 1720-1728* (London: HMSO, 1889), 29 August 1721. 'Mr·Manley's letter (of 10 Aug. 1721) to Edward Parsons, Esq., Secretary to the postmaster general, showing the abuses of the franking of letters.'

[113] For example, William A. Shaw (ed), *Calendar of Treasury Books and Papers, volume 5, 1742-1745* (London: HMSO, 1903), 20 July 1742.

[114] Cf., *Country Journal or The Craftsman*, 17 July 1742. Cf., also, Ellis, *The Post Office in the Eighteenth Century*, pp. 24-37.

[115] SP 36/21/130-1.

[116] The grand officers included Desaguliers and James Chambers.

was appointed grand treasurer in 1739, holding the office until his death in 1753.[117] With Fotherley Baker, the deputy grand master, and John Revis, the grand secretary, he was part of a triumvirate of bureaucrats that ran English Grand Lodge for much of the late 1740s in the absence of the grand master, the 5th Lord Byron, who attended Grand Lodge only twice – at his installation and to appoint a successor - during five years in office.

Jesse had followed his father into the Post Office, a succession confirmed in the press: 'we hear that Mr John Jesse, only son to Mr John Jesse who died last Tuesday, will succeed his Father in the Post Office, said to be worth £100 per Annum'.[118] His receipt of a £10,000 inheritance in 1733 provided a career boost,[119] and a year later following the death of Charles Peal, his immediate superior, Jesse was promoted to first clerk and undersecretary, with his salary doubling to £200.[120]

Jesse continued to be promoted, becoming deputy cashier in 1737 and then cashier.[121] He was now near the summit of the Post Office hierarchy

---

[117] Cf., *Schism*, pp. 144-8.

[118] *London Evening Post,* 12 June 1729 – 14 June 1729; *Daily Post,* 14 June 1729; et al. His father had been engaged in supervising 'mis-sent, overcharged and dead letters': cf., John Chamberlayne, *Magnæ Britanniæ notitia: or, the present state of Great Britain* (London: B. & S. Tooke et al, 1723), part II, p. 524.

[119] 'A few days since died at Deptford, Mrs Grace Jesse, a maiden lady, worth upwards of £10,000, the bulk of which she has left to her nephew and sole executor, Mr John Jesse of the General Post Office': *Read's Weekly Journal Or British Gazetteer,* 29 September 1733. Cf., also *Wills Proved at Prerogative Court of Canterbury,* 18 September 1733, LL ref: wills_1730_1739_2531215_642765. The legacy may have been worth upwards of £1-2 million in current money. Grace Jesse may have been the sister of the captain of the *Venetian* (cf., *Weekly Packet,* 10 - 17 May 1718 and *Weekly Journal or Saturday's Post,* 13 October 1722): 'a gentleman of great honour and integrity' who died in Messina, Italy, in 1724. Cf., *Daily Post,* 14 October 1724.

[120] *Grub Street Journal,* 6 June 1734.

[121] *Weekly Miscellany,* 15 January 1737; and John Chamberlayne, *Magnæ Britanniæ notitia: or, the present state of Great Britain* (London: D. Midwinter et al, 1741), part II, p. 82.

and his profile rose as his name appeared at the foot of numerous formal missives and in court proceedings in which he represented his employer.[122] Perhaps more significantly, in July 1742, following John Barbutt's dismissal from office as secretary to the postmaster generals, Jesse became the official channel through which warrants for mail intercepts were received by the Post Office and authorised to receive secret despatches.[123] Five years later in 1747, Jesse was promoted accomptant general, a position one rung below that of postmaster general.[124]

Jesse's life outside of work centred on freemasonry and a small number of associated charities. He was a supporter or 'governor' of at least two organisations sponsored or supported by senior members of Grand Lodge, including the London Infirmary[125] and the Small Pox Hospital.[126] He also served as a director of the Amicable Society with Fotherley Baker, the deputy grand master, and Edward Hody, another grand officer.[127] Grand Lodge's minutes for 6 March 1753 note Jesse's absence from the Quarterly

---

[122] For example, *London Daily Post and General Advertiser,* 7 September 1738; *Daily Gazetteer,* 11 September 1738. There were upwards of sixty such announcements over the next three years. Also cf. Middlesex Sessions: Justices' Working Documents - deposition on 1 October 1737; and signature appended to affidavit 13 October 1737; and City of London Sessions: Justices' Working Documents - signature on deposition at Justice Hall in the Old Bailey, 4 September 1746 and 15 October 1746.

[123] SP 36/55 f. 255.

[124] *Whitehall Evening Post or London Intelligencer,* 1 - 3 October 1747. Also, *Penny London Post or The Morning Advertiser,* 2 October 1747 - 5 October 1747. The position of Receiver General was regarded as being of equal status to that of Accountant General.

[125] Cf., *An Account of the ... London Infirmary* (London, 1742), p. 12; also, *Alexander's feast ... set to music by Mr Handel* (London: J. & R. Thomson, 1753), p. 22; *A Sermon Preached before the governors of the London Infirmary* (London: London Infirmary, 1743), p. 34; and *London Evening Post,* 18 - 21 July 1752.

[126] *General Advertiser,* 19 May 1750.

[127] Aviva Archives. Cf. also, *Whitehall Evening Post or London Intelligencer,* 5 - 7 May 1747; and *London Daily Advertiser,* 1 May 1752. Cf., also, *Schism,* chapter five.

Communication due to illness; those for the following meeting on 14 June record that 'the DGM acquainted the Brethren with the death of Bro John Jesse Esq'. Jesse's Will had been proved at the Prerogative Court of Canterbury the day before.[128]

George Shelvocke (1702-1760), Barbutt's successor as secretary, was the son of George Shelvocke (1675-1742), a naval officer and privateer. It has been assumed by some historians that Shelvocke senior was a member of the Horn Tavern lodge rather than his son, but this is less probable. Although Shelvocke junior would have been 21 in 1723 and thus below the age at which one was notionally permitted to be initiated a freemason, he was only a year younger than the Duke of Richmond, the master of the Horn, and within the Horn the age limit was not observed or enforced.[129]

The attraction to Richmond and other members of a bright young man who had travelled the world on a privateering voyage is obvious. And given the mores of the time, were Shelvocke senior the member of the Horn rather than his son, it remains the case that his son would almost certainly have followed in his steps and become a freemason himself. Additional evidence for Shelvocke being a freemason is found within those supporting his election as FRS in 1743. The application, which describes him as 'a gentleman skilled in mathematical and philosophical knowledge and other branches of polite literature', was signed by several prominent freemasons including Martin Folkes, John Machin, John Froeke and Desaguliers.[130]

---

[128] Jesse was probably Huguenot. The surname was relatively common in the Low Countries and France, and the family possibly descended from 'de Jessé Lévas' who emigrated from Languedoc to England after the Revocation. Cf., William and Susan Minet (eds.), *Register of Churches of the Tabernacle, Glasshouse Street and Leicester Fields, 1688-1783* (London: Huguenot Society, 1926), vol. XXIX, p. 100.

[129] George Shelvocke the younger was also a member of the Spalding Society (elected 1745) as were other freemasons including William Stukeley and Martin Folkes.

[130] Royal Society, Sackler Archives, EC/1742/36.

Martin Folkes (1690-1754)
William Hogarth (1697-1764)

Shelvocke worked closely with the Secret Department and was involved actively in conveying foreign intelligence to the secretaries of state. Among his correspondence is a letter dated 16 March 1746 from Robert Blanchflower in Gothenburg concerning a Swedish vessel transporting French soldiers to the Moray Firth. Shelvocke relayed the information that although the men held commissions in the French army they had sworn 'neither to fight with or against the Pretender' and wished to confirm that they would not be attacked by the Royal Navy.[131] At this point however the Jacobites had yet to be defeated and Culloden occurred only the following month.[132]

Much of Shelvocke's correspondence was directed through Andrew Stone who had succeeded Delafaye as under-secretary at the Southern Department in 1734 and in 1739 took over from Tilson as Keeper of the State Papers.[133] It is worth noting that Shelvocke's reports included detailed updates on the timing and location of the mail packet boats, information that continued to be relevant.[134]

THE POSTMASTERS GENERAL

The Secret Department may not have reported operationally to the post-master general, a position shared jointly by two appointees throughout the period, but the postmaster general nonetheless had access to the department and to its personnel.

Although sometimes portrayed as a political backwater, the potential influence attached to the position of postmaster general was considerable and political loyalty was a key test of fitness for office. It was no coincidence that many incumbents were related to or political allies of senior government ministers. James Craggs,[135] the first joint postmaster after the acces-

---

[131] SP 36/82/2/27, 16 March 1746.

[132] Cf., Goran Behre, 'Sweden and the Rising of 1745', *Scottish Historical Review*, 51 (1972), 148-71.

[133] Stone was under-secretary (to Newcastle) July 1734 - April 1751; Collector of State Papers May 1739 - June 1741; and Keeper of State Papers May 1741 -December 1773. Cf., SP 44/128. He resigned as under-secretary in April 1751 on being appointed tutor to the Prince of Wales.

[134] For example, SP 36/89/1/82, 10 November 1746.

[135] James Craggs (1657-1721). Cf., Stuart Handley, 'Craggs, James, the elder (*bap* 1657, *d*.1721)', *ODNB*, online edn, May 2006, accessed 5 March 2016.

sion of George I, was a close associate of the Duke of Marlborough and his son-in-law, Lord Sunderland.[136] More importantly, his son, also James, was secretary of state for the Southern Department from 1718 until his death in February 1721.[137]

Craggs the Elder resigned in 1720, tainted by financial scandal, and was replaced by Galfridus Walpole, formerly MP for Lostwithiel, Robert Walpole's youngest brother.[138] Following Galfridus's death in 1726 at the age of 43, the position went to Edward Harrison, a director of the East India Company and previously MP for Hertford.[139] He was the father-in-law of Charles Townshend, 3rd Viscount Townshend. He was also a possible member of the lodge at the Black Posts in Cockpit Court, Great Wild Street.[140]

Charles Cornwallis, 4th Baron Cornwallis, a political ally of Walpole and Townshend, sat as joint-postmaster general alongside Craggs but resigned in 1721 following promotion to the more lucrative position of paymaster of the forces.[141] His successor, Edward Carteret (*d.*1739), formerly MP for Bere Alston, was a nephew of Lord Carteret, secretary of state for the Southern Department from 1721 to 1724.[142]

---

[136] Charles Spencer, 3rd Earl of Sunderland.

[137] James Craggs, the younger (1686-1721).

[138] Galfridus Walpole (1683-1726), MP for Lostwithiel (1715-21). An appointment as postmaster general disqualified the holder from sitting in the House of Commons and each appointee, if an MP, was obliged to resign his seat before taking office.

[139] Edward Harrison (1674-1731), MP for Weymouth and Melcome Regis (1717-1722) and Hertford (1722-1726).

[140] Grand Lodge *Minutes*, p. 40.

[141] Charles Cornwallis, 4th Baron Cornwallis (1675-1722).

[142] Edward Carteret (1671-1739), MP for Huntingdon (1698-1700), Bedford (1702-05) and Bere Alston (1717-1721).

Like his predecessors, Carteret was aware of the purpose of the Secret Department and occasionally became involved.[143] A letter to Delafaye in April 1731, for example, requests a warrant for opening and copying 'correspondence from Rome addressed to one – Garden'.[144] In a postscript, Carteret advises Delafaye of a more personal matter, noting that 'We have a Lysbon mail come in just now and I am sorry to tell you, that I fear your old friend Capt. Cowper is lost, and his ship too, for we have no manner of news of him since he sailed from Falmouth'.

Sir John Eyles, a prosperous merchant, replaced Carteret.[145] Eyles had served on the commission to oversee estates forfeited to the crown after the abortive 1715 Jacobite Rising. He was a City stalwart, a director of the Bank of England, East India and South Sea companies, elected master of the Haberdashers' Company in 1716, and from 1737 until his death president of St Thomas's Hospital. Eyles was elected Lord Mayor in 1726 and served as colonel of the City of London's White Regiment of Militia. Following his death in 1745, he was replaced by Everard Fawkener, another merchant and a former ambassador to the Ottoman Empire.[146] Fawkener held office from 1745 to 1758 jointly with Thomas Coke, Lord Lovel, who had succeeded Edward Harrison in 1733.[147]

---

[143] Examples of Craggs' involvement include SP 35/17/109: Craggs to Delafaye regarding a matter which requires Lord Sunderland to draw up a warrant, 22 August 1719.

[144] SP 36/23/47.

[145] John Eyles (1683-1745), MP for Chippenham (1713-1727) and London (1727-1734).

[146] Sir Everard Fawkener was from 1735-1745 ambassador to the Ottoman Empire. Cf., Haydn Mason, 'Fawkener, Sir Everard (1694-1758)', *ODNB*, online edn, Jan 2015, accessed 14 December 2015.

[147] Thomas Coke (1697-1759), later Lord Lovel and from 1745 Earl of Leicester; MP for Norfolk (1722-28).

Coke, a wealthy Norfolk landowner, was Walpole's election manager for Norfolk. He was rewarded with a knighthood when the Order of the Bath was revived in 1725, and raised to the peerage as Lord Lovel at George II's coronation; he subsequently gained an earldom, becoming Earl of Leicester.[148] A prominent freemason, Coke was initiated in the 1720s and was grand master of English Grand Lodge from 1731 until 1732.[149]

Two questions remain. Were the masonic connections of Post Office officials and those within the Secret Department and the Deciphering Branch politically significant, and would or could operations have continued without them. The answers to both questions is 'yes'.

Peter Clark has noted that freemasonry 'provided a spinal element in social networking, helping to underpin contacts and communications in business, politics and local administration'.[150] In fact it did more. One need only read the text of Delafaye's *Fellowcraft's Song* to gain an insight into its emotional resonance:

The Fellow-Craft's Song

Hail Masonry! Thou Craft divine!
Glory of Earth! From Heav'n reveal'd,
Which dost with Jewels precious shine
From all but Masons Eyes conceal'd.

---

[148] A.A. Hanham, 'Coke, Thomas, Earl of Leicester (1697–1759)', *ODNB*. Lovel was installed as grand master of the Grand Lodge of England in 1731. Coke's name was pronounced 'Cook', and was often [mis]spelled the same way. Cf. Anderson, 1738 *Constitutions*, pp. 128, 142.

[149] *British Journal or The Censor,* 27 April 1728; also, *London Journal,* 27 April 1728.

[150] Peter Clark, *British Clubs and Societies 1580-1800: The Origins of an Associational World* (Oxford: OUP, 2000), p. 348

Chorus: *Thy Praises due who can rehearse*
            In nervous Prose or flowing Verse?

As Men from Brutes distinguished are
A Mason other Men excels;
For what's in Knowledge choice and rare
But in his Breast securely dwells.

Chorus: *His silent Breast and faithful Heart*
            Preserve the Secrets of the Art.

From scorching Heat and piercing Cold,
From Beasts whose Roar the Forest rends,
From the Affairs of Warriors bold
The Masons' Art Mankind defends.

Chorus: *Be to this Art due Honour paid*
            From which Mankind receives such Aid.

Ensigns of State that feed our Pride
Distinctions troublesome and vain!
By Masons true are laid aside:
Art's free-born Sons such Toys distain.

Chorus: *Ennobled by the Name they love*
            Distinguished by the Badge they wear.

Sweet Fellowship from Envy free,
Friendly Converse of Brotherhood,
The Lodge's lasting Cement be!
Which has for Ages firmly stood.

Chorus: *A Lodge thus built for Ages past*
        Has lasted and will ever last.

Then is our Songs be Justice done
To those who have enriched the Arts,
From Jabal down to Burlington
And let each Brother bear a Part.

Chorus: *Let noble Masons Healths go round,*
        Their praise in lofty Lodge resound.[151]

Within the Huguenot community and Whiggist lodges, freemasonry had become both an inward and outward sign of loyalty and trustworthiness. Of course the Secret Department could have functioned without the involvement of freemasons but the shared commonality of freemasonry aided its function. It was also the case that freemasonry provided a component of Britain's espionage endeavours at home and overseas, the subject of the next three chapters.

---

[151] Delafaye's masonic compositions extended beyond *The Fellow-Craft's Song*. A 1731 concert at the Theatre Royal in Lincoln's Inn Fields featured another work, 'a piece of vocal and instrumental music' given 'at the request of a great number of ... Free and Accepted Masons': *Daily Advertiser*, 20 April 1731.

CHAPTER FIVE

RUNNING HOT: THE SPIES IN THE COLD

What is called 'foreknowledge' cannot be elicited from spirits, nor from gods, nor by analogy with past events, nor from calculations. It must be obtained from men who know the enemy situation.[1]

Freemasonry was England's most popular and prominent fraternal association in the 1720s and 1730s.[2] In its new guise it rippled out from London across the English provinces and into Scotland, Ireland and Wales. It was transported internationally across Britain's burgeoning Empire by economic migrants, the military and merchants, for whom it became a means to expedite and strengthen trading relationships.[3] Freemasonry also took root elsewhere, with complementary and competing lodges and grand lodges created across Europe from Portugal in the west to Russia and Hungary in the east, and from Italy and Spain to Sweden. It developed a particularly devoted following among the European elites and continental aristocracy where the combination of mediaeval ritual and social exclusivity, allied to its association with Newtonian science and the Enlightenment, proved exceptionally attractive.[4]

English lodges in continental Europe provided a space where progressive elite Catholics might be introduced to and become comfortable with

---

[1] Sun Tzu, *The Art of War*.

[2] Peter Clark, *British Clubs and Societies 1580-1800* (Oxford: OUP, 2000).

[3] Jessica Harland-Jacobs, *Builders of Empire Builders of Empire: Freemasonry and British Imperialism, 1717-1927* (Chapel Hill, NC: University of North Carolina Press, 2012), pp. 1-20.

[4] Cf., *Foundations*, esp. chapter five. Also, Marsha Keith Schuchard, *Restoring the Temple of Vision* (Leiden: Brill, 2002) and Schuchard, *Emanuel Swedenborg, secret agent on Earth and in heaven: Jacobites, Jews, and Freemasons in early Modern Sweden* (Leiden: Brill, 2012).

Protestant British mores and cultural values. Freemasonry meshed with the social aspects of eighteenth-century diplomacy and politics, which allowed it to be deployed effectively by all sides.[5] The lodge was used by politicians who were devoted masons, and by others, including Walpole, for whom freemasonry was valuable principally for the political advantages it might bring. This latter aspect is discussed in more detail in the following two chapters. This chapter examines another by-product: how freemasonry was used covertly and overtly as a conduit for intelligence gathering.

Positioning freemasonry for intelligence purposes was not without risk. Freemasonry faced suppression and interdiction in Europe from the 1730s, with the Catholic Church and Catholic monarchs suspecting, sometimes with justification, that its lodges offered a forum for potential conspirators and thus a potential threat to the established order. This was accurate in the sense that private lodges could and did provide a private 'public sphere' for debate and discussion.[6] And academic research now accepts that masonic relational space was central to eighteenth and nineteenth-century sociability,[7] and that it could be and was used as a vehicle for sedition. Perhaps this added to its attraction, giving a frisson of danger.

This chapter highlights the activities of four secondary players on the European stage: John Coustos, William Dugood, Vincent La Chapelle and Charles Labelye. None were full-time government agents but rather informal spies, something common in the eighteenth century. Their intelligence reports were routed through intermediaries, such as Philipp von Stosch, a British agent resident in Rome, then Florence; via diplomats and merchants;

---

[5] Cf., Philip Woodfine, *The Duke of Newcastle's War: Walpole's ministry and the war against Spain, 1737-1742* (University of Huddersfield, PhD thesis, 1994), for examples of Walpole's cabinet meetings taking place over dinner.

[6] Jürgen Habermas, *transl.* Thomas Burger, *The Structural Transformation of the Public Sphere: An Inquiry into a Category of Bourgeois Society* (Cambridge: CUP, 1989).

[7] Pierre-Yves Beaurepaire, 'The Universal Republic of the Freemasons and the Culture of Mobility in the Enlightenment', *French Historical Studies*, 29.3 (2006), 407-31.

or in person, possibly through the lodge. Remuneration, if any, would not have been fixed but rather a function of the access and insights that were considered to be on offer; and payment was off-the-books from secret service monies.

JOHN COUSTOS

John Coustos (*c.*1703-*c.*1760?), is known best as one of the more prominent British victims of the Portuguese Inquisition and rather less as a small cog in Whitehall's network of European agents. The Coustos family had migrated to England in 1716 from Berne via The Hague, Leiden and Rotterdam, and were later naturalized.[8] It has been suggested that the family were originally Marrano, part of the quarter million Jews in Spain and Portugal who were forcibly converted to Christianity in the fifteenth century many of whom continued to practice Judaism in private.[9] 'Marrano' derives from the Arabic 'muharām' or 'harām', with a connotation of forbidden or unlawful.[10] It was used abusively and that it remained so in the eighteenth century is clear from the allusions to Coustos's supposed Jewish roots in accusations made against the lodge he founded in Paris in 1736. But notwithstanding this, there is no evidence that Coustos was other than what he professed to be - a practicing Protestant – as was his father, Isaac, a physician,[11] both of

---

[8] John Coustos, *The Sufferings of John Coustos ... in the Inquisition at Lisbon* (London: Coustos, 1746), p. 6. Isaac Coustos had at least four other children: Elizabeth, Marie, Joseph and Paul. Cf. William & Susan Minet, *Registers of the Churches of The Tabernacle Glasshouse Street and Leicester Fields*, p. 144.

[9] Cf., John Shaftesley, 'Jews in English Freemasonry in the 18th and 19th Centuries', *AQC*, 92 (1979), 25-62.

[10] Cf., http://www.jewishhistory.org/the-marranos, accessed 7 June 2016.

[11] Isaac Coustos probably practiced as an unregistered 'barber surgeon'. His name does not appear in *Monk's Rolls*, a list of members of the Royal College of Physicians.

whom were members of the Huguenot Church of Glasshouse Street and Leicester Fields.[12]

John Coustos, *Sufferings*
Portrait on Frontispiece, 1746

Coustos trained as a jeweller and diamond cutter. He became a free-mason in his early twenties, a member of the lodge at the Rainbow Coffee

---

[12] *Registers of the Churches of The Tabernacle Glasshouse Street and Leicester Fields*, pp. 129, 131, 134 & 144-6.

House and subsequently a founder of that at the Prince Eugene's Head Coffee House.

Coustos left London just over a decade later, explaining in *Sufferings* that this was at the 'solicitation of a friend … in order to work in the galleries of the Louvre'.[13] The friend is unnamed and unintentionally or otherwise the date is incorrect. Coustos had left for Paris in 1736, some two years earlier. And the motivation, at least in part, was espionage. Anti-English sentiment in France had been building with mounting support for the exiled Stuarts one of its corollaries. Through Waldegrave and other sources Whitehall was aware that Charles Radcliffe, the titular Earl of Derwentwater,[14] a committed Jacobite, was engaged in securing support for the Stuart cause at the French court and beyond. Derwentwater had fought in the 1715 Jacobite Rising. Captured, he had been tried, found guilty and sentenced to death, but escaped Newgate prison while awaiting execution. He fled to Italy and later moved to Paris where he married[15] and took a commission in Charles Fitz-James's regiment.[16]

The time and place of Derwentwater's initiation into freemasonry is uncertain but he co-founded a masonic lodge in Paris in 1725 or 1726 whose

---

[13] Coustos, *Sufferings*, p. 6.

[14] Charles Radcliffe, the titular 5th Earl of Derwentwater (*c.*1693-1746), in Leo Gooch, 'Radcliffe, James, styled third earl of Derwentwater (1689-1716)', *ODNB*. Radcliffe had been convicted of treason and attainted, and the title was thus no longer recognised in Britain.

[15] Derwentwater wed Charlotte Clifford, a Jacobite sympathiser and widow of Thomas Clifford, second son of Lord Clifford of Chudleigh. She was the daughter of Charles, 2nd Earl of Newburgh. The marriage was solemnised at Brussels on 24 June 1724.

[16] A grandson of James II through his father, the Duke of Berwick, Charles de Fitz-James, 4th Duke of Fitz-James (1712-1787); he was awarded a French title and later became a Marshal of France. Cf. Gooch, 'Derwentwater', *ODNB*.

membership was drawn mainly from the exiled Jacobite community. He was later installed grand master in France.[17]

Historians take opposing views of Jacobite freemasonry. Some argue that it functioned as a fraternal association of exiled Jacobites and a private space for those of similar social status; others hold that it was a well-spring of Stuart conspiracies. It was both, and its members' political views ranged from overtly revolutionary to more moderate dinner-party Jacobites. Despite many paying lip service to the Stuart cause, only a minority were ever active insurgents and for many, if not most, loyalty to James Stuart ebbed and flowed in accord with fashion, as well as Jacobite failure and success.

Outwardly, French freemasonry had a similar structure to that in England.[18] One of its principal functions was to provide a forum for gentlemanly association, conversation and dining. The right lodge also validated one's status in polite society. Despite Cardinal Fleury's disquiet and opposition from within the Catholic Church, freemasonry achieved traction within the French aristocracy and among the affluent upper middling to the extent that in September 1737 the *Daily Advertiser* could publish a report from its correspondent in Paris that 'the Order of Freemasons lately established here meets with great success; everyone is desirous of being admitted a member, and numbers are daily taken in at the expence [sic] of ten Louis d'Ors each. Among them are the P. of Conti, all the young dukes, M. de Maurepas, M.

---

[17] As grand master, Derwentwater issued a charter to Baron Carl Fredrik de Scheffer, allowing him to establish masonic lodges in Sweden and issue a set of masonic regulations - Règles générales de la Maçonnerie. The latter relied heavily on Anderson's 1723 *Constitutions* other than in one respect: it insisted that freemasonry should be exclusively Christian. Scheffer became grand master of Swedish Freemasons in 1753.

[18] Cf., Monod, *Jacobitism and the English People, 1688-1788*, for a discussion of the point. Also Jessica Harland-Jacobs, *Builders of Empire: Freemasons and British Imperialism, 1717-1927*.

St. Florentin, etc. There are nineteen lodges already constituted'.[19] Indeed, according to the press, so successful was freemasonry that 'the ladies are about to establish a counter order in imitation'.[20]

Where French freemasonry differed from its Anglo-Saxon counterpart was in its embrace of a more complex, theatrical and quasi-spiritual chivalric ritual. This found adherents among the aristocracy and court circles elsewhere in Europe, including the German states, Austria and also Sweden, where it was transformed by Charles XIII into the Swedish Rite.[21]

The oration given at Paris in December 1736[22] by Andrew Michael Ramsay - 'Chevalier Ramsay' - at Derwentwater's lodge had much in common with the *Old Charges* and Anderson's 1723 *Constitutions*, but embellished them.[23] Ramsay inflated the Craft's lineage, tracing it back to Abraham and the Jewish patriarchs, and to ancient Egypt. He placed freemasonry within a medieval context, dating the origins of modern freemasonry to the Crusades when 'many princes, lords and citizens associated themselves and vowed to restore the Temple of the Christians in the Holy Land, to employ themselves in bringing back their architecture to its first institution'.

---

[19]   *Daily Advertiser*, 23 September 1737.

[20]   Ibid.

[21]   Swedish Rite was designed and formalised by Charles XIII in the late eighteenth century. An exclusively Christian order, it contains ten principal degrees: three St John's or Craft degrees; two St Andrew's or Scottish degrees; and five Chapter or Templar degrees. Members of the Grand Council take an 11th degree, becoming Knight Commanders of the Red Cross.

[22]   The date of the Oration was probably 27 December 1736, although Gould specifies the date as 21 March 1737. Both were technically correct since Ramsay delivered the Oration on more than one occasion. It was also printed and circulated widely.

[23]   For a detailed exposition cf. C.N. Batham, 'Chevalier Ramsay – A New Appreciation', *AQC*, 81 (1968), 280-315. There are various versions of Ramsay's *Oration*. Bernheim suggests that he plagiarised material from English and French sources. Cf. *inter alia*, Berheim, *Etudes Maçonniques* 'Ramsay and his Discours Revisited': http://www.freemasons-freemasonry.com/bernheim_ramsay03.html#c, accessed 20 August 2016.

Ramsay contended that the knight crusaders had 'agreed upon several ancient signs and symbolic words drawn from the well of religion in order to recognize themselves amongst the heathen and Saracens', and that 'these signs and words were only communicated to those who promised solemnly, even sometimes at the foot of the altar, never to reveal them'. The masonic promise was a 'bond to unite Christians of all nationalities in one confraternity', and the essence of Ramsay's chivalric, muscular freemasonry was 'after the example set by the Israelites when they erected the second Temple who, whilst they handled the trowel and mortar with one hand, in the other held the sword and buckler'.[24]

Alongside praise for freemasonry's chivalric and mediaeval origins, Ramsay argued that it epitomised all that was virtuous: a sense of humanity, good taste, fine wit, agreeable manners, and a true appreciation of the fine arts, science and religion. He advanced a holistic concept that appealed to Europe's elites and validated their self-worth. Ramsay also posited that 'the interests of the Brotherhood are those of mankind as a whole' and that 'the subjects of all kingdoms shall learn to cherish one another without renouncing their own country'. In common with Desaguliers, he saw freemasonry as a movement that could unite individuals 'of all nations' and actively proselytised it as such.

Monod and others have proposed that Ramsay's oration fired the starting gun for the introduction of higher degrees and complementary masonic 'side orders'. This is partly true, although such side orders and higher degrees were already in use in Scotland and Ireland. But one cannot ignore European aristocracy's abiding obsession with chivalric orders, something that dated at least to the Crusades. Among many examples are the Knights Hospitallers (formed in 1099), the Order of Saint Lazarus (1100), the Knights Templars (1118), and the Teutonic Knights (1190). Other degrees

---

[24] Quotations from Dudley Wright, *Gould's History of Freemasonry throughout the World*, (New York, NY: Charles Scribener's Sons), volume III, pp. 13-4. For a more detailed exposition cf. Batham, op. cit.

and orders were even more select, among them the Order of the Golden Fleece, founded in Bruges in 1430 by Philip III, Duke of Burgundy, and limited to fifty knights plus the sovereign. It remains active today. Knowingly or not, Ramsay's approach allowed him to push at an already open door.

Externally, French freemasonry initially copied London's masonic lodges and offered entertainments, and dining and drinking, alongside masonic liturgy. Margaret Jacob comments that the lodges were in essence replicas of those in England with shared norms of governance and behaviour.[25] This is not wholly accurate. Leaving to one side Jacobitism and a more elaborate ritual and greater religiosity, there was another key difference: the context in which the lodges met. Where Britain's constitutional structure allowed debate and balanced parliamentary and royal authority, in France the crown lay at the centre of political power and its influence was virtually absolute.

Freemasonry in England was not a constitutional threat, more the opposite. But in France it was perceived by the Catholic Church as a subversive if not potentially heretical movement. It was an organisation whose leaders were openly elected, that advanced deism, and that evangelised the natural liberties of justice. Freemasonry also advocated education, arguably the ultimate threat to autocracy.[26] There was also the absence of any obligation to adhere to Roman Catholicism; indeed, the opposite was the case: 'As Masons we only pursue the universal Religion or the Religion of Nature. This is the Cement which unites Men of the most different Principles in one sacred Band and brings together those who were most distant from one another'.[27]

---

[25] Margaret C. Jacob, *Living the Enlightenment: Freemasonry and Politics in Eighteenth-Century Europe* (Oxford: OUP, 1991), p. 4.

[26] Under the terms of the fourth masonic charge: 'All preferment among Masons is grounded upon real Worth and personal Merit only; that so the Lords may be well served, the Brethren not put to Shame, nor the Royal Craft despised ... no Master or Warden is chosen by Seniority, but for his Merit...'

[27] William Smith, *A Pocket Companion for Freemasons* (London, 1735), pp. 43-5.

The success of Ramsay's oration and the imprimatur of France's aristocratic and mercantile elites led to an influx of new members - 'the Order [in France] increases so fast that it now takes up nine lodges'.[28] With Derwentwater grand master of French freemasonry, Waldegrave's concerns that he was lobbying on the Stuarts' behalf and that French ministers were increasingly evasive about the approaches being made to them by those who supported Jacobite interests were passed to London.[29] It is this which explains Coustos's move to Paris and his establishment of a lodge within days of Ramsay's oration.[30]

There would have been concern in London that Derwentwater could and would use freemasonry to advance the Jacobite cause. Freemasonry had been organised in a similar manner in support of the Hanoverians, and Richmond and Desaguliers had only two years earlier established lodges at Paris and Aubigny[31] to promote a Whig political agenda.

It may be ironic but Richmond had initiated Ramsay in 1730.[32] Whether this was despite or because of Ramsay's suspected Jacobite allegiances is

---

[28] *The Leeds Mercury*, 22 March 1736, quoted in J.A.M. Snoek, *Initiating Women in Freemasonry* (Leiden: Brill, 2012), p. 15. To place this in context, Derwentwater's lodge reputedly had 500 members.

[29] SP 78/213/76.

[30] Ramsay delivered his Oration on 27 December, an event that would have been advertised in advance; Coustos's lodge met formally for the first time the following day. Marsha Keith Schuchard, unpublished manuscript made available privately.

[31] His grandmother, Louise Renée de Penancoët de Kérouaille, Duchess of Portsmouth (1649-1734) a mistress of Charles II of England and a French spy; she was later made duchess of Aubigny.

[32] Ramsay was initiated at the Horn on 9 March 1730. He had been elected FRS in November 1729 and in April 1730 received a doctorate from Oxford, the first Catholic to do so since the Reformation. Ramsay was a prominent Jacobite and had briefly acted as tutor to the young Charles Edward Stuart.

uncertain, but Townshend had ordered Delafaye to maintain surveillance on Ramsay and the initiation may have been part of that process.[33]

With Derwentwater's freemasonry gaining traction within Paris, Whitehall would have sought to add to its intelligence gathering capability, a goal achieved by Coustos virtually immediately. Less than two months after forming his lodge, the Duc de Villeroy,[34] one of Louis XV's most senior courtiers, was initiated by Coustos. There is no proof that this was at Louis XV's request, something indicated by Coustos, but that is a secondary issue. Villeroy's admission gave the lodge status which was reflected in it being renamed 'Villeroy-Coustos Lodge', with Villeroy installed as worshipful master on 17 February 1737 and Coustos appointed his deputy.

Louis Bontemps,[35] the hereditary 'Premier Valet', was another prominent initiate. The Bontemps family had been ennobled in the mid-seventeenth century and Louis, one of whose godparents was Louis XIV, held the title alongside other royal offices including Governor of the Tuileries, Captain of the Varenne Hunt and Superintendent of the Royal Buildings and Gardens.[36]

A list of members of Villeroy-Coustos lodge is given in the appendices but two names should be mentioned here: Johan Christoph Baur, a German-born Lutheran banker who was later appointed deputy grand master of France; and Count Czapski, a loyal supporter of Stanislau of Poland. Schuchard suggests that Baur provided a secret conduit for Louis XV through which monies were transferred to finance Swedish troops in Poland, and

---

[33] Cf., Jeremy Black, 'A Failed Attempt at Censorship: the British Diplomatic Service and Pöllnitz's Histoire secrette de la Duchesse d'Hanover', *Quaerendo* 18.3 (1988), 211-27, esp. 211. I am grateful to Marsha Keith Schuchard for this reference.

[34] Louis de Neufville, Duc de Villeroy (1695-1766).

[35] Louis Alexandre Bontemps (1669-1742).

[36] Premier Valet de chamber du roi; Gouverneur des Tuileries; Capitaine des Chasses de la Varenne du Louvre.

that he engaged with French diplomacy and intelligence on a broader level.[37] Luthy is cited to advance the argument that 'when Fleury came to power, he entrusted Baur with ... secret transactions, especially concerning Polish affairs', and that 'Baur ... encouraged the support of German Lutherans who were crucial to Stanislaus's campaign'.[38] Set against this view it should be noted that Baur is not mentioned by Perrault in his *Le Secret du Roi*, an exhaustive account of Louis XV's secret foreign policy in Poland.[39] Regardless, Baur's relationship with Swedish diplomats in Paris facilitated the expansion of freemasonry into Sweden and the issuance of warrants authorising the establishment of Swedish lodges.[40]

Count Czapski was equally well-connected and well-informed about the French court and diplomatic matters. He was a first cousin to Marie Leszczynska (1703-1768), one of King Stanislau's daughters,[41] who had married Louis XV in 1725. Czapski was later elected master of Villeroy-Coustos lodge and subsequently founded one of the first lodges in Poland at Warsaw.

Notwithstanding his masonic access to these and other influential figures, and his position as a jeweller of repute, a role parallel to that of a private banker, the effectiveness of Coustos as an intelligence agent is unknown. There is no evidence of any intelligence product supplied in his own name, and Derwentwater made it plain within months that he was unhappy to see lodges operating in France that were loyal to English Grand Lodge. French freemasons heeded his call and many left English-warranted lodges to join those that recognised Derwentwater.

---

[37] Schuchard, *Emanuel Swedenborg*, p. 205.

[38] Ibid., p. 233. Herbert Luthy, *La Banque Protestante en France* (Paris: SEVPEN, 1961).

[39] Gilles Perrault, *Le Secret du Roi - La Passion Polonaise* (Paris: Fayard, 1992).

[40] Schuchard, *Emanuel Swedenborg*, pp. 205 & 340.

[41] Czapski had also fought at Königsberg alongside General Johan Stenflycht, one of Stanislau's principal backers.

Freemasonry's growing influence substantiated concerns within the French government, police and secret service, and in 1737 Cardinal Fleury moved to curb the perceived threat despite protests from Derwentwater, Ramsay and others. But the police ban on freemasonry effectively drove the lodges underground: 'all the Taverns and Eating Houses are forbid, by an Order of the Lieutenant de Police, to entertain the Free-Masons'.[42]

Nonetheless, Villeroy-Coustos lodge was the subject of a police raid later that year and the lodge ceased to operate thereafter.[43] The section of the lodge's records that deal with its denunciation and closure were later redacted – 'cancelled by the advice (and order) of the brethren [for] reasons known to the brethren'.[44] The reason is not clear but it is likely that its demise was hastened by depositions made to the authorities in which Coustos and Thomas Le Breton, the master of Louis d'Argent and a member of Villeroy-Coustos, were accused of improper and heretical behaviour:

> Thomas Le Breton, with his kindred spirits (La Confederation), as well as the man called *Jean Meyers Custos*, and others, in defiance of the laws of God and man, held a meeting in the Rue du Four, and another at Dassy, both absolute orgies - and that too during Lent, in fact during Passion Week. The whole progeny of turpitude and excess evidently ran riot in the streets: drunkenness, gluttony, fireworks, revelry; the entire village of Dassy turned out. And all this on the pretence of holding a masonic meeting.[45]

---

[42] *The Leeds Mercury*, 29 March 1737.

[43] The raid led to the lodge Minute Book and other records being confiscated. They are now held at the Bibliothèque Nationale, Paris.

[44] W. McLeod, 'More Light on John Coustos', *AQC*, 95 (1982), 118.

[45] Ibid., 117-9. My italics. McLeod also refers to a press report in August 1744 following Coustos's arrest in Lisbon which described him in similar terms as a 'Lent breaker'.

The emphasis on Coustos's alleged middle name - 'Meyers' - was designed to draw attention to his supposed Jewish roots. Shaftesley in *AQC* 92 proposes that Coustos was Jewish but can only advance anecdotal evidence, including the similarity of 'Coustos' to 'de Costa', a common Portuguese Jewish surname, and the prevalence of Jews in the diamond trade.[46] However there is no evidence that Coustos's religious convictions were other than as stated in *Sufferings*: 'baptised according to the form used by the Protestants ... "In the name of the Father and of the Son and of the Holy Ghost"'.

Fleury's move against freemasonry was nonetheless nuanced. Despite raids on specific lodges, France's Parlement did not impose a blanket ban nor was the Papal Bull fully implemented. And although Waldegrave was correct to warn that the Jacobites were lobbying Louis XV and his ministers to support the Stuarts, and that freemasonry had become integral to that process, Fleury did not believe that the Jacobites had the support in Britain that would guarantee a Stuart Restoration. It explains not only his ambivalence towards Jacobite freemasonry but also his unwillingness to offer material support to the Stuarts.[47]

Coustos remained in Paris until late 1740 or early 1741, when he left for Lisbon.[48] He states that the move was inspired by the discovery of diamonds in Brazil, a Portuguese colony, and that he travelled to Lisbon to obtain the necessary travel permissions 'in hope of finding an opportunity [to] make my fortune'.[49] The Portuguese authorities ignored his petition and 'having lost all hope', Coustos instead decided to settle in the city, becoming a diamond cutter and dealer 'to support my family with decency [and] to lay up a competency for old age'.

---

[46] Shaftesley, 'Jews in English Freemasonry in the 18th and 19th Centuries', *AQC*, 92.

[47] Cf., Guite, *The Jacobite Cause, 1730-1740: the International Dimension.*

[48] Coustos states that he left for Lisbon five years after arriving in Paris.

[49] Coustos, *The Sufferings of John Coustos*, p. 6.

Once again the stated reasons may be disingenuous. Almost immediately after arriving in Lisbon Coustos established another lodge. His fellow members were mainly non-Portuguese nationals, principally merchants and jewellers. Were Coustos engaged in intelligence gathering, such men were an ideal source of information and offered a means of dissemination.

Coustos was denounced to the Portuguese Inquisition in October 1742. According to the Inquisition his lodge included at least fourteen other members. Nine were French nationals: four were merchants (Messrs Brulé, Felix, Julian and Bolange); three were jewellers (Messrs Charmoa, Pietre, Villanova); one a gunsmith (Lambert Blanger); and the last, Alexandre Mouton, either a diamond cutter or tailor to the French ambassador.[50] There were two English members (Messrs Fose and Ivens), a book seller and watchmaker, respectively; a Scot, a Mr Gordon, whose occupation is not stated; and a Dutchman, Mr Vandervel, another jeweller.[51]

Coustos argues in *Sufferings* that he and his fellow masons were not aware that freemasonry had been prohibited in Portugal and, in any event, the lodge met at 'private houses of chosen friends' rather than in public taverns. His disavowal may have been untruthful. It is unlikely that Coustos would not have known that *In Eminenti* had proscribed freemasonry across Catholic Europe, including Portugal, even if the interdict was not always observed, and that freemasonry had been banned elsewhere for political reasons.[52]

Quite apart from the Papal Bull, European governments - Protestant and Catholic - were wary of potentially subversive organisations, especially where members took oaths and elected their officers at meetings which the authorities were unable to monitor. The United Provinces proscribed

---

[50] Ibid. Different descriptions are given on pp. 109 and 116.

[51] 'Trial of John Coustos by the Inquisition. Original documents of the Inquisition at Lisbon.' *AQC*, 67 (1954), 107-23.

[52] The conventional practice was that papal Bulls required the approval of local legislative bodies, secular and religious, before they could be enforced.

freemasonry, albeit temporarily, in the late 1730s, as did Poland. This also affected Saxony and Lithuania, where the king was respectively Elector and Grand Duke. And other countries followed. An edict from Charles VI briefly prohibited freemasonry in the Austrian Netherlands, and in 1740 Philip V approved the Bull, decreeing that those in Spain who were proved or deemed to be freemasons would be condemned to the galleys. France didn't implement the Bull nationally but masonic meetings were banned in certain cities in the mid-1740s. And freemasonry came under threat in Germany and Switzerland, with the city of Hanover, the Canton of Geneva and the Council of Berne all issuing interdictions.

There are several possible explanations for Coustos's response to the Inquisition but the most likely is that it would have been self-defeating for him to have admitted either in *Sufferings* or before the Inquisition that he was willing to flout the law and the Bull either covertly in the 'private houses of chosen friends' or otherwise. And an argument that freemasonry continued elsewhere in Europe despite ecumenical and national bans would have been inflammatory and irrelevant.

WILLIAM DUGOOD

Coustos's move to Lisbon can be compared with that of William Dugood (*fl.*1715-1767), another jeweller, freemason and spy. Some twenty-five years earlier, Dugood, a Scottish Catholic, had been employed in Italy as a secretary and factotum to Thomas Coke, later Earl of Leicester,[53] then on the Grand Tour.[54] While in Rome, Dugood gravitated towards the exiled Jacobite court where he was recommended to the exiled Earl of Mar, John

---

[53] As Lord Lovel, grand master of English Grand Lodge, 1731-2. Cf., A.A. Hanham, 'Coke, Thomas, earl of Leicester (1697–1759)', *ODNB*. His Grand Tour lasted from 1712 to 1718 and he was in Rome from 1714.

[54] Marina Belozerskaya, *Medusa's Gaze: The Extraordinary Journey of the Tazza Farnese* (Oxford: OUP, 2012), p. 117.

Erskine. Mar introduced him to James Stuart, and Dugood, then around thirty and regarded as 'the most excellent jeweller in Europe', was engaged as court jeweller.[55]

Dugood's access to the exiled Jacobites made him a target for Philip von Stosch (1691-1757), a Prussian resident in Italy who was subsequently recruited as a spy by Lord Carteret.[56] His reports to London were written using the alias 'John Walton'.[57] Stosch persuaded Dugood to become an informer however Dugood came under suspicion of spying a year later in 1722 and was arrested by the authorities on the pretext of being a heretic. Fearing that his own position would be compromised, Stosch used his influence with Cardinal Albani,[58] with whom he shared an obsession for antiquities, to obtain Dugood's release and facilitate his retreat from Rome to London.

Stosch's letters of recommendation to Carteret and others helped Dugood become established as a jeweller in London and he later traded from the Sadler's Shop in the Haymarket.[59] It is not known whether Dugood received payment from secret service funds but it is a probability, especially since Delafaye was a principal conduit for Stosch's intelligence.[60]

---

[55] NA SP 85/14, f. 162. The description is given credence by his later work for the Duke of Devonshire.

[56] Dorothy MacKay Quynn, 'Philipp von Stosch: Collector, Bibliophile, Spy, Thief (1611[sic]-1757)', *The Catholic Historical Review*, 27.3 (1941), 332-44. Quynn suggests that Stosch was recruited by Carteret in 1721.

[57] SP 85/13/61; SP 85/16; SP 98/32; SP 105 et al.

[58] Alessandro Albani (1692-1779), a leading collector of antiquities and art patron. Although a Roman Catholic (and a cardinal from 1721), he was generally supportive of Austrian and Britain interests against those of the French and Spanish.

[59] *Daily Post*, 1 November 1727.

[60] For example, SP 78/187/21, f. 67, 14 October 1727.

Dugood was initiated into freemasonry in London at the Goose and Gridiron on 15 March 1725[61] and is also listed as a member of the middling Three Tuns lodge in Billingsgate.[62] He was elected to the Royal Society in March 1728, with two prominent freemasons, Desaguliers and Folkes, acting as his sponsors.[63] He subsequently played an active role in the Society and contributed to experiments into optics, electricity and magnetism.[64]

Dugood returned to Italy in 1731. He had been recruited by Countess Palatine Dorothea Sophie of Neuburg,[65] Regent of the Duchy of Parma from 1731 to 1735,[66] to value the family's collection of gems, coins and Greek and Roman antiquities.[67] His arrival in Parma was noted by the British Resident, who informed Delafaye accordingly.[68] It is unclear how long Dugood remained in Parma but it is thought that Jacobite pressure was brought to bear

---

[61] *AQC*, 25, p. 214.

[62] Grand Lodge *Minutes*, p. 176.

[63] Royal Society, Sackler Archives, Dugood, William. Also, Royal Society, CM0/3/6: Minutes of a meeting of the Council of the Royal Society, 18 April 1728. Dugood's modest financial standing and connections within the Council of the Royal Society may have exempted him from paying the Society's admission fee. Cf., Royal Society, CM0/3/8: Minutes of a meeting of the Council of the Royal Society, 24 October 1728. His professional reputation as the 'former Chevalier's Jeweller' was advertised at the time. Cf., *Daily Journal*, 14 May 1728.

[64] The Royal Society, RBO/12/62.

[65] Dorothea Sophie (1670-1748), Princess of Neuburg and Duchess of Parma from 1695 to 1727. The sixth daughter of the Elector of the Palatinate, Philip William of Neuburg, her sisters included the Queen of Spain, the Queen of Portugal and Empress of the Holy Roman Empire.

[66] The Countess ruled until 1735, when the duchy was ceded to Austria after the War of the Polish Succession.

[67] David Connel, 'Recently identified at Burton Constable Hall: The collection of William Dugood FRS - jeweller, scientist, freemason and spy', *Journal of History Collections* (2009) 21.1, 33-47; cf., also, *The Yorkshire Post*, 24 May 2006.

[68] NA SP 98/33, Francis Colman to Duke of Newcastle, 28 December 1731.

to force his departure from service.[69] Dugood left for Florence in around mid-1733 to join Stosch who had relocated to the city.

Stosch had been exposed as a spy in 1731 and had fled Rome for sanctuary in Tuscany. His case was taken up by Lord Chesterfield who wrote from The Hague to his cousin, Lord Harrington, secretary of state, 'to lay before your Lordship the case of Monsieur Stosch whose preservation or ruin depends entirely on the immediate payment of what is due him from England'.[70] Chesterfield was conscious of Stosch's value as an agent and despite leaving Rome he had continued to provide intelligence, most recently 'acquaint[ing] the Greffier ... that the Pretender has left Rome and that the Duke of Ormonde is expected in Italy'.[71]

Chesterfield confirmed that Stosch remained a useful asset and that his last report had been validated 'by a letter I received last post from Mr Colman'.[72] Harrington replied positively. Stosch was granted a pension and shelter in Florence, then under the jurisdiction of the progressive Gian Gastone de Medici, the seventh and last Medici to hold the title before its assumption in 1737 by Francis Stephen, Duke of Lorraine. The degree to which Stosch's information was sourced through his masonic connections is unknown but he formed a lodge in Florence soon after arriving and made Dugood a member during his time in the city.

While in Florence, Dugood was arrested on a spurious charge of theft. Stosch once again secured his release but instead of leaving Italy, Dugood and his family travelled south to Rome believing they were protected by an assurance of passage issued by Countess Dorothea Sophie. In the event the countess could not offer protection and Dugood was arrested on entering Rome.

---

[69] Belozerskaya, *Medusa's Gaze,* p. 180.

[70] Chesterfield to Harrington, 13 April 1731. Bonamy Dobree, *Letters of Philip Dormer Stanhope, Fourth Earl of Chesterfield* (New York, NY: Kings Printers Eyre & Spottiswoode, 1932), volume 2, p. 195.

[71] Ibid. A 'greffier' was a clerk, presumably at the secretary of state's office.

[72] Ibid. Francis Colman was Britain's diplomatic envoy in Tuscany; he also acted as a conduit for Stosch in his communications with London.

His freedom was secured only with difficulty and to guarantee his safe departure from Italy he was given passage on the *Dolphin*, a British warship sailing for England via Portugal. His escape was arranged by the British agent in Rome and agreed with Delafaye. The understanding was that Dugood would be debriefed in London where 'there might be gathered some useful knowledge from him relating to the Jacobites and their affairs abroad, and particularly of persons in England, and Scotland most attached to the Pretender'.[73] If nothing else, it suggests that Dugood had continued to be active and to provide intelligence, and that there was an expectation in Whitehall that he would continue to do so. Regardless, Dugood disembarked at Lisbon where he used letters of introduction from Dorothea Sophie to obtain entré to the Portuguese court. Maria Anna, her sister, was Queen of Portugal and Dugood secured employment as a court jeweller to John V.

Dugood was resident in Lisbon in the 1740s when Coustos arrived in the city. He was almost certainly one of the 'several substantial jewellers and other persons of credit' referred to by Coustos in *Sufferings* and possibly a 'chosen friend' in whose house 'we used to dine together and practice the secrets of freemasonry'.[74] Indeed, Coustos mentions Dugood specifically in his testimony to the Inquisition:

> I afterwards referred them to Mr Dogwood [Dugood], an Englishman [sic], who was born a Roman Catholic and was a freemason. This gentleman had travelled with and was greatly beloved by Don Pedro Antonio, the king's favourite, and who, having settled a lodge at Lisbon fifteen years before,[75] could acquaint them, in case he thought proper, with the nature and secrets of masonry.[76]

---

[73] NA SP 98/35, Brinley Skinner to Delafaye, 1 May 1734.

[74] Coustos, *Sufferings*, pp. 10-11.

[75] Some sources state that Dugood visited Lisbon in 1728, however, there appears to be no supporting evidence.

[76] Coustos, *Sufferings*, p. 32.

Why Coustos would call out Dugood in this way is unclear although there are several possible reasons. The disclosure may have been designed to deflect attention away from Coustos's own position[77] and to demonstrate that freemasonry was accepted in Portugal on a *de facto* basis, notwithstanding the Bull.[78] Or it could have been retribution. It is not known whether Dugood's decision to remain in Portugal was contrary to Whitehall's wishes or at their behest.

COUSTOS (ONCE AGAIN)

Coustos's ill-treatment by the Inquisition is detailed at length in *Sufferings*. A translation of the Inquisition's files and a transcript of the arrest, examination and torture, and his legal hearing and sentencing, are transcribed in Vatcher's 'John Coustos and the Portuguese Inquisition',[79] where it is suggested that the arrest was purely a function of his freemasonry and deemed heresy, rather than because Coustos was suspected of spying. But while this may be the case, it may be significant that Coustos's trial featured in

---

[77] The same argument can be applied to another of Coustos's acts: at his arrest Coustos 'called aloud to one of my friends (Mr Richard) who had been at the coffee-house with me and was a free-mason, conjuring him to give notice to all the rest of our brethren and friends of my being seized by command of the holy office in order that they might avoid the misfortune which had befallen me, by going voluntarily to the Inquisitors, and accusing themselves': *Sufferings*, p. 17.

[78] Clement XII's papal Bull against freemasonry, *In Eminenti*, in April 1738, forbade Catholics to become masons and condemned existing masons to excommunication. It was however applied unevenly across Europe. In France, many lodges continued to meet privately and although Derwentwater resigned as grand master he did not leave freemasonry. He was replaced as grand master by Louis de Pardaillan de Gondrin, Duc d'Antin (1707-1743), a nobleman and courtier.

[79] S. Vatcher, 'John Coustos and the Portuguese Inquisition', *AQC*, 81 (1968), 9-87.

diplomatic despatches between de Beauchamp, the French ambassador to Lisbon, and the French Foreign Ministry in Paris.[80]

John Coustos, *Sufferings*
Engraving of Coustos's torture by the Portuguese Inquisition, 1746

In his testimony before the Inquisition, Coustos declared his respect for Portugal and its king. He claimed that that 'every freemason is obliged at his admission to take an oath on the holy gospel, that he will be faithful to the king and never enter into any plot or conspiracy against his sacred person, or against the country where he resides, and that he will pay obedience to the magistrates appointed by the monarch'. Coustos pleaded that freemasonry's purposes were charitable and designed to enhance the ethics

---

[80] Ibid., p. 83. It is also doubtful whether Portugal would have wished to publicise suspected espionage.

of its members and that no acts were undertaken by freemasons 'repugnant to decency and morality, to the dictates of the Roman faith or to the obedience which every good Christian owes to the injunctions of the monarch in whose dominions he lives'.

Coustos's entreaties failed and 'the Inquisitors commanded me to be taken back to my dismal abode'. *Sufferings* records how Coustos was tortured to force him to abjure and embrace Catholicism, writing that his interrogators offered that 'if I turned Roman Catholic it would be of great advantage to my cause, otherwise that I perhaps might repent of my obstinacy when it was too late'. But Coustos refused their offers. He was charged with heresy and sent for trial, found guilty and sentenced to four years in the galley,[81] 'a prison standing by the river side ... it being the receptacle not only of such as are condemned by the Inquisitors but likewise by the lay judges'.[82] He was relatively fortunate; eight of his fellow lodge members were sentenced to execution by burning; another three had already been executed.[83]

Early into his sentence and while recovering in hospital from injuries, Coustos spoke with an intermediary who would 'write to my brother-in-law, Mr Barbu, to inform him of my deplorable state; and to entreat him, humbly to address the Earl of Harrington in my favour; my brother-in-law having the honour to live in his lordship's family'. The appeal succeeded and Harrington 'was so good as to endeavour to procure my freedom [and] spoke to his grace the Duke of Newcastle ... with a view to supplicate for leave from our sovereign that his minister at Lisbon might demand me as a subject of Great Britain. His Majesty interposing in my favour and his commands being dispatched to Mr Compton, the British minister at Lisbon, that gentleman demanded my liberty of the king of Portugal, in his Britannic

---

[81]   Coustos was sentenced on 21 June 1744.

[82]   Anthony Gavin, *The Mysteries of Popery Unveiled in the Unparalleled Sufferings of John Coustos...* (Enfield: R. Reynolds & H. Thompson, 1821), pp. 133-4.

[83]   H.W. Coil & W.M. Brown, *Coil's Masonic Encyclopedia* (Richmond, VA: Macoy, 1996), p. 56.

Majesty's name, which I accordingly obtained the latter end of October, 1744'.[84]

Harrington was secretary of state for the Northern Department.[85] Newcastle, secretary of state for the Southern and responsible for diplomatic relations with Portugal. Compton, the Hon. Charles Compton (1698-1755), the youngest son of the 4th Earl of Northampton, had been made ambassador to Lisbon in 1727.[86] Harrington was a freemason,[87] as was his brother, Charles Stanhope,[88] and his cousin, Lord Chesterfield, as was Newcastle himself.

Coustos was released at the latter end of October 1744 and obtained passage on a Dutch man-of-war 'as there was at this time no English Ship in the Port of Lisbon'. He arrived in England in December having enjoyed 'the civility of every person in the ship which continued until our arrival at Portsmouth where we landed without having been put to a farthing expense.'[89]

Coustos's release had hinged on the actions of his brother-in-law. But 'Barbu' is an incorrect spelling. Coustos's marriage to Alexis *Barbut* took place at the French Church at Glasshouse Street and Leicester Fields on 7 December 1723. It was witnessed by Catrine Barbut, Isaac Coustos and Pierre Chapeau.[90] And as noted above, Alexis's brother, John, was the former secretary to the Post Office.

---

[84] Coustos, *Sufferings*, pp. 50-1.

[85] Harrington was secretary of state for the Northern Department from 1730 until 1742, the year of Barbutt's dismissal, and again from 1744 until 1746.

[86] *Daily Journal*, 17 May 1727.

[87] He was present at the meeting of Grand Lodge on 24 June 1721 when the Duke of Montagu was chosen grand master.

[88] Charles Stanhope was a member of the Bear & Harrow in Butcher's Row.

[89] Coustos, *Sufferings*, p. 76.

[90] William & Susan Minet (eds.), *Registers of the Churches of The Tabernacle Glasshouse Street and Leicester Fields, London 1688-1783* (London: Huguenot Society, 1926). Also, Susan Broomhall (ed), *Spaces for Feeling: Emotions and Sociabilities in Britain, 1650-1850* (London: Routledge, 2015), p. 36.

Sufferings was published in 1746 in the wake of the Jacobite Rising. It was dedicated to Harrington and Newcastle and thanked them for their intercession. The book was edited before publication, probably at Newcastle's behest, and additional anti-Catholic material included so that it might play a propagandist anti-Jacobite role. It did. The print was handled by William Strahan,[91] later the king's printer, and its subscribers filled fourteen pages of the second edition and included Lord Cranston, the grand master of English Grand Lodge.

But although *Sufferings* was later a publishing success with editions printed throughout the eighteenth and nineteenth centuries,[92] the first edition was unprofitable: 'the sale not being sufficient to defray the charge'.[93] Coustos was forced into debtors' prison from where he petitioned Newcastle for financial assistance. Aid was granted, with payment made allegedly from secret service funds.[94]

Most biographies including Musgrave[95] record that Coustos died in 1746, although there is no record of probate nor any contemporary obituary, an unusual omission given that *Sufferings* had garnered considerable attention. They are wrong. Coustos died at a later date. A declaration on oath by Rebecca Clements quoted in the *Chelsea Settlement and Bastardy Examinations, 1733-1766*[96] stated that 'she is pregnant of a bastard child or children which was or were unlawfully begotten on her body by one Mr John Coustos, a jeweller, who now lodges at a house in Tibals [Theobalds] Row near Red Lyon [Lion]

---

[91]   William Strahan (1715-1785).

[92]   Classified advertisements announcing the re-publication of the book appeared in many newspapers including the *Public Advertiser*, 9 June 1757; and *Star*, 14 December 1791 and 13 January 1792.

[93]   Newcastle, Add. MS. 33,054, f. 313, John Coustos, *Prisoner in the Inquisition at Lisbon: Petition for assistance*, c.1746.

[94]   Ibid. Schuchard claims the payment was made from secret service accounts: cf., *Emanuel Swedenborg*, p. 237, fn. 140.

[95]   William Musgrave, *Obituary, Prior to 1800* (London, 1900), volume 14, p. 85.

[96]   Tim Hitchcock and John Black (eds), *Chelsea Settlement and Bastardy Examinations, 1733-1766* (London: London Records Society, 1999), pp. 57-63.

Square, London... he had carnal knowledge of her body the first time about two years ago at the Angel Inn behind St Clements Church, London, and several times after at the said inn'. The statement was sworn on 29 April 1748.[97] The record does not refer to Coustos's sons: James, Jean-Paul and David.[98]

An entry in the *Biographical Dictionary of Actors, Actresses, Musicians, Dancers, Managers & Other Stage Personnel in London, 1660-1800* also points to a later date, recording that Coustos, 'long confined in the Inquisition in Portugal upon the account of Free Masonry', flourished as a singer from 1747 until 1750.[99]

Vatcher's comment on Coustos is also telling: 'our first impression was that he probably lived to a ripe old age, this was because in his edition of 1790 there is a print of him obviously of more mature years'.[100]

VINCENT LA CHAPELLE

Vincent La Chapelle (*c*.1700-*c*.1746), another member of the Rainbow Coffee House,[101] was similarly a founder of the lodge at the Prince Eugene's Head Coffee House, having migrated to London in around 1722. Kwaadgras suggests that La Chapelle was Roman Catholic rather than Protestant,[102]

---

[97]   Sworn before Peter Elers, Justice of the Peace for Middlesex: Middlesex Sessions' Papers, General Orders of the Court, 1743-1753 et al.

[98]   His sons were James [Jacques], Jean Paul and David, who, like his father, was also imprisoned for debt. Cf., *Registres de Eglises de la Savoye de Spring Gardens et des Grecs*, 10 December 1725; also *Public Advertiser*, 28 August 1769.

[99]   Philip H. Highfill, Kalman A. Burnim, Edward A. Langhans, *A Biographical Dictionary of Actors, Actresses, Musicians, Dancers, Managers & Other Stage Personnel in London, 1660-1800* (Carbondale: Southern Illinois Press, 2006), volume 4, p. 12.

[100]   Vatcher, 'John Coustos and the Portuguese Inquisition', *AQC*, 81, 9-87, quote from 11.

[101]   Recorded as Vincent de la Cappell.

[102]   Evert Kwaadgras, 'Masonry with a Message and a Mission. Some remarks on the history of Freemasonry in The Netherlands', Address to Internet Lodge, Kingston-upon-Hull, 8 August 2002.

and this is possible in that many Huguenots were forced to convert to Catholicism, albeit that they later abjured. But while the name 'La Chapelle' is not limited to Huguenots, there were numerous Protestant 'La Chapelles' in London at that time including Armand Boisbeleau de la Chapelle, a minister at the French L'eglise de l'Artillerie and later the L'eglise Wallonne de la Haye;[103] Amos de la Chapelle, a Huguenot émigré naturalized in 1706;[104] Marie Chapelle of the French Church at Glasshouse Street and Leicester Fields; and Anne, Antoine, Charlotte, Helène, Jean, Jérémie, Marie, Pierre, Thomas and Vincent La Chapelle, all congregants at the French Church at Savoy Spring Gardens, the last being the 'maître d'école' of the French School in Grosvenor Street.[105]

Philip and Mary Hyman describe La Chapelle as one of the most influential chefs in the eighteenth century and the author of one of the era's best-selling cookery books - *The Modern Cook*.[106] His reputation endured, with Escoffier terming him masterful and a chef who almost single-handedly transformed English and French cuisine.[107] Although knowledge of La Chapelle's personal life is limited, one of the more important aspects appears to have been his freemasonry and in addition to his membership of at least two London lodges he was pivotal in establishing freemasonry in the Low Countries.

---

[103] Andreas Flick, 'The dubious affair of Laurent de Saumery', *Proceedings of the Huguenot Society*, XXVII.1 (1998), 81-96.

[104] Graham C. Gibbs, 'Abel Boyer: the making of a British subject', *Proceedings of the Huguenot Society*, XXVI.1 (1994), 14-45.

[105] *Registres des Eglises de la Savoye de Spring Gardens at des Grecs*, 29 September 1726.

[106] Philip Hyman, Mary Hyman, 'La Chapelle, Vincent (fl. 1733–1736)', *ODNB*. Dedicated to Chesterfield, *The Modern Cook* was published in 1733 in three volumes at a guinea per copy; a second edition was produced in 1736 and a third in 1744. A French language edition, *Le cuisinier moderne*, was self-published in 1735, with a second French edition in 1742, now upgraded to five volumes.

[107] Auguste Escoffier, *Le guide culinaire* (Paris, 1903).

THE

MODERN COOK:

C O N T A I N I N G

INSTRUCTIONS

For Preparing and Ordering Publick Entertainments for the Tables of Princes, Am-
baſſadors, Noblemen, and Magiſtrates.

As alſo the leaſt Expenſive Methods of providing
for private Families, in a very elegant Manner.

New Receipts for Dreſſing of Meat, Fowl, and Fiſh; and
making Ragoûts, Fricaſſees, and Paſtry of all Sorts, in
a Method, never before publiſh'd.

Adorn'd with COPPER-PLATES,

Exhibiting the Order of Placing the different Diſhes, &c.
on the Table, in the moſt polite Way.

By Mr. *VINCENT LA CHAPELLE*,
Late Chief Cook to the Right Honourable the Earl
of CHESTERFIELD:

And now Chief Cook to his Highneſs the
Prince of ORANGE.

In THREE VOLUMES.

The SECOND EDITION.

V O L. I.

L O N D O N:
Printed for THOMAS OSBORNE, in *Gray's-Inn.*
MDCCXXXVI.

Vincent La Chapelle, *The Modern Cook*
Frontispiece, 1736 edition

La Chapelle was propelled into prominence as chef de cuisine to Phillip
Dormer Stanhope, 4th Earl of Chesterfield, Britain's ambassador at The
Hague. He had been recommended by the Duke of Richmond:

Scarcely had the Duke arrived in France than he received an urgent entreaty from the illustrious Lord Chesterfield, ambassador to The Hague, beseeching him to find him a chef de cuisine. His Lordship would seem to have been most exacting in this respect, in fact he would be satisfied with none but a veritable cordon bleu, and, placing complete reliance in his friend's sound judgment and fastidious palate, he addressed him thus:

Dear Duke,

I believe you will easier pardon the trouble I am going to give you, than you would the excuses that I ought to make you for it. So I'll proceed directly to the business.

You must know then, that I have a cook that was sent to me about two months ago from Paris who, though he is not a bad one, yet is not of the first rate, and as I have a mind, de faire une chere exquise, I should be glad to have a Maitre Cuisinier d'un Genie Superieur, who should be able not only to execute but to invent des morceaus friands et parfaits, in short such a one as may be worthy to entertain your distinguishing palate, if you should come to The Hague. If you can find such a one, I beg of you make the best bargain you can for me and send him to me here. But unless you can find one who is allowed by all Paris to be at the top of his profession, don't send me any, those I have already being tolerable ones. Though this may be a very troublesome employment for you, yet you will allow that it would have been wronging your taste if while you were at Paris I had addressed myself to anybody but you, en fait de Cuisine...

Your obedient humble Servant
Chesterfield[108]

---

[108]   Earl of March (ed.), *A Duke and his Friends* (London: Hutchinson & Co., 1911), pp. 156-8.

How Richmond knew La Chapelle is unknown but Delafaye provides a possible link. And it is arguable that Delafaye would have wished to have a reliable independent agent in the ambassador's household.

Chesterfield had been sworn to the Privy Council and appointed ambassador to the United Provinces in 1728; his younger brother, John Stanhope, became his secretary. His principal task at The Hague was to keep the Dutch informed and amenable while William Stanhope, his cousin, led negotiations in Madrid to conclude a peace treaty with Spain.[109] At the same time Chesterfield assisted in building an entente with Austria as British foreign policy tilted east.[110] The process was concluded with the Treaty of Vienna and enhanced by the initiation of the Duke of Lorraine, the future husband of Marie Theresa and prospective Holy Roman Emperor, discussed in chapter seven. Chesterfield also negotiated the terms on which Princess Anne, the Princess Royal, would wed William Fris, the Prince of Orange.[111]

Chesterfield grew bored of The Hague and was permitted to return to London in February 1732. La Chapelle accompanied him but left his service shortly afterwards to accept a position as master chef to the Count of Montijo, the Spanish envoy in London.[112]

While La Chapelle may have been lured by the prospect of a higher salary, it is more feasible that he entered Montijo's service for other reasons. Spain had allied with France against the Habsburgs and become overtly hostile to British interests in Europe and Ireland. Montijo was an influential

---

[109] At their conclusion he was granted a peerage as Lord Harrington and appointed secretary of state. Stanhope (c.1683-1756), was secretary of state for the Northern Department, 1730-42, and again 1744-6. He was appointed president of the Privy Council in 1742.

[110] John Cannon, 'Stanhope, Philip Dormer, 4th earl of Chesterfield (1694–1773)', (Oxford: OUP, 2004; online edn, Sept 2012), accessed 11 June 2016.

[111] The future William IV of Holland, hereditary Stadtholder of the United Provinces. The marriage was solemnised in London in 1734.

[112] Cristóbal Gregorio Portocarrero y Funes de Villalpando, the 6th Count of Montijo (1692-1763).

diplomat and a senior member of the Spanish court with links to the opposition in Britain.[113] Black notes Montijo proclaiming his political sympathies 'by providing free beer to those who demonstrated against the ministry during the Excise Crisis'.[114] And in 1741 a letter to Walpole reported 'an honest English chapman' overhearing two Jacobites at The Hague talking 'with great intimacy of Count Montijo'.[115]

France's invasion of the Duchy of Lorraine commenced in 1733, accompanied by Spanish, French and Savoyard troops attacking and recapturing Naples and Sicily. Although the Secret Department had covert access to Spain's diplomatic mail, it would have been advantageous for Delafaye, Newcastle and Walpole to have had a clear insight into Spanish thinking, something that La Chapelle may have been able to provide. There is no evidence within the National Archives that La Chapelle was a British agent but this is not surprising. He would have reported verbally through intermediaries or in person as part of Delafaye's circle in London, not least through the church and his lodge memberships.

La Chapelle left Montijo's service in 1734. Britain and the United Provinces had begun to broker peace talks that year and a preliminary treaty between the warring parties was negotiated and signed in 1735.

Prince William of Orange married the Princess Royal at St James's Palace in March 1734 and a few months later La Chapelle joined their

---

[113] There is an oblique (later) masonic link: the first Grand Lodge of Spain (the 'Gran Logia Española') was formed in 1767 when Spanish Freemasonry became independent of England. It changed its name in 1780 to the Gran Oriente Española and adopted the French system of ritual. Spain's first grand master, the Count of Aranda, was also Spain's Prime Minister. He was banished under Charles IV and succeeded as grand master of Spanish Freemasonry by Eugenio Eulalio de Palafox y Portocarrero, the 7th Count of Montijo.

[114] Black, *British Politics and Foreign Policy, 1727-44*, p. 122.

[115] Robert Trevor to Sir Robert Walpole, 22 August 1741 in *The Manuscripts of the Earl of Buckinghamshire* (London: HMSO, 1895), HMC, 14th report, appendix, part IX, p. 76.

household, returning to The Hague as the royal couple's chef de cuisine.[116] On 8 November the same year, he set up the first Dutch masonic lodge in the United Provinces, Lodge 'L'Union Royale', at the Lion d'Or tavern at The Hague, becoming its first master. The founding members were La Chapelle; Phillipe Fluvet [or Fiufet], the senior warden; Daniel Friard, the junior warden, and François Liégois, Salomon Noch and Jean Fache. Four candidates were initiated at the first meeting: Antoine Maillet, the innkeeper; Louis Dagran, a wealthy draper or cloth merchant; and William Constant and N. de St. Genevieve, whose occupations are unknown.[117] The names are predominantly French rather than Dutch, which points to a Huguenot connection.

Dagran's journal, *Annales et Archives des Francs-Macons*,[118] indicates that the Duke of Richmond was also involved with the lodge, albeit at the periphery. On 22 November 1734, Liégois, reportedly a former employee of Richmond, was asked to obtain a 'legitimate constitution' from the duke. The request was granted and a warrant was despatched from London to the lodge secretary in March 1735, accompanied by a copy of Anderson's *Constitutions*.[119]

---

[116] When La Chapelle published *The Modern Cook* in 1733, he was described as 'Chief Cook to the Right Honourable the Earl of Chesterfield'. A year later an advertisement for the book described him as cook to the Count of Montijo (*Gentleman's Magazine and Historical Review*, volume 4, p. 55); in 1736, the title page (and contemporary classified advertisements) announced that he was 'now Chief Cook to his Highness the Prince of Orange'.

[117] A narrative of the event appears in *Annales et Archives des Franc Maçons*. Friard may have been the same person who was a member of the Prince Eugene's Head lodge.

[118] Louis Dagran, *Annales et Archives des Franc Maçons sous la Grande Maîtrise des Provinces Unies et du Ressort de la Généralité en Forme de Journal*. It is held in the Bibliotheek voor de Nederlandse Letteren. Cf., http://www.dbnl.org/tekst/_doc003198601_01/_doc003198601_01_0007.php.

[119] Ibid. Cf., also, *AQC*, 83, p. 150.

> They write from the Hague, that on Monday the 24th of October, N. S. there was open'd, a Dutch Lodge, at the *New Doole*, of the Noble and Antient Society of Free Mafons, with all the Order, Regularity and Magnificence, due to that illuftrious Society. The Solemnity was honour'd with the Prefence of their Grand Mafter Mr. John Cornelis Rademaker, Treafurer to his Highnefs the Prince of Orange, and their Deputy Grand Mafter Mr. John Geunen, with the Wardens and Brothers of the French Lodge; there were receiv'd feveral Brothers, in the Dutch Language : After which the Grand Mafter and Society were pleas'd to elect Mr. Lowis Dagran to be Mafter of the faid Lodge, Mr. Van Loon and Mr. Crawford Wardens, and Mr. Ruremonde Secretary ; when Mr. Lowis Dagran, Mafter, was pleas'd to give a moft fplendid Entertainment to the Society.

Extract from the *General Evening Post*, 4 - 6 November 1735

A second lodge, 'Le Véritable Zèle', was founded at The Hague a year later on 24 October 1735, with Dagran its first master. Its consecration was recorded in the press by *Amsterdamsche Saturdagsche Courant* on 3 November 1735, which printed that the Treasurer General, Johan Cornelis Rademacher, had been made grand master of the United Provinces. (The lodge afterwards acquired the name 'Loge du Grand Maître des Provinces Unies et du Ressort de la Généralité'.) The reaction in the United Provinces was profoundly negative. Fearing that improper influence could or would be exerted, the provinces lobbied successfully for freemasonry to be proscribed. It was interdicted until 1744, although the ban was not widely enforced.

In the late 1730s or early 1740s, La Chapelle relocated to Lisbon as head chef to John V. Portugal's national wealth had expanded as capital flowed in to the country from Brazil and other colonies. And with increased national income came a corresponding rise in international influence. Britain had maintained intelligence resources in Lisbon for decades and the National Archives contains multiple reports, more than a hundred of which were directed to Delafaye. Given the precedence of George Gordon, William Dugood, John Coustos and others, it is tempting to place La Chapelle's role in Lisbon in the same context notwithstanding the lack of corroboratory evidence.

On leaving Lisbon, La Chapelle was employed in Paris as executive chef to Jeanne Antoinette Poisson, Madame de Pompadour (1721-1764), from March 1745 mistress and confidante to Louis XV. La Chapelle died shortly afterwards. There is no extant obituary and the cause of death is unknown. He is commemorated at The Hague by a lodge established and named in his honour.[120]

CHARLES LABELYE

Charles de Labelye (1705-62), was one of the youngest members of the French lodge at Solomon's Temple in Hemming's Row. Although born in Vevey, Switzerland, his father was a French Huguenot refugee, described in 1709 as 'Monsieur François Dangeau Labelye, Sieur de la Bélye, refugié en cette ville par sa Religion'.[121] Labelye moved to London in the early 1720s and studied and lodged with Desaguliers at Channel Row, becoming his protégé and assistant. Desaguliers' description of Richard Newsham's fire engines - a 'water engine for quenching and extinguishing fires' - was based on measurements and drawings made 'at my Desire by Mr Charles Labelye'. And it was Labelye rather than Desaguliers who wrote the account of the

---

[120] Cf., www.vincentlachapelle.nl.

[121] Roger Bowdler, 'Labelye, Charles (*bap*.1705, *d*.1762)', *ODNB*, online edn, Oct 2009, accessed 12 June 2016. Cf., also, Alec Skempton et al, *A Biographical Dictionary of Civil Engineers in Great Britain and Ireland* (London: Institute of Civil Engineers, 2002), pp. 389-91.

then novel method of transporting stone in Bath, the first documented use of a railway.[122]

Labelye began to achieve commercial success in his own right in the 1730s when he was appointed architect and principal engineer for Westminster Bridge, a project that would take twelve years to complete and require the demolition of Channel Row. Labelye was confirmed in the position in 1738 and awarded an annual salary of £100 and a daily expense allowance of 10s.[123] His selection caused resentment amongst his rivals who were aggrieved that a foreigner had been appointed to such a prestigious post.[124] Batty Langley, a rival architect and freemason, lambasted Labelye in his *A survey of Westminster Bridge as 'tis now sinking into ruin*. The work was published in 1748 when construction was at a nadir and one illustration depicts Labelye hanging from a gibbet under the arches. Langley had produced his own designs for the bridge in 1736 and considered that Labelye had plagiarised his work.

There was also resentment at Labelye's masonic links to the commissioners overseeing the project. The commission was chaired by Henry Herbert, 9th Earl of Pembroke,[125] and contained several prominent freemasons including Nathaniel Blackerby, George Payne and Thomas Brereton MP, all

---

[122] Desaguliers, *Course of Experimental Philosophy* (London, 1744), pp. 178, 274-9.

[123] Labelye was not the highest paid employee. Richard Graham received £300 per annum as Surveyor and Comptroller. The total cost of construction amounted to around £198,000: Skempton, *A Biographical Dictionary of Civil Engineers*, p. xxv.

[124] The foundations for the first pier were laid in January 1739: *Country Journal or The Craftsman*, 13 January 1739. Cf., Charles Labelye, *The Present State of Westminster Bridge* (London, 1743), 2nd edn.

[125] Herbert had attended the Duke of Montagu's installation as grand master and succeeded him as captain and colonel of the 1st Troop of Horse Guards. He was probably a member of Martin Folkes's lodge at the Bedford Head in Covent Garden. Cf., *Foundations*, p. 103.

members of the Horn.[126] John La Roche, a fellow Huguenot and member of Prince Eugene's Head, sat on both the Westminster Bridge Commission and that overseeing the rebuilding of Brentford Bridge (1740-42) where Labelye was similarly chief engineer.[127]

Westminster Bridge was completed in 1750 and Labelye received a gratuity of £2,000 and an ongoing consultancy of £150 per annum. He was also invited to undertake other schemes, including improvements to the harbour and dock facilities at Sandwich, Great Yarmouth and Sunderland, and engineering projects for the Coastguard and Royal Navy.[128]

Like his mentor, Desaguliers, Labelye combined his engineering consultancies at home and abroad with freemasonry. A project at Exeter in 1732 gave him the opportunity to attend the St John the Baptist lodge at the New Inn on the High Street. The lodge had been constituted recently and Labelye's 'zealous endeavours to promote masonry' were noted approvingly by the lodge secretary.[129] And on a return visit to the West Country Labelye was appointed senior warden of the Bear Tavern lodge in Bath, albeit that he later resigned, apologising that his workload precluded him from visiting

---

[126] The project for a bridge was revived by a 'Society of Gentlemen' meeting at the Horn Tavern. Cf., Christa Jungnickel and Russell McCormack, *Cavendish* (Philadelphia, PN: American Philosophical Society, 1996), p. 90. Freemasons employed on the bridge included Samuel Tuffnell, a member of the Bell Tavern lodge. His firm, Jelfe & Tufnell, obtained a £155,000 contract for the stonework.

[127] *Read's Weekly Journal Or British Gazetteer*, 3 April 1736; and *Order concerning the rebuilding of Brentford Bridge & receiving proposals for the same and appointing a Committee for the Bridges*: General Orders of the Court, Middlesex Quarter Sessions, 13 September 1739. Also LMA, City of London: MJ/SP/1743/01/03.

[128] Kent History & Library Centre: Sa/P/1 & 11Cf; Norfolk Record Office: Y/TC 84/1 & 3; Y/PH/100; Y/PH/2401; ADM 354/127/175; ADM 106/1012/254; ADM 106/1021/312; ADM 106/1021/173 et al. Also Wiltshire and Swindon History Centre: 2057/F6/12; Cambridgeshire Archives: R/59/31/40/61/iii & iv.

[129] G. Norman, 'Early Freemasonry at Bath, Bristol and Exeter', *AQC*, 40 (1927), 244.

with any frequency.[130]   Labelye was already a member of at least one other London lodge, the White Bear in King Street, Golden Square, where he was senior warden in 1730 and presumably master thereafter.[131]

Labelye's most notable masonic connection was not in England however but in Spain. In 1728 when working on a hydraulic project in Madrid, Labelye established the first masonic lodge in Spain and became its first master. The petition to constitute the lodge had been presented to the Grand Lodge of England in April:

> The Deputy Grand Master acquainted the Brethren that he had received a Letter from several Masons at a Lodge at Madrid in Spain, which he read to them, and the Grand-Lodge unanimously agreed to what was prayed for in their Letter, which is as follows -
>
> *Right Worshipful Master*
>
> *We here undersigned Masons, free and accepted, residing at present in Madrid and other places of the Kingdom of Spain, take the Liberty of this Letter as our Duty oblige us to acquaint our Most Right & Worshipful Grand Master, his Worthy Deputy, the Grand Wardens, and all the Lodges of Masons now constituted in England, that having been always very desirous to see our Ancient Society propagated, its true and virtuous Designs encouraged, and the Craft flourish in every place where our Affairs have called us, Resolved accordingly to propagate it in this Kingdom whenever it could be done in a lawful manner. And as we had some time ago the Opportunity of the presence of his Grace the Duke of Wharton, we petitioned him to Constitute a Lodge in this Town, the which he readily granted and executed, and after our Lodge was formed we accepted and made Masons three persons here under mentioned, and Just After it was Resolved unanimously to acquaint with our Proceedings our Grand Master and the General Officers in England, to all which his Grace submits himself entirely having acted in this Occasion as a second Deputy.*

---

[130]   Cf. Grand Lodge *Minutes*, p. 228.

[131]   His name appears as 'Cha. De La Belle'.

Be pleased therefore to acquaint our Grand-Master and all the Lodges in general at the next Quarterly Communication with the Contents of this Letter, and we expect the favour to be inserted in the Book under the name of the Madrid Lodge, our Meetings being fixed at present on the first Sunday in every Month. We hope to send at the Quarterly Communication that shall be held about St John Baptist's day of this present Year, a longer List of Members of our Lodge and a Copy of such By Laws as we Resolve upon as they are thought proper for the Country wherein we are at present for the Union amongst us and the Charity to the poor, so much recommended and exercised in Our Ancient Society, upon which in general we pray God Almighty to shed his most precious favours and blessings.

We are, Sir and Right Worshipful Master,
Your most dutiful Brethren and humble Servants.

Dated in our Lodge at Madrid
15th February 1728 N.S.

By his Grace's Orders
Philip Duke of Wharton &c. Deputy Grand Master

sic subscribitur
Charles De Labelye   Master}
Richards[132]   Senior Warden} pro tempore
Thomas Hatton   Junior Warden}
Eldridge Dinsdale
Andrew Gallwey[133]

---

[132] A Michael Richards, possibly the same person, was later a member of the University Lodge.

[133] Possibly Andrew Galloway.

Then the Grand Lodge drank prosperity to the Brethren of the Lodge at Madrid, and desired the Grand Master to write them word of their being acknowledged and received as Brethren, or in what manner he shall think proper.[134]

Labelye received Grand Lodge's formal thanks for his efforts following his return to London the following November:

Mr Labelle the present Master of the Lodge held at Madrid in Spain stood up and confirm'd what was some time past delivered in a Letter from the said Lodge to the Grand Master and Grand Lodge in England (concerning their Regularity and submission to us etc.) and acquitted himself in a handsome manner like a Gentleman and a good Mason. Then the Health to the Brethren of the Madrid Lodge was propos'd and drank with three Huzzas.[135]

Labelye's involvement with the lodge is notable not because it was the first to be constituted in Spain and the warrant the first to be issued outside the British Empire but because of the presence of the exiled Duke of Wharton, a Jacobite.[136] Indeed, the lodge met initially at Wharton's rooms at the Fleurs de Lis in St Bernard's Street in Madrid.[137] It is tempting and legitimate to believe that Labelye had been asked to seek out Wharton and that the lodge was constructed in part as a means of gathering intelligence on his activities and those

---

[134] Grand Lodge *Minutes*, 17 April 1728.

[135] Grand Lodge *Minutes*, 26 November 1728.

[136] Cf. Lawrence B. Smith, 'Wharton, Philip James, duke of Wharton and Jacobite duke of Northumberland (1698-1731)', *ODNB*, online edn, Jan 2008; also Lewis Melville, *The life and writings of Philip, Duke of Wharton* (London: John Lane, 1913).

[137] The lodge is now Matriteuse Lodge, No. 1, on the Register of the Grand National Orient of Spain.

of other Jacobite sympathisers.[138] There are no extant records but the request may have been passed to Labelye by Delafaye directly or via Desaguliers, whom Delafaye knew well. Not only were they colleagues at the Horn and the Royal Society,[139] and fellow Huguenots, but Delafaye's wife, Elizabeth, was godmother to Desaguliers' daughter of the same name.[140] Desaguliers would also be instrumental in establishing other politically significant lodges including the Duke of Richmond's lodges in Paris and Aubigny, and Lord Chesterfield's at The Hague at which the Duke of Lorraine was initiated.

Philip, Duke of Wharton
Unknown artist, c. 1722

---

[138] Audrey Carpenter comments that Wharton established the Madrid lodge 'for reasons of expediency and after yet another change of loyalties': Carpenter, *John Theophilus Desaguliers*, p. 91. This is possible but implausible; but even if correct, it does not counter the argument that Delafaye would have wished to ensure that he had up-to-date intelligence on Wharton.

[139] Royal Society, Sackler Archive: NA 2468.

[140] Carpenter, *John Theophilus Desaguliers*, p. 231.

Following his departure from Britain, Wharton had been publicly associated with the exiled Jacobite court. James Stuart invested him with the Order of the Garter when the duke visited him in Rome and in 1725 Wharton became Jacobite ambassador to the Holy Roman Empire in Vienna. Wharton subsequently returned to Spain and in 1727 fought as a lieutenant colonel in the Spanish army, appearing before the British at the siege of Gibraltar. His action led to him being charged with high treason and in 1728 the Privy Council demanded his return to England to face the charge. Wharton reportedly 'scornfully threw the letter out of his coach window'.[141]

Wharton's reply was published in the Jacobite-leaning *Mist's Weekly Journal* in August 1728. Using a pseudonym, 'Amos Drudge', he penned a literary analogy depicting the loss of liberties and government corruption in a fictional Persia following a usurpation. The piece, a companion to *Reasons for Leaving his Native Country* published in 1726, was modelled on Montesquieu's *Persian Letters*. In his narrative Wharton lauded James Stuart as 'a Prince whose gracious behaviour is sufficient to win, his majesty to awe, and his courage to face the most inveterate of his enemies, [whose] sufferings have added experience and patience to those endearing qualities in order to complete the greatest character that ever Eastern monarch bore … the misfortunes of his subjects grieve him even more than his own such is his public spirit'. In contrast, George I and George II were painted as vain and avaricious tyrants.[142]

The government was outraged and Wharton's missive censured as 'an infamous, scandalous and treasonable libel, calculated to poison the minds of His Majesty's subjects with groundless jealousies, to sow sedition and overturn the peace of this kingdom, and in favour of a spurious, abandoned

---

[141] George L. Craik and Charles Macfarlane, *The Pictorial History of England: 1688-1760* (London: Charles Knight, 1841), volume 4, p. 401.

[142] Monod, *Jacobitism and the English People, 1688-1788*, p. 37.

and abjured Pretender'.[143] More to the point, publication gave Walpole the excuse to order the destruction of Nathaniel Mist's presses and arrest some twenty people connected to the paper. The move was significant. Delafaye considered *Mist's Weekly* more harmful than other opposition publications because of its broad circulation and appeal to the lower middling.[144] The opportunity to take it down was grasped with both hands.

Despite Wharton's absence overseas a 'judgment of outlawry for high treason' was pronounced against him in April 1729 and the Treasury Solicitor, Anthony Cracherode,[145] instructed to seize his assets.[146] In contrast to his bravado in public, Wharton had sought a reconciliation, approaching Horatio Walpole in Paris in 1728 and offering intelligence in return for a pardon. The offer was rejected. Wharton was discredited and there was no need for his information. Britain's representative at the Spanish court, Sir Benjamin Keene,[147] provided comprehensive reports on Jacobite activities as did Delafaye's agents. Having failed to reach an accommodation, Wharton returned to Spain. A second attempt at reconciliation also failed[148] and in ill-health and with limited resources Wharton succumbed to alcoholism. He died a pauper at Poblet in May 1731 at the age of 33.

---

[143] *The Gentleman's Magazine*, July 1731, p. 287. The quote is from the Grand Jury of Devon and Exeter.

[144] Paul Chapman, 'Jacobite Political Argument in England, 1714-1766 (Cambridge: PhD Thesis, 1983), p. 22.

[145] Anthony Cracherode, Treasury Solicitor, 1715-30. Sainty, *Office-Holders in Modern Britain: volume 1: Treasury Officials 1660-1870*.

[146] William A. Shaw (ed), *Calendar of Treasury Books and Papers, volume 1, 1729-1730* (London, 1897), p. 382, 2 June 1730.

[147] Appointed consul-general at Madrid in 1724; minister-plenipotentiary in 1727; and envoy-extraordinary at the Spanish court in 1734-9. Ambassador in Lisbon and thereafter to Madrid (1749-57). Cf., Jean Mclachlan, *Trade and Peace with Old Spain* (Cambridge: CUP, 2015). Also, M. J. Mercer, 'Keene, Sir Benjamin', *ODNB*.

[148] Cf. Norman Milne, *Libertines and Harlots* (Bath: Parragon Publishing, 2014), p. 87-9.

Relatively little is known of Labelye's later years. He was naturalised in 1746 but left England in the early 1750s. He travelled to the South of France in 1752 and to Naples the following year. His final home was Paris, where he died in 1762.[149]

---

[149] Bowdler, *ODNB*.

CHAPTER SIX

FRENCH CONNECTIONS - THE HORN TAVERN LODGE

*Men are so stupid and concerned with their present
needs, they will always let themselves be deceived.*[1]

At around the same time that Derwentwater and others were positioning
freemasonry in France to advocate Jacobitism, a politically opposite exercise was underway at the Richmond's lodge at the Horn Tavern in London
and in the 1730s at his lodges in Paris and Aubigny. The Horn was the most
influential lodge in England and the largest of the four that had founded the
Grand Lodge of England.[2] Its early membership returns to Grand Lodge list
more than seventy names,[3] but by the early 1730s this had tripled to around
two hundred and fifty.[4]

The Horn dwarfed the three other founding lodges. That at the Goose
and Gridiron in St Paul's Churchyard had just over twenty members; the
lodge at the Queen's Head in Knaves Acre (formerly of the Apple Tree
in Covent Garden), had around the same number; and the lodge at the
Queen's Head in Holborn (formerly of the Crown Ale House near Drury
Lane), held a mere fourteen. But this was not the only difference.

---

[1] Niccolò Machiavelli (1469-1527), *The Prince.*

[2] Formerly the Grand Lodge of London and Westminster.

[3] Originally established at the Rummer & Grapes in Channel Row; the lodge
probably moved to the Horn to accommodate its growing membership.

[4] Christopher Powell, 'The influence of the members of Lodge IV on
Freemasonry between 1717 and 1740', *AQC*, 128 (2015), 225-54.

The Horn was the only founding lodge to be based in Westminster, located in New Palace Yard, a few yards from Parliament and the offices of state. And unlike its three companion founding lodges, the Horn's connections were distinguished and more than substantial. In the mid-1720s at least thirteen members of the lodge were English or continental aristocrats; some twenty were Fellows of the Royal Society; over twenty were magistrates, several serving as chairmen of the bench;[5] and almost a third were Members of Parliament. Many held active or honorary military rank, with two general officers and at least ten colonels, while others were senior officials at the departments of state and the Exchequer.

At the Horn's social summit were five men with a direct blood link to the crown. Four were the grandsons of Charles II: Charles Lennox, 2nd Duke of Richmond (1701-1750); Charles FitzRoy, 2nd Duke of Grafton (1683-1757); Henry Scott, Earl Delorraine (1676-1730); and Francis Scott, Earl of Dalkeith, 2nd Duke of Buccleuch (1705-1751). The fifth, James Waldegrave (1684-1741), was the grandson of James II; he was created Earl Waldegrave by George II in 1729.

---

[5] William Cowper, Nathaniel Blackerby and Leonard Streate.

Charles Lennox, 2nd Duke of Richmond & Lennox
Jonathan Richardson the Elder (1667-1745), c. 1726

Aside from Delafaye, the lodge's masonically-influential non-aristo-
cratic members included Desaguliers and George Payne. Their reworking
of masonic ritual identified freemasonry with Enlightenment ideology and
Newtonian science and positioned it as a proselytiser of constitutional government and religious toleration. Desaguliers had been the third grand
master of Grand Lodge in 1719 and served as deputy grand master in 1722,
1723 and 1725. More broadly he was a member or master of several other

significant lodges, including the Huguenot lodge at Solomon's Temple in Hemming's Row; the Bear and Harrow near Temple Bar; and the University Lodge. He also presided at several occasional lodges, including that at Richmond-on-Thames when Frederick, Prince of Wales, was initiated.

George Payne was grand master in 1718 and 1720, and one of Desaguliers' most effective colleagues.[6] He was close to Richmond, serving as his deputy master at the Horn and as his grand warden in 1724. Payne was in addition an acting grand officer on numerous occasions and deputy grand master in 1735.

Another member of the Horn, William Cowper, held senior administrative office at the House of Commons and House of Lords as Clerk to the Parliaments. He was appointed the first grand secretary and in 1726 was selected to be deputy grand master.[7] Among other lodge members were Alexander Chocke, a senior magistrate, Clerk of the Debentures of the Exchequer and deputy grand master in 1727; Edward Wilson, grand secretary in succession to William Cowper; and Nathaniel Blackerby, a senior magistrate, public and parliamentary official, deputy grand master (1728-30) and grand treasurer.[8]

---

[6] George Payne (1685?-1757). Cf., *Foundations*, esp. chapter three.

[7] *Foundations*, esp. chapter three.

[8] Ibid., appendix one.

Alexander Chocke, Receiver of Excise
Deputy Grand Master, 1728
Joseph Highmore (1692-1780)   Engraved by John Pine (1690-1756)

The Horn's association with the evangelising of English freemasonry in France was driven by Richmond directly and expedited as a result of his French ducal title – Duc d'Aubigny - to which he succeeded in 1734 following the death of his grandmother, Louise de Kéroualle.[9] Kéroualle had been despatched to England by Louis XIV in the anticipation that she would

---

[9]   Louise Renée de Penancoët de Kéroualle (1649-1734).

become a royal mistress and promote French interests. She succeeded and was created Duchess of Portsmouth by Charles II and rewarded by Louis XIV with jewellery, a pension, and a title and estate at Aubigny-sur-Nère, 40 kilometres south-east of Orléans.

The Horn's members included several French nationals, two of whom were related to Richmond: the Marquis de Thais, a first cousin;[10] and the Comte de Sade, the father of the notorious Marquis de Sade, a second cousin.[11] Others included Jean Erdman, Baron Dieskau, a soldier and diplomat;[12] and Charles François de Cisternay du Fay, a member of the French Royal Academy of Science.[13] But of greater importance were Richmond's later initiates, especially the courtier, politician and philosopher Baron Montesquieu,[14] and Louis XV's secretary of state, Comte de St. Florentin.[15]

PARIS & AUBIGNY

Richmond convened his first English lodge in France in 1734. Meetings were held at Louise de Kéroualle's house on the Rue des Saints-Pères in Paris close to the Seine, and later in a private room at the Hôtel Bussy in Rue Bussy. It also met at Aubigny. Both locations were popular and the

---

[10] Francis Louis de Gouffier, Marquis de Thais (c.1687-1753).

[11] Jean-Baptiste-François-Joseph, Comte de Sade (1702-1767).

[12] Jean Erdman, Baron Dieskau [Jean-Armand Dieskau] (1701-67), a diplomat and soldier. A professional soldier, he was later wounded and captured fighting against British colonial forces in Canada in 1755. He was repatriated after eight years in captivity.

[13] Charles du Fay (1698-1739), later director of the French Royal Academy of Science. Du Fay was elected FRS, proposed by Richmond, Martin Folkes, later PRS, and Hans Sloane, PRS.

[14] Charles-Louis de Secondat, Baron de La Brède et de Montesquieu (1689-1755).

[15] Louis Phélypeaux, Comte de St Florentin (1705-1777).

lodge attracted more than twenty members in the first year.[16] Its success can be attributed principally to Richmond. Whether in London or Paris, the duke was a celebrity. His installation as grand master in London in 1724 was marked by a lavish feast at the Merchant Taylors' Hall in the City, one of the few venues of sufficient size to accommodate the many hundreds who wished to attend. Anderson describes the event in his 1738 *Constitutions*,[17] detailing the 'expressions of joy, love and friendship' and 'orations, music and mason songs'.[18]

Richmond had been born at the family estate at Goodwood in West Sussex in 1701 and was married at The Hague at the age of eighteen, allegedly to satisfy a gambling debt incurred by his father. On his return to England from the Grand Tour in 1722 he bought a captaincy in the Horse Guards and was elected MP for the family seat at Chichester. His father's death the following year advanced him to the title and from the Commons to the House of Lords.[19]

Richmond's Sussex estate and connections allowed him to influence if not dominate local politics. Newcastle described him as 'the most solid support of the Whig interest in Chichester' and Richmond himself enthused that he had been 'bred up from a child in the Whig principles'.[20] The two became allies,[21] and with Newcastle's assistance Richmond ensured that Sussex

---

[16] 'Nous y avons une loge de plus de vingt frères': Richmond to Montesquieu, Chanteloup, 31 July 1735; cf., René Pomeau, 'Une correspondance inédite de Montesquieu', *Revue d'Histoire Littéraire de la France*, 2 (1982), 217-8.

[17] 1738 *Constitutions*, pp. 118-9.

[18] One of the earliest masonic songs is Matthew Birkhead's 'The Free Masons' Health' (London, 1720). The vocal score is at UGLE Library & Museum, M/10 BIR.

[19] Timothy McCann, 'Charles Lennox, second duke of Richmond, second duke of Lennox, and Duke of Aubigny in the French nobility', *ODNB*.

[20] British Library, Add. MS 32700, f. 264.

[21] 'Newcastle to Bishop Bowers, 6 June 1723': McCann, *Correspondence of the Dukes of Richmond and Newcastle*, pp. xxiii, xxvi.

returned only government supporters.[22] His reward for loyalty was installation as a Knight of the Bath in 1725 and a Knight of the Garter in 1726, and Lord High Constable and a Lord of the Bedchamber in 1727. Richmond was appointed Master of the Horse in 1735 and raised to the Privy Council the same year. But the clearest indication of his 'staunch defence of the Hanoverian succession'[23] was his elevation to Lord Justice in 1740.[24]

Richmond's freemasonry was in a similar vein to his politics and designed to promote Whig interests. From London's standpoint, sympathetic French aristocrats and intellectuals were a potentially influential faction that could be exploited for political gain and who might knowingly or unknowingly provide useful intelligence. Richmond was highly personable and had the ability to charm. Lord Hervey, a friend, wrote that 'there never lived a man of more amiable composition ... thoroughly noble in his way of acting, talking and thinking',[25] while Fielding described Richmond as both 'excellent company' and 'one of the worthiest of magistrates, as well as the best of men'.[26]

In September 1734 the press reported that a lodge had been held in Paris where 'the Duke of Richmond assisted by another English nobleman of distinction there [Earl Waldegrave], President Montesquieu, Brigadier Churchill, Ed. Yonge Esq. and Walter Strickland, admitted several persons of distinction into that most ancient and honourable society'.[27] The presence of Waldegrave is significant. A long-standing member of the Horn,

---

[22] Ibid., p. xxxi.

[23] McCann, 'Charles Lennox, second duke of Richmond', *ODNB*.

[24] Richmond also had a military career. He was appointed ADC to George I in 1724 and appointed to the same role by George II. 'A conscientious officer', Richmond was promoted brigadier general in 1739, major general in 1742 and lieutenant general in 1745. He made full general later the same year.

[25] Romney Sedgwick (ed.), *Lord Hervey's Memoirs* (London, 1931), vol. III, p. 12.

[26] Henry Fielding, *An Enquiry into the Causes of the late increase in Robbers* (London, 1751), 2nd edition, p. 107.

[27] *St James's Evening Post*, 7 September 1734.

Waldegrave had rejected his Catholic Jacobite upbringing as an exile in Paris and allied himself with the Hanoverian succession and Protestantism. His access to Louis XV's court circles and knowledge of the Jacobite community in France proved invaluable during his ambassadorship, especially in intelligence gathering.

Waldegrave monitored Jacobite intrigue assiduously, expanding Britain's spy networks in France and enlisting François Bussy, whom he had met while in Vienna, as a principal intelligence agent. Bussy, codenamed '101', had access to confidential government correspondence and his recruitment provided exceptional political and diplomatic intelligence for a decade.[28] Waldegrave also established a working relationship with Cardinal Fleury through which he sought to counter (not always successfully) anti-Hanoverian sentiment within the French administration. The combination ensured that Waldegrave would become one of Britain's most important diplomats.[29]

Fleury was at the centre of power in France for seventeen years until the early 1740s. He had been tutor to the future Louis XV, appointed when the latter was five, and the two developed a personal bond such that in 1723 when Louis came of age, Fleury was asked to attend private meetings between the king and his first minister, the Duc de Bourbon. When Bourbon objected to the arrangement and asked that Fleury be dismissed he was obliged to back down. Although Fleury later refused to accept the title of 'premier ministre', his elevation to Cardinal in 1726 made clear his position and authority within France, as did his actions.

Notwithstanding his age - he was seventy when Louis XV acceded - Fleury exercised almost unrestricted power in the king's name and was so pivotal to decision-making that Britain's foreign policy sometimes hinged on fathoming his intentions. Indeed, Waldegrave reported to London that other ministerial level officials were more like functionaries than men with

---

[28] Ibid.

[29] The National Archives contain some 600 items of relevant correspondence.

responsibility for policy.[30] Fleury's reliance on the king's favour made him an obvious subject for intrigue and his age invited speculation as to his health. Both themes feature in Waldegrave's reports to Whitehall.[31]

One of Richmond and Waldegrave's more significant masonic catches was Charles Louis de Secondat, Baron Montesquieu, président à mortier du parlement de Bordeaux.[32] While en route to Vienna in 1727 to take-up his first diplomatic posting as ambassador to the Habsburg court, Waldegrave was asked to pause his journey in Paris to await instructions; George I's death required that his position as ambassador be reconfirmed. But although his place in Vienna was approved, Waldegrave was placed in temporary charge of the Paris embassy for three months from January to March 1728 while Horace Walpole was summoned to London.

Waldegrave took the opportunity to resume his social and family connections in Paris and through his Jacobite uncle, Lord Berwick, was introduced to Montesquieu. They became friends, and Montesquieu accompanied Waldegrave to Vienna. Waldegrave stopped at The Hague en route where Montesquieu was introduced to Chesterfield, who invited him to visit London on his return. They sailed on Chesterfield's yacht in October 1729. Montesquieu was presented at court and the following year, a few months before Chesterfield returned to Holland, Montesquieu was initiated into freemasonry at the Horn:

> We hear that on Tuesday night last night at a Lodge held at the Horn Tavern in Westminster, when the Duke of Norfolk, Grand Master, Nathaniel Blackerby, Esq., Deputy Grand Master, and other grand officers, as also the Duke of Richmond, Master of the Lodge ... and several other persons of distinction were present; the following foreign noblemen,

---

[30] NA SP 78/223 f. 226.

[31] For example, NA SP 78/200/26 f. 34; SP 78/222/71 f. 185; SP 78/217/29 f. 75 et al. Waldegrave communicated with London on at least a weekly basis.

[32] A hereditary legal office, head of a panel of judges.

Francis-Louis de Gouffier, Charles-Louis President de Montsquier [sic], Francis Comte de Sade ... were admitted members of the Ancient and Honourable Society of Free Masons.[33]

Montesquieu remained in London for another two years. His election as a Fellow of the Royal Society on 26 February 1730, shortly before his initiation into the Horn, was proposed by Hans Sloane, George Teissier[34] and Paul de St. Hyacinthe,[35] the latter Huguenots. There was a connection. Montesquieu was married to a Protestant and his stance on the separation of powers within government and the progressive political and religious views expressed in *Lettres Persanes* marked him out as a useful ally.[36] Indeed, far from being a devout Catholic, Shackleton comments that Montesquieu held Deist views and saw God as a monarch 'to whom all nations bring tribute, each with its own religion',[37] an approach that chimed with English masonic ritual with its obligation to respect 'that Religion in which all Men agree'.

Montesquieu felt an affinity with the Horn, freemasonry and its adherents, and his letters confirm that he bonded with Montagu and Richmond. He gave Richmond the nickname *chiarissimo*, an appropriate aphorism,[38] and was familiar with his masonic circle, especially Montagu, Folkes,[39]

---

[33] *British Journal*, 16 May 1730. Cf. also Melvin Richter, *Charles de Secondat Montesquieu, The Political Theory of Montesquieu* (Cambridge, 1977), p. 15.

[34] George Teissier was physician to George I and George II, and to the Chelsea and St George's Hospitals.

[35] St Hyacinthe, a soldier, rake and author, also co-founded the influential *Journal littéraire* with Willem Jacob 'sGravesande in 1713: cf., Sackler Archives.

[36] Published in 1721.

[37] Robert Shackelton, *Montesquieu: a critical biography* (Oxford: OUP, 1961), p. 353.

[38] *AQC*, 81, pp. 96-7. The Duke of Montagu was nicknamed 'magnifico', an equally appropriate aphorism.

[39] Montesquieu to Martin Folkes, 10 November 1742, quoted in *AQC*, 81, p. 97.

Arbuthnot, 'Le docteur Misaubin'[40] and of course Desaguliers,[41] whom he described as 'la première colonne de la maçonnerie'[42] Montesquieu noted satirically that 'je ne doute pas que sur cette nouvelle tout ce qui reste encore à recevoir en France de gens de mérite ne se fasse maçon' [I don't doubt that Desaguliers' visit to France will be the catalyst for all those in France who are worthy now becoming freemasons].[43]

John Montagu, 2nd Duke of Montagu
Grand Master, 1721
Sir Godfrey Kneller (1646-1723)

---

[40] Montesquieu to Richmond, 20 May 1734: op. cit., 327.

[41] Cf., Goodwood Archives, West Sussex County Record Office, Box 36, bundle IX; re-printed in Robert Shackleton, 'Montesquieu's Correspondence' *French Studies*, XII.4 (1958), 324-45.

[42] 'The first pillar of freemasonry.'

[43] Montesquieu to Richmond, 2 July 1735, op. cit., 328.

Chesterfield remained in touch with Montesquieu and was affected deeply by his death two decades later. He published a personal notice in the *Public Advertiser* on 10 February 1755 to mark his friend's passing:

His Virtues did Honour to human Nature, his Writings Justice. A Friend to Mankind, he affected their undoubted and unalienable Rights, with Freedom, even in his own Country, whose Prejudice in Matters of Religion and Government he had long lamented, and endeavoured (not without some Success) to remove. He well knew and justly-admired the happy Constitution of this Country, whose fixed and known Laws equally refrain Monarchy from Tyranny, and Liberty from Licentiousness. His Works will illustrate his Name, and survive him as long as right Reason, Moral Obligation, and the true Spirit of Laws shall be understood, respected and maintained.[44]

Whether in London or Paris, the combination of lodge ritual and fraternalism provided routes by which British Protestant politicians and statesmen could bring open-minded French Catholics (and others) into their social and cultural milieu.[45] It opened a bridge across the religious divide and presented progressive, reformist European Catholics with a mechanism to understand the Enlightenment values and social mores of Whig Britain. At the same time, freemasonry opened a door to diplomatic advances. It may not

---

[44] *Public Advertiser*, 20 February 1755. Cf., also *London Evening Post*, 18 - 20 February 1755; and *Whitehall Evening Post or London Intelligencer*, 18 - 20 February 1755.

[45] I am grateful to Paul Monod who lent greater clarity to my thinking on this issue.

always have worked but the significance of English freemasonry to men such as Montesquieu was evident, not least from his decision to initiate his son.[46]

General Charles Churchill's presence at Richmond's lodge in Paris signposts that the event had a political side and that it was worthwhile for one of Walpole's most trusted agents to monitor the lodge. The presence of Walter Strickland speaks to the same purpose. Both were involved with masonic diplomacy on other occasions. Churchill participated in the raising of the Duke of Lorraine at Houghton Hall and Strickland was present at his initiation at The Hague.[47] Delafaye would also have been kept apprised of what was planned. Waldegrave was in touch with him on a weekly and sometimes daily basis up to and including August 1734 when Delafaye retired from office.[48]

Alongside Montesquieu's son, the principal initiate that September was the Marquis de Brancas, a celebrated French aristocrat and diplomat.[49] He had served twice as France's ambassador to Madrid and in 1713 had been

---

[46] Jean Baptiste Montesquieu (1716-1796). Cf., *Whitehall Evening Post*, 5 September 1734.

[47] The Strickland family had substantial influence in Yorkshire and in the eighteenth century represented a series of parliamentary constituencies in the Whig cause. Sir William Strickland (1665-1724), the 3rd Bt., was MP for the quintessentially rotten borough of Old Sarum in Wiltshire (1716-22), with ten electors, and thereafter Malton in Yorkshire (1722-24). His son, also William (1699-1735), was MP for Malton (1708-15), then Carlisle (1715-21) and finally Scarborough (1722-35), with an electorate of some forty-four voters. One of his patrons was Horace Walpole. Walter Strickland's son, also William (1714-1788), was MP for Beverley in Yorkshire (1741-47), a seat controlled by the Pelhams. Cf., Sedgwick, *The History of Parliament: the House of Commons 1715-1754*.

[48] Cf., NA SP 78/205 Waldegrave to Delafaye, Dispatches from Paris, 1734. In particular, SP 78/205/109 21 July 1734 regarding Jacobites and SP 78/205/70 f. 90 24 June 1734 regarding espionage.

[49] Louis de Brancas de Forcalquier (1672-1750), the Marquis de Brancas and Marquis de Cereste. Cf., for example, *Daily Courant*, 27 January 1730; *Daily Journal*, 11 August 1730.

appointed a Chevalier de la Toison d'Or.[50] Underlining his importance was the role he played in the negotiations between France and Sweden in the mid-1720s that sought to conclude an alliance.[51] He was also head of a confidential mission to Austria in the 1730s.[52] In this context it is not surprising that de Brancas was one of those named on the list of diplomats, politicians, aristocrats and other 'persons of interest' whose mail was intercepted by the Secret Department of the Post Office and its agents, a warrant having been issued to that effect on 15 May 1730.[53]

De Brancas's penchant for mediaeval ritual is seen in his membership of the Order of the Golden Fleece, an exclusive aristocratic body headed jointly by the king of Spain and the Holy Roman Emperor. He was also a nominal Prince of Nisyros, a principality created by Pope Boniface IX and associated with the Knights Hospitallers. De Brancas later held office as governor of Provence and in 1740 was elevated to a Marshal of France.

Richmond's lodge at Paris was complemented by that at Aubigny. The prelude to its first meeting is recorded in a letter to Richmond dated 23 August 1734 from Thomas Hill, the duke's former tutor and now a friend and member of his household.[54] It emphasises how Desaguliers altered lodge ritual – 'the production' - to provide a 'greater air of antiquity and consequently make it more venerable' and thus more appealing to its aristocratic French audience:

> I have communicated to the new, if I am not mistaken, right worshipful …
> Dr J[ohn] Theophilus Desaguliers, your Grace's command relating to the

---

[50] *Echo or Edinburgh Weekly Journal*, 11 March 1730.

[51] *Daily Courant*, 1 September 1725.

[52] *General Evening Post*, 16 - 18 October 1735; *Daily Gazetteer*, 18 October 1735; *Old Whig or The Consistent Protestant*, 23 October 1735.

[53] SP 36/18/211, ff. 211-2.

[54] Hill was later appointed secretary to the Council of Trade and Plantations (the Board of Trade); he held the office from 19 October 1737 - 20 September 1758. Cf. Sainty, *Office-Holders in Modern Britain*, volume 3, pp. 28-37.

brotherhood of Aubigny sur Nere. I need not tell you how pleased he is with this further propagation of masonry... When I mentioned the diploma he immediately asked me if I had not Amadis de Gaula[55] or some of the old Romances. I was something surprised at his question, and begun to think as the house was tiled[56] our brother had a mind to crack a joke. But it turned out quite otherwise. He only wanted to get a little of the vieux Gaulois[57] in order to give his style the greater air of antiquity and consequently make it more venerable to the new lodge. He went from me fully intent on getting that or some other such book. What the production will be you may expect to see soon.[58]

It became customary for Richmond to travel to France annually and in September the following year he convened a lodge in Paris once again:

They write from Paris that His Grace the Duke of Richmond and the Rev. Dr Desaguliers (formerly Grand Masters of the Ancient and Honourable Society of Free and Accepted Masons and now authorised by the present Grand Master under his Hand and Seal, and the Seal of the Order) having called a lodge at the Hotel Bussy, His Excellency the Earl of Waldegrave, his Majesty's Ambassador to the French King; the Right Hon. the President Montesquieu; the Marquis de Lomaria;[59] Lord Dursley, son of the Earl of

---

[55] *Amadis de Gaula* is a sixteenth-century Spanish tale of knight errantry. It was the subject of an opera by Handel in 1715: *Amadigi di Gaula*.

[56] 'Tyled': the reference is to a closed and guarded masonic lodge.

[57] Literally the 'Old Gaul', probably 'ancient or historical French'.

[58] A copy of the letter is at the UGLE Library: HC/8/F/3. The text suggests that Desaguliers may have attended The Hague in 1734 in connection with La Chapelle's lodge. Richmond visited The Hague in May and September 1734.

[59] A French nobleman and military commander; cf., *Daily Courant*, 31 January 1707.

Berkeley;[60] the Hon. Mr Fitz-Williams;[61] Messrs. Knight, father and son; Dr Hickman,[62] and several other persons, both French and English, were present; and the following noblemen and gentlemen were admitted to the Order, viz., His Grace the Duke of Kingston; the Rt. Hon. the Count de St. Florentin, Secretary of State to his most Christian Majesty; the Right Hon. The Lord Chewton, son to the Earl of Waldegrave; Mr Pelham; Mr Herbert; Mr Armiger;[63] Mr Cotton[64] and Mr Clement.[65] After which, the new Brethren gave a handsome Entertainment to all the Company.[66]

The names and standing of those present similarly confirms freemasonry's diplomatic and espionage potential. The central figure at the initiation was the Comte de Saint-Florentin, senior advisor to Louis XV and the minister

---

[60] Augustus Berkeley, later 4th Earl of Berkeley (1715-1755). He succeeded his father in 1736.

[61] The son of the Irish peer Lord Fitz-Williams, the Hon. Mr Fitz-Williams succeeded as Page of Honour to George II in 1726: *London Journal*, 26 November 1726. Cf., also *Gentleman's Magazine and Historical Review*, volume 1, pp. 352-3.

[62] Dr Nathan Hickman (c.1695-1746), FRS (1725) and tutor to the Duke of Kingston. He was a Fellow of Merton College, Oxford (1722) and later of University College, Oxford (1731-35).

[63] Among several possibilities are Isaac Armiger, a justice of the peace for Middlesex (Middlesex Sessions Papers - Justices' Working Documents, April 1749: LL ref: LMSMPS503940060); and Gabriel Armiger, a Sworn Clerk in the Office of His Majesty's Remembrancer: NA E 134/6Geo1/Mich33.

[64] There are several possible candidates including Thomas Cotton, a justice of the peace for Middlesex. Cf., General Orders of the Court, 9 April 1730, LL ref: LMSMGO556000493 et al.

[65] Pierre Clément (1707-1767), a Huguenot cleric from Geneva, author of *Les Fri-Maçons: Hyperdrame* (1740) and James Waldegrave's tutor.

[66] *Old Whig or The Consistent Protestant*, 25 September 1735. Cf., also, *General Evening Post*, 18 September 1735, and George Kenning and A.F.A. Woodford, *Kenning's Masonic Encyclopedia and Handbook of Masonic Archaeology, History and Biography*, (Oxford, 2003), p. 233.

with responsibility for the Huguenots in France.[67] He would have been an appropriate figure to cultivate and the concurrent initiation of the Duke of Kingston[68] and Waldegrave's eldest son, James, Lord Chewton, was designed to flatter Phélypeaux much as Newcastle's raising had honoured the Duke of Lorraine at Walpole's Houghton Hall.

Among the various attendees, 'Mr Pelham' was Thomas Pelham Jr. (*c*.1705-1743), Newcastle's reliably loyal second cousin. He was MP for Hastings (1728-41), and succeeded his father as MP for Lewes and as a member of the Board of Trade, in both cases from 1741 until his death. Pelham had been secretary to the British ambassador at the Congress of Soissons (1728-30) and at the time of the meeting was secretary to Waldegrave.[69]

---

[67] Louis Phélypeaux (1705-77), Comte de Saint-Florentin, Marquis (1725) and later duc de La Vrillière (1770).

[68] Evelyn Pierrepont, 2nd Duke of Kingston (1711-73), had succeeded to his grandfather's title in 1726. He spent a decade in Europe whoring and gambling but was nonetheless a loyal Hanoverian, raising his own regiment - 'Kingston's Light Horse' - which fought at Culloden against the Jacobites in the 1745 Rising. He was honoured personally by George II, becoming Master of Staghounds (1738) and invested a Knight of the Garter (1741).

[69] Sedgwick, *The History of Parliament: the House of Commons 1715-1754*. In 1738 he married Sarah Gould, the sister of the wealthy merchants John and Nathaniel Gould, directors of the Bank of England and the East India Company, and Members of Parliament.

CHAPTER SEVEN

DIPLOMACY AND THE LODGE

Bella gerant alii, tu felix Austria nube.[1]
Let others wage war; you, happy Austria, marry!

The House of Habsburg had provided Holy Roman Emperors in a continuous line of father to son, brother or grandson, from Frederick III[2] in the mid-fifteenth century to Leopold I[3] in the eighteenth. Towards the end of his reign and two years into the War of the Spanish Succession, Leopold formulated a Mutual Pact of Succession with his sons.[4] Signed on 12 September 1703, the pact agreed that his elder son, Joseph, later Joseph I,[5] would succeed to the core Habsburg dominions of Austria, Hungary, Croatia and Bohemia, while Charles,[6] his younger son, would claim Spain and its territories in Europe and Spanish America. The pact also specified their respective line of succession with each committing to being succeeded by his own son; however, should there fail to be a male heir in either line, the surviving brother would

---

[1] Matthias Corvinus, king of Bohemia (1443-1490).

[2] Frederick III (1415-1493), Holy Roman Emperor from 1452 until his death, the first emperor of the House of Habsburg.

[3] Leopold I (1640-1705). The second son of Ferdinand III by his first wife, Maria Anna of Spain, Leopold became Holy Roman Emperor in 1658, his older brother, Ferdinand, having died in 1654.

[4] The death of Charles II in 1700, the last Habsburg ruler of Spain, brought to an end the senior line of the House of Habsburg. There were no heirs and the War of Spanish Succession (1701-14) set Louis XIV of France, who claimed Spain and its empire for his grandson, Philip, against Leopold I, who claimed them for Charles.

[5] Joseph I (1678-1711), Holy Roman Emperor from 1705 until his death.

[6] Charles VI (1685-1740).

succeed instead. If neither brother produced a male heir, Joseph's daughters would take precedence and inherit the Habsburg estates as a whole.[7]

Joseph I died in 1711 with no male heirs. Charles inherited and subsequently was elected Holy Roman Emperor as Charles VI. Two years later the War of the Spanish Succession ended with the Treaties of Utrecht and Rastatt signed respectively in 1713 and 1714. Spain was not absorbed by either the French or Habsburg Empires; it was instead settled that Philip, Duc d'Anjou, Louis XIV's grandson,[8] would be crowned king of Spain with the proviso that he renounce his right to the French throne and thereby void the possibility of a single monarch uniting Spain and France. He was also forced to relinquish territory. Austria gained the kingdoms of Naples and Sardinia, and the major part of Milan and the Spanish Netherlands. Sicily went to the Duke of Savoy. And Gibraltar and Minorca were ceded to Britain which in addition obtained trading access to Spain's colonies in Latin America.

In the wake of the post-war pan-European settlement, Charles VI formally abandoned the Mutual Pact of Succession and promulgated a decree that established new parameters. Known as the Pragmatic Sanction, it dictated that the Habsburg estates would be inherited by his eldest son but should there be no male heir the estates would pass not to Joseph I's daughters but to his own. Only if such daughter or daughters died without issue would the estates revert to Joseph I's daughters and their descendants. In the event that a daughter succeeded, her husband would be eligible for election as Holy Roman Emperor.

The hereditary territories that comprised the Habsburg dominions were governed separately with different laws of succession and Charles VI wished the Pragmatic Sanction to be recognised in each. They were advised of the

---

[7] Gustav Turba, *Die pragmatische Sanktion, authentische Texte samt Erläuterungen und Übersetzungen* (Vienna: K-K Schulbücher-Verlage, 1913). Cf., http://www.heraldica.org/topics/royalty/ps1713.htm#Family accessed 3 June 2016.

[8] Philip V of Spain (1683-1746).

terms formally in March 1720 and each signified their consent with the last, Fiume, signing an agreement in 1725.[9] Notwithstanding the problems raised by Salic law, the mediaeval Germanic legal code that allowed only male inheritance,[10] the German states also conformed, albeit that Saxony and Bavaria later reneged. The Prince Elector of Saxony had married Maria Josepha, Joseph I's elder daughter, in 1719, and in 1722 the Prince Elector of Bavaria wed Maria Amalia, his younger. Despite renouncing their claims, both would later seek to assert a right of inheritance.

Charles VI and his wife, Elisabeth Christine,[11] had a son in 1716, but he died within a year of birth. Their next two children were daughters: Maria Theresa,[12] born in 1717; and Maria Anna, in 1718. Royal conception was thereafter more problematic and with an increasingly slim prospect of a male heir, Charles VI became obsessed with getting the agreement of Europe's major powers to uphold the Pragmatic Sanction. His fixation opened Austria to political blackmail not only from France but also Prussia and Spain, which wanted the return of the territories it had ceded to Austria.

The Pragmatic Sanction was not a simple matter of Habsburg inheritance. It had a direct impact on the balance of political power in Europe. Austria, the seat of Habsburg influence, ruled or controlled a swathe of territories from the Austrian Netherlands, Milan, Tuscany and Naples, to a stretch of Central and Eastern Europe from the Tyrol, Bohemia and Silesia to Hungary and Transylvania. And although the various prince-electors, lords and bishops within the German states who owed their allegiance to the Holy Roman Emperor had *de facto* independence within their territories, Vienna's influence was nonetheless sizable.

---

[9] Cf., http://www.heraldica.org/topics/royalty/ps1713.htm#Pragmatic.

[10] *But of Salic land no portion of the inheritance shall come to a woman: but the whole inheritance of the land shall come to the male sex*: http://avalon.law.yale.edu/medieval/salic.asp, accessed 2 March 2016.

[11] Elizabeth Christine (1691-1750), Princess of Brunswick-Wolfenbüttel.

[12] Maria Theresa (1717-1780).

Notwithstanding that Britain had no territorial claims in continental Europe (although Hanover had its own interests), Whitehall saw an opportunity to press its advantage.[13] Intercepted despatches and conventional guidance from Austria's diplomats provided an indication of what Charles VI would be willing to sacrifice to achieve his policy goals.[14] By 1727/8 Austria's position was transparent[15] and London manoeuvred to reach an accord that transformed what had been an uneasy political relationship with Vienna into one of mutual accommodation.[16]

Waldegrave was instrumental in the negotiations. He had presented his credentials to Austria in April 1728 and remained in Vienna through to mid-1730, when he relocated to Paris to succeed Horace Walpole as ambassador.[17] The Anglo-Austrian negotiations culminated in the 1731 Treaty of Vienna. It marked a new accord and at the same time brought to a close the Anglo-French consensus of the prior decades.

---

[13] This was of course separate from Hanover's foreign policy interests, although the two tended to converge for obvious reasons.

[14] NA SP 78/188/137, f. 302: a précis of the Emperor's proposals to the Congress presented verbally by Kinski and Fonseca and comprising *inter alia* the abolition of the Ostend Company and acceptance of the Pragmatic Sanction.

[15] For example, NA SP 78/193/124, f. 373: a report from Count Kinski, Austria's ambassador to London, to the secretary of state, Lord Townshend, advising that the Holy Roman Emperor would be prepared to be accommodating on various points were the Pragmatic Sanction to be accepted.

[16] NA SP 78/191/140, f. 403: Horace Walpole to Delafaye, Paris, 24 June 1729. The dispatch noted that Count Kinski had expressed hopes for a political and diplomatic reconciliation.

[17] Waldegrave corresponded with Delafaye regarding foreign policy and intelligence matters throughout the 1720s and 1730s in letters that underline their strong personal relationship and mutual respect. Although voluminous, the archival records are not complete with an unknown number of confidential letters destroyed after reading. Cf., NA SP 78/185/115, 26 June 1727; NA SP 78/185/122, 9 July 1727; NA SP 78/186/18, 30 August 1727; NRA 28249 Waldegrave; NA SP 78/199/43, February 1731.

Part of London's price for pivoting its foreign policy was Austria's consent to abolish the Ostend Company, an Austro-Flemish trading house that competed directly with British interests in Asia, most especially the East India Company. The initial impact was however muted. As the secretary to the British ambassador at The Hague, Charles Holzendorf,[18] noted presciently, 'the Ostend Company will certainly make use of all sorts of artifices to prolong their East India trade, and though their charter may be abolished they are pretty sure that if they are not protected by the Imperial Court they will not be prosecuted by them so that at least for some years we must expect they will hurt our trade everywhere'.[19]

The Pragmatic Sanction was in due course accepted by most European states, albeit in some instances only nominally. And in recognition that the person most likely to succeed Charles VI as Holy Roman Emperor would be Maria Theresa's consort, diplomatic attention focused on the sole candidate, Francis Stephen, the surviving younger son of the Duke of Lorraine.[20] He had been selected by Charles following the death of his older brother,

---

[18] Holtzendorf was naturalised English in April 1732, cf., *Journal of the House of Lords*, volume 24, 1732-1737 (HMSO), p. 79. He had worked for the British government since at least 1718 ('Treasury Warrants: 15 April 1718', *Calendar of Treasury Books*, volume 32, 1718, p. 312). Holtzendorf received a pension of £400 per annum before other emoluments in consideration of his service at Madrid where he had been secretary to the British ambassador. Cf., for example, *London Gazette*, 17-21 June 1721; 'Warrants for the Payment of Money: 1720, October-December' in William A. Shaw (ed), *Calendar of Treasury Books and Papers*, volume 1, 1729-1730 (London: HMSO, 1897), pp. 592-606; 'Warrants for the Payment of Money: 1742, October-December' in *Calendar of Treasury Books and Papers*, volume 5, 1742-1745 (London: HMSO, 1903), pp. 196-207; and D.B. Horn, 'The Cost of the Diplomatic Service, 1747-52', *English Historical Review*, 43.172 (1928), 606-11, esp., 609.' Holzendorf later served in Vienna (*London Gazette*, 5-9 February 1754); he died in 1779 (*General Evening Post*, 27-30 November 1779).

[19] NA SP 84/316 f. 128: Charles Holzendorf to George Tilson, 5 February 1732.

[20] Francis Stephen (1708-1765), later Francis I as Holy Roman Emperor and Grand Duke of Tuscany.

Léopold Clément,[21] and in 1723 was summoned to live and be educated at the Habsburg court in Vienna.

FRANCIS STEPHEN, DUKE OF LORRAINE

Lorraine had been occupied by France from 1669 until 1697 when the Treaty of Ryswick forced a French withdrawal. Although the then Duke of Lorraine[22] was married to Elisabeth d'Orléans, the daughter of the Duke of Orléans, Louis XIV's younger brother, and had instigated a policy of good relations with France, he also had connections to the Habsburgs. The duke's mother was Eleonora Maria Josefa,[23] a daughter of Ferdinand III[24] and half-sister to Leopold I,[25] both Holy Roman Emperors.

Vienna viewed Lorraine as a strategic buffer that safeguarded Austria's sphere of influence in the west and limited French territorial ambitions. France saw Lorraine through the opposite side of the same prism. An independent Lorraine raised a barrier to French expansion and any marriage that would tie Lorraine to the Habsburgs posed a military threat that could bring Austrian influence directly to France's borders. The prospect of Francis Stephen's marriage to Maria Theresa raised a menace that haunted French foreign policy for two decades and catalysed two pan-European

---

[21] Léopold Clément Charles (1707-1723), died in the smallpox epidemic that swept across Europe that year.

[22] Léopold Joseph Charles Dominique Agapet Hyacinthe (1679-1729), Duke of Lorraine; son of Charles V and Eleanora Maria Josefa.

[23] Eleonora Maria Josefa of Austria (1653-1697), Queen of Poland (1670-73) following marriage to Michael I of Poland. She married the then Duke of Lorraine in 1678, five years after her first husband's death.

[24] Ferdinand III (1608-1657), King of Hungary and Croatia, King of Bohemia and Archduke of Austria. Holy Roman Emperor from 1637-death.

[25] Leopold Ignaz Joseph Balthasar Felician (1640-1705), King of Hungary and Croatia, King of Bohemia and Archduke of Austria, elected Holy Roman Emperor in 1658.

conflicts: the 1733 War of the Polish Succession and the War of the Austrian Succession that followed in 1740.

Francis Stephen was in Vienna in 1729 when his father died unexpectedly. Granted leave of the Habsburg court, he left for Lunéville, the capital of the Duchy of Lorraine. Six months later in January 1730, continuing his father's policy of accommodation,[26] the duke travelled to France for his first formal state visit accompanied by a retinue of 'forty horses and attended by the principal lords of his court'.[27] The duke was housed at the Royal Palace in Paris and subsequently received by Louis XV at Versailles[28] where 'waterworks, both ordinary and extraordinary, played for his diversion'.[29]

Lorraine's state visit was punctuated by receptions and dinners hosted by the nobility and diplomatic corps, including the Russian ambassador.[30] The many entertainments included theatrical evenings, formal balls and a stag hunt; and the duke was granted admission to the Académie Royale des Sciences, a body whose honorary membership was limited to ten.[31] He received a parting gift of eight gold-embroidered tapestries valued at 150,000

---

[26] *Daily Courant*, 20 January 1730. Leopold Joseph's rapprochement with France had not always succeeded: an attempt to marry his daughter, Anne Charlotte, to King Louis XV had been rebuffed, as was a second proposal that she marry the widowed Louis, Duc d'Orléans.

[27] *Daily Courant*, 27 January 1730.

[28] *London Journal*, 24 January 1730.

[29] *Daily Post*, 6 February 1730.

[30] *London Journal*, 7 February 1730.

[31] The Duke of Richmond had been made a member in 1728. Cf., 'Letter from Richmond to Folkes, Aubigny, 3 October 1728' in Charles Richmond, Earl of March (ed.), *A Duke and his Friends: The Life and Letters of the Second Duke of Richmond* (London, 1911), pp. 154-6.

livres; Louis's generosity spoke not only to the political significance of Lorraine but also underlined the extent of French wealth and power.[32]

The duke next toured Lorraine and then the Austrian Netherlands and United Provinces.[33] In a report from The Hague, *The London Gazette* noted that that 'the Duke of Lorraine, who goes by the name of the Count of Blamont,[34] arrived at Brussels some days ago and is expected [at The Hague] in fifteen days designing to see this country; it is even reported that his Highness intends to go to England'.[35] Later the same month the *London Evening Post*, *Fog's Weekly Journal* and much of London's press picked up the same story, declaring enthusiastically that 'the Duke of Lorraine is hourly expected here incognito'.[36] They were premature. Francis Stephen remained in Brussels where his hosts entertained him lavishly: 'great preparations ... for several feasts which are still to be given to the Duke of Lorraine whose departure from hence is not yet fixed'.[37] Public excitement in Britain nonetheless continued fed by a torrent of press reports[38] that described balls,

---

[32] *Daily Post*, 9 February 1730. Equivalent to *c.*£7 million. There are two principal but different mechanisms to measure the current value of historic money. One is based on a retail price deflator and the second on an arguably more realistic tax-adjusted average earnings deflator. The actual value is probably somewhere between the two. In the 1720s £1 was equivalent to *c.*23 livres.

[33] The territories comprised much of present-day Luxembourg, Belgium and Holland.

[34] It was conventional for royalty to travel 'incognito', notwithstanding that the person behind the assumed identity would be known. Doing so was a means of negating the requirement for formal diplomatic protocol and the concomitant expense of formal ceremonies, exchanges of gifts and costly entertainments. The practice was pragmatic with no implication of dishonour on either side. Cf., Ulrik Langen, 'The Meaning of Incognito', *The Court Historian*, 7.2 (2002), 145-55.

[35] *London Gazette*, 24 - 27 April 1731.

[36] *London Evening Post*, 18 - 20 May 1731.

[37] *Daily Journal*, 31 May 1731.

[38] For example, *Daily Advertiser*, 2 June 1731.

dinners, shooting parties and a myriad of other entertainments comprising 'whatever else is remarkable'.[39]

A few days later the London press proclaimed that Lorraine had sailed from Holland to Dover and was travelling by road to the capital accompanied by the twenty-one year old Viscount Weymouth, Thomas Thynne.[40] Once again they were mistaken. The duke was now in Flanders visiting Mons, Namur and Charleroi. He returned to Brussels later the same month, returned to cross the Low Countries in July and was back in Brussels in August.[41] A month later[42] he left for Antwerp and The Hague,[43] where he attended lectures given by Desaguliers,[44] 'the best mechanic in Europe',[45] one of Europe's most highly regarded scientific lecturers and a flag-carrier for Britain's commercial and political standing.

Holzendorf wrote from The Hague to George Tilson, under-secretary at the Northern Department,[46] Delafaye's counterpart, to inform him of Lorraine's arrival, describing the duke as 'an excellent, sober character, generally applauded by everybody here [and] the pattern of a complete young prince and gentleman'. He reported that Lorraine had met Desaguliers

---

[39] *Daily Journal*, 7 June 1731.

[40] For example, *Daily Post*, 9 June 1731 & *Grub Street Journal*, 10 June 1731.

[41] *Daily Post*, 10 September 1731.

[42] *London Gazette*, 18 - 21 September 1731.

[43] *Daily Advertiser*, 14 September 1731.

[44] This was Desaguliers' second visit to the Low Countries; he had travelled to Zeeland two years before. On this occasion he lectured at Rotterdam, The Hague and Amsterdam.

[45] James Brydges to William Mead, 16 June 1718, Huntington Library: Stowe MS, ST 57, XV, 252.

[46] George Tilson (*c.*1672-1738), under-secretary of state to Boyle, 1708-10; Bolingbroke, 1710-14; Townshend, 1714-16; Methuen, 1716-17; Sunderland, 1717-18; Stanhope, 1718-21; Townshend, 1721-30; and Harrington, 1730-38. Tilson was elected FRS in 1735; his proposers included J.T. Desaguliers (Horn Tavern), Roger Gale (lodge unknown), and Alexander Stuart (Rummer, Charing Cross), as well as Philip Zollman, who had that year joined the Secret Department.

and attended his 'public lectures ... without any constraint and ... very attentively', and passed on the intelligence that Lorraine 'professes himself a great admirer and friend of the English Nation and is learning the English tongue with such an application that he carries an English Grammar in his pocket'.[47]

Lorraine's presence at Desaguliers' lectures was also noted by the Dutch press which wrote that 'the learned and renowned Dr Desaguliers is now presenting a complete course of lectures on Mechanical and Experimental Philosophy which has been attended not only by persons of the first rank, but which has also been honoured on several occasions by the presence of the Duke of Lorraine'.[48]

Desaguliers was not only a 'learned and renowned' scientist but also a past grand master and deputy grand master of the Grand Lodge of England whose freemasonry was infused with themes from the scientific and philosophical Enlightenment. Margaret Jacob terms this the 'mentality of official masonry' and explained it as a 'taste for science ... craving for order and stability ... worldly mysticism [and] rituals, passwords and mythology, [and a] religious devotion to higher powers, be they the Grand Architect, the king or the Grand Master'.[49] It had particular appeal to Europe's elites.

Lorraine's initiation into English freemasonry was effected within days with a private lodge convened at Lord Chesterfield, the British ambassador's residence in the city. Desaguliers presided as master, with John Stanhope, Chesterfield's younger brother, and Holzendorf serving as senior and junior wardens respectively.[50] It is significant that on his return to London a year later Holzendorf was selected as a grand steward.[51] Other attendees aside

---

[47] NA SP 84/314, ff. 188-7.

[48] *Amsterdamse Courant*, 4 October 1731.

[49] Margaret Jacob, *The Radical Enlightenment*, p. 102.

[50] James Anderson, *Constitutions* (London: Anderson, 1738), p. 129.

[51] Grand Lodge *Minutes*, 7 June 1733.

from Chesterfield included Walter Strickland,[52] the nephew of the Bishop of Namur;[53] Benjamin Hadley;[54] and an unnamed 'Hollandish brother',[55] possibly Vincent La Chapelle.

Despite his Catholicism, Thomas Strickland, the Bishop of Namur, was a British intelligence agent. He later entered Charles VI's service in Vienna from where he provided information on the Habsburg court.[56] Walter Strickland, his nephew, probably attended the lodge as a proxy for his uncle and for the same purpose. He was also present at Richmond's lodge in Paris in September 1734 when a number of senior French politicians were brought into the lodge.

Lorraine's initiation at The Hague was a small but significant component of the preparations for the duke's visit to England. It was principally political and it is hard to conceive that it would have occurred without Whitehall's sanction. Lorraine's subsequent invitation to Walpole's Houghton Hall to be raised to a master mason was the second act in the same masonic play. Although neither Walpole nor Newcastle were active freemasons, they were aware of its potential influence. Delafaye and Richmond had used freemasonry for political purposes for close to a decade to cement support for the Hanoverians and successive Whig administrations, and to prevent the organisation from falling under Jacobite influence. Their Jacobite counterparts had done the same on behalf of the Stuarts.

---

[52] The name is sometimes given as 'Jeremy Strickland' rather than 'Walter'.

[53] Namur was in the Austrian Netherlands; it is now the capital of the Wallonia region of Belgium.

[54] Benjamin Hadley [poss. Headley or Hudley] has not been identified. Contenders include a merchant and a ship's captain (ADM 106/869/77). There is one mention in *Burney* in 1767: 'On Sunday died in Queen Anne Street, Cavendish Square, Benjamin Hadley of the county of Salop': *London Evening Post*, 28 - 30 April 1767.

[55] Anderson, *Constitutions* (1738).

[56] John Callow, 'Strickland, Thomas John Francis (*c.*1682-1740)', *ODNB*, online edn, Oct 2008, accessed 29 March 2015.

In the second week of October the press reported that the duke was 'hourly expected', that 'his baggage and some saddle horses' had arrived, and that 'the Blue Guards lie ready to receive him at Greenwich and conduct him through the City to Hanover Square' and the residence of Count Kinski.[57] The 'great preparations' and the 'quality and distinction' of those invited to attend the duke's various engagements[58] were publicised widely, as were the prospective diversions, with the *Daily Journal* making much of Lorraine's invitation to Newmarket for the racing and the supposed order that the Prince of Wales's servants stand 'in readiness' for the event.[59]

Lorraine arrived at Greenwich on 13 October less than two weeks after his initiation at The Hague. His visit was scripted and formed part of Whitehall's diplomatic ballet with Austria. The Treaty of Vienna had been signed only six months before and recognition of the Pragmatic Sanction and Maria Theresa's right to inherit had eased the path to Lorraine's future election as Holy Roman Emperor.[60] He would have been aware of the import. Even the British public knew that Lorraine 'is designed to marry the Emperor's eldest daughter and even to succeed to the Empire' and thus 'his reception will be the more extraordinary'.[61]

The duke's itinerary was similar to that of his state visit to France: a formal welcome at court; stag hunting in Windsor Forest with the royal family in the hunting party; and a sequence of dinners, with Newcastle hosting a 'most magnificent' entertainment at Claremont House, his estate in Surrey, and Count Kinski reciprocating at Hanover Square.[62] There was a display of naval power, with the duke invited to Woolwich to launch *Somerset*, the

---

[57]   Count Philip Kinski of Wchinitz and Tettau (1700-1749), ambassador to Britain. The name is also written as 'Kinsky'.

[58]   For example, *Daily Advertiser*, 14 October 1731.

[59]   *Daily Journal*, 11 October 1731.

[60]   The Treaty of Vienna was signed on 16 March 1731.

[61]   *The Norwich Gazette*, 9 - 16 October, 1731.

[62]   *London Gazette*, 19 - 23 October 1731.

Royal Navy's most advanced 80-gun warship, and *Grampus*, a 16-gun sloop.[63] It was followed by a tour of Greenwich Hospital and a dinner hosted by the Lords of the Admiralty at the Queen's House. Over the next several days Lorraine visited Sloane's botanical gardens in Chelsea; the Royal Society, where Lorraine and Kinski were elected FRSs; and the Royal Exchange and East India Company in the City.[64] There were also tours of St Paul's and the Law Courts.

In the last week of October Lorraine's party left for Newmarket to be entertained by a series of high stakes races with a side excursion to Cambridge University. The party then returned to London for the investiture of the Lord Mayor and a second round of balls, dinners and theatrical evenings. A month later at the beginning of November Lorraine and Kinski left London again, on this occasion for Walpole's country estate at Houghton Hall in Norfolk. They travelled via Suffolk, staying at the Duke of Grafton's Euston Hall,[65] and arrived at Houghton in the second week of November.

Lorraine was accompanied on the journey by members of Walpole's inner circle,[66] and the visit was held away from the press and designed to allow an opportunity 'to confer ... on some important affairs ... which are said to be the chief inducement of his Highness's coming to this Court'.[67] Lorraine would remain at Houghton for nearly a week. Preparations for the visit had been placed in train by Walpole over a month earlier and extended to procuring the services of an army of catering staff – 'twenty cooks have been at work for some time past in getting everything ready for the grand entertainment of the Duke of Lorraine', and London's foremost confec-

---

[63]   Rif Winfield, *British Warships in the Age of Sail, 1714-1792* (Barnsley: Seaforth Publishing, 2007).

[64]   *Daily Courant*, 5 November 1731.

[65]   *Universal Spectator and Weekly Journal*, 6 November 1731.

[66]   *Daily Courant*, 12 November 1731 et al.

[67]   *Echo or Edinburgh Weekly Journal*, 10 November 1731.

tioner, Edward Lambert, a member of the French lodge at the King's Head in Pall Mall: 'Mr Lambert, the confectioner who has prepared most of the deserts for the nobility who have hitherto entertained the Duke of Lorraine is going, with several of his servants, down to the seat of Sir Robert Walpole in Norfolk to prepare a most magnificent one there for the entertainment of that Prince'.[68]

Adding to the sense of purpose, 'eight carriages are constantly passing night and day between this City [London] and Houghton ... with necessaries for the entertainment of his serene highness the duke of Lorraine'.[69] And pointing to the nature of what would be discussed, 'most of the Clerks of the Treasury [had been invited] in order to serve as waiters, that none but gentlemen may attend upon that occasion'.[70]

Delafaye was involved with Lorraine's visit and reported on its progress to Waldegrave in Paris:

> The Duke of Lorraine is come at last, under the travelling name of Count Blamont. Count Kinsky brought him hither. They came to court [then at Hampton Court] in chairs (having alighted at Baron Hattorf's lodgings upon the Green).[71] The guards took no notice of them, I mean by the way of being drawn up or saluting. They alighted at the first gate and walked through the court, upstairs, through the guard chamber and the next room, into the cartoon gallery, at the door of which the house keeper was placed to keep everybody else from going in. My lord Harvey [a court favourite and the vice-chamberlain to the king] waited in the cartoon gallery and carried him that way into his Majesty's private apartment. Then I saw my lord chamberlain conducting his highness through the Admiral Gallery to the Queen's apartment, where he saw (in private) her Majesty

---

[68] *London Evening Post*, 28 - 31 October 1731.

[69] *Grub Street Journal*, 4 November 1731.

[70] *Daily Advertiser*, 2 November 1731.

[71] Baron Hattorf (d.1737), was George II's secretary of state for Hanover.

and the royal family, except the Prince of Wales, to whom he afterwards paid a visit, being carried also the private way.

I imagined Count Blamont would from thence have slunk away, but he was more gallant, went to the Queen's circle, and saw the dining in public, standing behind their Majesties, or rather in some measure between their chairs. After about a quarter of an hour's stay there, he went and dined at Count Kinsky's at Isleworth [the ambassador's country house west of London], and so back to London to Count Kinsky's house there [at Hanover Square], whither all the ministers went early this morning to pay their court to his Highness, before they came to the king's levy here. The duke of Lorraine was not here this day but tomorrow he is to meet their majesties and the royal family at the hunting in Windsor Forrest and they are to dine together, as I hear, at Cranborn lodge. The duke of Newcastle will give his highness a great entertainment next week at Claremont. They talk of Count Blamont's going to Newmarket at the end of next week and that we shall then remove to town, but that is not certain.[72]

A few days later Delafaye provided Waldegrave with another update:

The hunting was last Saturday … and the dinner was here. There sat at table the King, the Prince of Wales on his majesty's right hand and Count Blamont on his left, and the ministers and such other great officers and such others as his Majesty was pleased to appoint who sat péle melé without any distinction. They were about fourteen in all… A play is now acting here to which Count Blamont is come from Count Kinsky's. Tomorrow the Duke of Devonshire entertains his Highness at supper in town. Wednesday is to be another hunting and another dinner

---

[72] Delafaye to Earl Waldegrave, 15 October 1731 in William Coxe, *Memoirs of the Life and Administration of Sir Robert Walpole* (London: Cadell & Davies, 1798), vol. III, pp. 122-3.

here. Thursday Count Blamont goes to see a ship launched and will be entertained by the Admiralty. Friday he dines with my lord the Duke of Newcastle at Claremont and is to be a ball here at court. Saturday another hunting. This day sev'night his Highness goes to Newmarket and comes back to town for his birthday after which the Duke of Grafton will entertain him at Euston and Sir Robert Walpole at Houghton.[73]

Shortly after Lorraine's arrival, Walpole's neighbour, Lord Lovel, a political ally and grand master of Grand Lodge, convened a lodge at Houghton where he 'made Brother Lorrain and Brother Thomas Pelham, Duke of Norfolk, Master Masons'.[74] The minutes of the nearby Maid's Head Lodge at Norwich note the initiation of Newcastle, Essex, General Churchill and others by its master, Thomas Johnson,[75] in order to regularise their attendance at Houghton and allow Newcastle to be raised alongside the duke as a mark of respect. The *Norwich Gazette* also recorded the initiation of Walpole and Count Kinski,[76] as did the London press: 'during the stay of the Duke of Lorraine at Sir Robert Walpole's seat Houghton in Norfolk, a Lodge of Free and Accepted Masons was held by the Lord Lovel, grand master, in which Sir Robert Walpole and Count Kinski were admitted Brethren'.[77] Among those present in the lodge were Richmond, the Earl of Albemarle, Lord Baltimore and the Earl of Scarbrough.

---

[73] Ibid., Delafaye to Earl Waldegrave, 18 October 1731, p. 123.

[74] Anderson, 1738 *Constitutions*, p. 129. Monod has put forward the suggestion that the raising may have occurred in the bedroom at Houghton designed and decorated with an astrological ceiling by William Kent (1685-1748). (Private communication, 20 August 2016.) Kent had co-designed Lord Burlington's Chiswick Villa which includes a similar zodiac-based decoration.

[75] Cf., G.W.G. Barnard's response to Gilbert Davies, 'The Duke of Lorraine and English Freemasonry in 1731', *AQC*, 37 (1924), 137-8.

[76] *The Norwich Gazette*, 27 October, 1731; cf., Davies, 'The Duke of Lorraine and English Freemasonry in 1731', 120.

[77] *London Evening Post*, 25 - 27 November 1731 et al.

Although it has been posited that the lodge was convened at Houghton principally as an entertainment rather than to raise the duke, this is improbable.[78] A masonic ceremony at the Palladian home of the Prime Minister attended by the political elite would have had a substantial emotional and diplomatic impact. And any comparable masonic event in London in which the duke was involved would have been reported. Indeed, this is precisely what happened when he attended the Devil's Tavern:

> Last night his Serene Highness the Duke of Lorraine, the Prince of Wales and several of the nobility were at a lodge of Free Masons at the Devil Tavern near Temple Bar where they were handsomely entertained by the brethren.[79]

This was probably a masonic dinner since Frederick, Prince of Wales, was not initiated into freemasonry until 1737.[80] Regardless, the aristocracy vied to entertain the duke and his presence at such a masonic feast was

---

[78] Cf., Davies, 'The Duke of Lorraine and English Freemasonry in 1731', esp. 125.

[79] *London Evening Post*, 2 - 4 December 1731, *Daily Post*, 4 December 1731. This was probably Lodge No. 8 and not a dinner in advance of the Quarterly Communication. Lorraine's presence and that of the Prince of Wales was not detailed in Anderson's 1738 *Constitutions*. Davies (pp. 131-2) speculates that Lorraine's visit may have been omitted had he attended a dinner but not the meeting of Grand Lodge. This is inconceivable. Any visit by the Prince of Wales, the Duke of Lorraine 'and several of the nobility' was noteworthy. The day had also included a boxing match between Britain's bare knuckle champions, Mr Figg and Mr Sparks. Cf., *The Daily Advertiser*, 4 December. Cf., also, Alfred Robbins, 'Frederick, Prince of Wales as a Freemason', *AQC*, 29 (1916), 326-9.

[80] *London Evening Post*, 5 November 1737. Cf., also, *London Spy Revived*, 9 November 1737.

understandable. Lorraine's hosts were freemasons and an invitation to participate in a private lodge was a courtesy.[81]

Lorraine's entry into freemasonry had political resonance. Although it would be wrong to interpret it as an implicit or explicit endorsement of Whiggist mores, it was a means to bind Lorraine more closely to the British political establishment. Richmond's involvement is particularly telling. Highly personable, fluent in French and soon to be a French aristocrat in his own right, Richmond had been an exponent of political freemasonry for a decade. A former grand master, he was a member of Lorraine's retinue on his journey to Houghton, was present at his raising, acted as his host on several occasions in London and proposed Lorraine as an FRS.[82]

Unlike the majority of his earlier engagements, Lorraine's meeting with Walpole was purely political and many of those present that November had attended Houghton before. It was standard practice for Walpole to travel to Norfolk immediately after the celebrations in London that marked the king's birthday.[83] Around thirty colleagues would normally attend to discuss the government's agenda and although no complete list survives, they were generally a mixture of government ministers and confidantes. Foremost were the Duke of Newcastle and his brother, Henry Pelham, Secretary at War[84] from 1724 until 1730 and now Paymaster General.[85] Others included Sir William Yonge, a Lord of the Treasury and later Secretary at War, an

---

[81] 1723 *Constitutions*, pp. 151-2.

[82] Royal Society, Sackler Archives, NA 940.

[83] The king's birthday was on 30 October.

[84] In the eighteenth century the title was 'Secretary at War'. The secretary was concerned principally with the administration of the Army rather than military policy. The position was subordinate to the secretaries of state for the Northern and Southern Departments.

[85] Cf., P.J. Kulisheck, 'Pelham, Henry (1694-1754)', *ODNB*, online edn, Jan. 2008, accessed 20 June 2016.

effective Commons operator;[86] Archibald Campbell, 3rd Duke of Argyll, Lord Keeper of the Privy Seal in Scotland and Walpole's parliamentary manager for Scotland;[87] Charles FitzRoy, 2nd Duke of Grafton, lord chamberlain and a Lord Justice,[88] and Arthur Onslow, the influential Speaker of the House of Commons. Also at Houghton were Richmond's brother-in-law,[89] William Keppel, 2nd Earl of Albemarle,[90] an aide-de-camp to the king; Charles Calvert, Lord Baltimore, a close friend of Richmond whose family owned Maryland; and General Charles Churchill.[91]

Charles Churchill (1679-1745), the natural son of General Charles Churchill and a younger brother of the Duke of Marlborough, was one of Walpole's most trusted intimates and one of the least known but most intriguing figures at Houghton. He was a professional soldier and having entered the army as an ensign in the 3rd Foot in 1688, he acquired a captaincy in 1697, served as ADC to his father at Blenheim, and was promoted major in 1706/7. Churchill obtained the colonelcy of the regiment two years later and became colonel of his own regiment of dragoons, the 10th, in 1722/3.

---

[86] Cf., H.T. Dickinson, 'Yonge, Sir William, fourth baronet (*c*.1693-1755)', *ODNB*.

[87] Cf., Alexander Murdoch, 'Campbell, Archibald, third duke of Argyll (1682-1761)', *ODNB*, online edn, Oct 2006, accessed 20 June 2016.

[88] Cf., A.A. Hanham, 'FitzRoy, Charles, second duke of Grafton (1683-1757)', *ODNB*, online edn, May 2008, accessed 20 June 2016.

[89] Albemarle was married to Anne Lennox, Richmond's sister.

[90] Jonathan Spain, 'Keppel, William Anne, second earl of Albemarle (1702-1754)', *ODNB*.

[91] Other attendees included Sir Charles Turner, MP for the neighbouring Norfolk seat of King's Lynn; Richard Lumley, 2nd Earl of Scarbrough, in 1727 appointed Master of the Horse; William Capell, 3rd Earl of Essex, a Gentleman of the Bedchamber and Lord Lieutenant of Hertfordshire; George Cholmondeley, 2nd Earl of Cholmondeley, Lord Lieutenant for Cheshire, Anglesey, Caernarvonshire, Denbighshire, Flintshire, Merionethshire and Montgomeryshire; and Lord Hervey, a Whig loyalist and court favourite.

He was promoted brigadier general in 1727, major general in 1735 and lieutenant general in 1739.

Churchill's political loyalty to Walpole was compensated with the seat of Castle Rising, a constituency controlled by Walpole following his father's acquisition of twenty-five rental properties - burgages - that endowed the owner with the right to vote. The total electorate numbered around sixty. Churchill held the Norfolk seat from 1715 until his death, voting with Walpole throughout. Hervey describes him as a 'worthy and good-natured, friendly and honourable man',[92] and confirms that he was an 'intimate friend for many years and through all the different stages of [Walpole's] power and retirement, prosperity and disgrace'.[93] That they were more than political allies is suggested by Churchill's presentation to Walpole of two Alexander Albani busts and a painting – *Architecture* – by Polydore Vergil, the latter valued at £300 when the Houghton collection was sold in 1779.[94]

Churchill was one of relatively few men trusted by Walpole to undertake secret diplomatic duties. His missions included an assignment in Vienna in 1721 'to make the most pressing Instances in His Majesty's Name to the Emperor, that Mr Knight ... Prisoner in the Citadel of Antwerp,[95] may be forthwith delivered up, together with all his Papers and Effects;[96] and at the height of the Atterbury Crisis it was Churchill who was tasked with travelling to Paris to obtain intelligence on the extent of French support for the Jacobites.

---

[92]   John, Lord Hervey, *Memoirs of the reign of George II* (New York: Scribner & Welford, 1884), volume I, p. 24.

[93]   Hervey, op. cit. Churchill followed Walpole into opposition in 1717 and was a firm supporter in 1727 and throughout the 1733 Excise Crisis. Capping this, Churchill's illegitimate son, also Charles, was engaged to Walpole's natural daughter, Maria. They married in 1746.

[94]   Davies, 'The Duke of Lorraine and English Freemasonry in 1731', esp. 130. The collection forms the basis of that in the Hermitage, St Petersburg.

[95]   Antwerp was within the Austrian Netherlands.

[96]   *The London Gazette*, 14 February 1721.

Horace Walpole's critique of Churchill as 'ignorant' - his correspondence so 'ill spelled that Sir Robert Walpole used to keep them unread till he saw him, and then he often could not read them himself'[97] - was ironic. Churchill had a justifiable reputation for intellect and wit. Horace Walpole offers several examples but the best is from Charles Hanbury-Williams who recalls that when Churchill came to vote in the Commons while on crutches he passed near to the Prince of Wales who jested 'Mr Churchill, I see even the lame and the blind come to vote'. 'Yes, Sir', Churchill responded, 'the lame of our side, and the blind of theirs'.[98] The two knew each other well. Churchill had been a Groom of the Bedchamber to the prince since 1718 and retained that position when the prince succeeded as George II in 1728; his regiment of dragoons was honoured with a royal inspection the following year.[99]

Lorraine left England in early December. He was accompanied to Greenwich on the last leg of his journey by the royal family, Count Kinski, the ever-present Duke of Richmond, and the Earl of Albemarle, and dined with Richmond the evening before he boarded the royal yacht – *Fubbs* – for the return journey to Holland,[100] and then the German states and Austria.[101]

The duke retained a commitment to freemasonry throughout his life and was later a member of the Aux Trois Canons lodge in Vienna, consecrated in 1742 by a lodge from Breslau. It survived only six months before being closed at the order of his wife, Maria Theresa. Although the Bull was not in effect in Austria, Maria Theresa was turned against freemasonry by her Jesuit advisers who considered it subversive and under the influence of

[97] *Horace Walpole's Correspondence* (Yale edition), volume 30, p. 289, fn. 13.

[98] Charles Hanbury-Williams, *The Works, of the Right Honourable Sir Chas. Hanbury-Williams* (London: Jeffrey & Son, 1822), i. 74-6.

[99] *The London Gazette*, 4 May 1729.

[100] *The London Gazette*, 7 - 11 December 1731.

[101] *London Evening Post*, 1 - 4 January 1732; *Daily Journal*, 5 January 1732; Ibid, 6 January 1732; *Grub Street Journal*, 20 January 1732 et al.

foreign governments. Given the circumstances of the duke's initiation and raising, it can be argued that they had a point, and the political instability within the Habsburg Empire compounded the perceived threat:

> The Queen, having received certain intelligence of a Society of Freemasons, sent a detachment of soldiers in order to invade the Lodge. The Commanding Officer called upon those present in the name of the Queen, to deliver up their swords, which were delivered up by all her subjects to the Master, who gave them to the officer, so as to show their obedience to the Queen... Persons of any quality were brought to the Rumorhaus. The princes and foreigners were set free at once and other persons of rank received private confinement. But on her son's birthday the Queen forgave them all, but forbade them very severely to meet again. This persecution was occasioned by the clergy ... who had great influence with Maria Theresa.[102]

The sanctions against freemasonry in Austria were short-lived and over the following decades with the duke now Holy Roman Emperor, freemasonry became an extension of polite society and the number of lodges expanded.[103] Freemasonry had also taken root elsewhere with lodges established in the Austrian Netherlands, Bohemia, Galicia, Bratislava, Hungary and elsewhere from the early 1730s. Many were exclusive and dominated by the nobility

---

[102] *History of Freemasonry throughout the World* (New York, NY: Charles Scribner's Sons, 1936), vol. III, p. 164.

[103] For example, a diplomatic lodge was formed in Vienna in 1754, 'Aux Trois Coers', and a military Lodge, 'Die Freimütigen', in the 1760s. Cf., Malczovich, 'A Sketch of the Earlier History of Masonry in Austria and Hungary, cont'd', *AQC*, 6 (1893), 85-91.

and wealthy merchants. Bradley's examination of Zur Wohltätigkeit[104] suggests that the profile of freemasonry in Vienna remained as such for at least four decades when the lodge's members tallied a prince, thirty-six counts, one marquis, fourteen barons and a collection of over forty court officials, aristocrats and ambassadors.[105]

In addition to Francis Stephen, the most prominent proponents of freemasonry in Austria were members of the Esterházy family. At least seven were active in the order: Count Emerich,[106] a member of Zur gekronte Hoffnung in Vienna; Count Franz,[107] a member of Aux Trois Canons; Count Franz Seraphin,[108] a member of Zur gekronten Hoffnung and De le Union in Brussels; Count Johann Baptist,[109] master of lodge Zur gekronten Hoffnung; Count Johann Nepomuk,[110] master of Zur gekronten Hoffning; Prince Nikolaus I,[111] deputy master of Zur gekronten Hoffnung; and Count Nikolaus,[112] a member of Nur neugekronten Hoffnung.

---

[104]   An amalgam of Zur gekrönten Hoffnung, Zur den drei Feuern and Zur gekrönten Hoffnung. Joseph II had issued a decree in 1785 that reduced the number of Viennese lodges from eight to two, ostensibly to provide a measure of protection for the Catholic Church. The decree was rescinded four years later.

[105]   Herbert Bradley, 'Bro. Mozart and some of his Masonic Friends', *AQC*, 26 (1913), 241-70. On a related note, Ladislas de Malczovich charts the introduction of esotericism, side orders and symbolism in Austria and the German states, features favoured by Europe's aristocracy: C. Kupferschmidt, 'A Glimpse at Early Freemasonry in Germany', *AQC*, 9 (1896), 160-5.

[106]   Emerich Graf Esterházy von Galanta (1722-1792).

[107]   Franz Graf Esterházy von Galanta (1715-1785).

[108]   Franz Seraphin Graf Esterházy von Galanta (1748-1815).

[109]   Johann Baptist Graf Esterházy von Galanta (1747-1800).

[110]   Johann Nepomuk Graf Esterházy von Galanta (1754-1840).

[111]   Nikolaus I Joseph Furst Esterházy von Galanta (1714-1790).

[112]   Nikolaus Graf Esterházy von Galanta (1741-1809).

The Esterházys also commissioned three of their directors of music, 'kapellmeisters', to perform in lodge: Joseph Haydn;[113] Paul Wranitzky;[114] and Ignaz Pleyel.[115] All became freemasons as a necessity. Haydn was initiated in 1785 into Zur wahren Eintracht.[116] Wranitzky into Zur gekronten Hoffnung.[117] And Pleyel into an unnamed lodge in Eberau, Hungary. But the best known composer to be associated with freemasonry was Mozart,[118] initiated in 1784 into Zur Wohltätigkeit.[119]

PRINCE ANTHONY ESTERHÁZY

The Esterházys' association with freemasonry began a half-century earlier in 1733:

> On Tuesday last Prince Anthony Esterházy, lately arrived here, and another German Nobleman, a relative to the Elector of Mentz,[120] were admitted Free and Accepted Masons at the French Lodge, held the first and third Tuesday of every Month, at the Duke of Lorraine's Head in Suffolk Street.[121]

---

[113] Franz Joseph Haydn (1732-1809).

[114] Paul Wranitzky (1756-1808).

[115] Ignace Joseph Pleyel (1757-1831), from 1772 Haydn's pupil at the Esterhazys' principal seat at Eisenstadt.

[116] 'True Harmony' lodge.

[117] 'Crowned Hope' lodge, also translated as 'Just and Perfect' lodge.

[118] Wolfgang Amadeus Mozart (1756-1791), court musician at Salzburg from 1773 until 1777, and a freelance musician and composer in Vienna from 1781.

[119] 'Beneficence' or 'Charitable' lodge.

[120] A mid-size ecclesiastical state and archbishopric on the Rhine.

[121] *Daily Advertiser*, 9 August 1733. The lodge had met formerly at Prince Eugene's Coffee House in St Albans Street.

Prince Anthony Esterházy was Prince Paul II Anton Esterházy de Galántha, a Hungarian nobleman.[122] Unlike most other Hungarian and Magyar aristocrats, the Esterházys had been loyal to the Habsburgs and when the Ottomans were pushed back at the Battle of Vienna, a decisive battle in the Austro-Ottoman war, the family was rewarded with land, sinecures and titles, with Leopold I in 1687 raising the Esterházys from counts to hereditary princes.[123]

The family's estates were enhanced through judicious marriages and by the eighteenth century the Esterházys were the largest landowners in Hungary with estates exceeding 1,850 square miles (*c*.4,800 square kilometres) and a fortune that rivalled that of the Habsburgs.[124] Within the remit of their lands, Esterházy authority was absolute and their tenants remained feudal serfs until the late nineteenth century.

The Esterházy estates were strewn with palaces including Schloss Esterházy at Eisenstadt, south of Vienna, occupied since 1622; Forchtenstein Castle to the south-west of Eisenstadt, the family treasury, acquired the same year; and Lackenbach Palace, from 1625 the seat of the Hungarian viceroy, a position held by a member of the family.[125] The Esterházys also owned Galanta in Slovakia, Pápa in Hungary and a hunting lodge, Süttör, at Fertöd, also in Hungary. The last was rebuilt in the eighteenth century as a 126-room Hungarian version of Versailles. The family's home in Vienna was a palace on Wallnerstrasse completed at the turn of the seventeenth century to maintain their status at the Habsburg court.

---

[122] Prince Paul II Anton Esterházy de Galántha (1711-1762).

[123] Also known as the Great Turkish War or the War of the Holy League (1683-1699), between a coalition headed by the Holy Roman Empire and the Ottoman Empire. The war concluded with the Treaty of Karlowitz in 1699 with some 60,000 square miles of territory ceded to the Habsburgs.

[124] Peter Wilson (ed.), *A Companion to Eighteenth-Century Europe* (Oxford: Blackwell, 2008), p. 94.

[125] The first to hold the position was Count Miklós Esterházy (1583-1645).

Paul Esterházy,[126] the first member of the family to be ennobled, was succeeded by his son, Michael,[127] and briefly by his brother, Joseph, who ruled for barely two months. Paul Anton inherited at the age of ten. His mother, Maria Octavia, and Count Georg Erdődy, an Imperial Privy Councillor, managed the family estates as co-regents until Paul Anton reached the age of maturity and took control in 1732. His visit to London occurred the following year.

The nobleman accompanying Esterházy to the Duke of Lorraine's Head - 'the relative of the Elector of Mentz' - was similarly significant. The Electorate of Maintz was the largest ecclesiastical province in Germany and the most prestigious of the princely states that made up the Holy Roman Empire. Its ruler, the Archbishop-Elector, was one of seven prince-electors and ranked second in political precedence to the Emperor. He was simultaneously Germany's primate, a key religious figure, and as arch chancellor headed the imperial chancellery. He was also head of the Electoral College, the body that chose the Emperor, and had responsibility for crowning him.[128]

The Electorate of Mainz had been close to the forefront of British foreign policy concerns since 1729 and the death of Lothar Franz von Schönborn.[129] His successor, Count Palatine Francis Louis of Neuburg, Prince-Bishop of Breslau,[130] was in office for only three years before his own death in 1732, and the succession and its ramifications led to diplomatic scheming across Europe.[131] Newcastle appears to have indicated that the government would support French proposals[132] and wrote accordingly to Schlienitz, Poyntz and

---

[126] Pál (Paul) Esterházy (1635-1713).

[127] Prince Mihály (Michael) (1671-1721).

[128] Cf., A. Hamilton, *The Town and Country Magazine* (London, 1769), volume 1, p. 433.

[129] Lothar Franz von Schönborn (1655-1729), Archbishop-Elector of Mainz from 1694 to 1729 and Bishop of Bamberg from 1693 to 1729.

[130] Franz Ludwig von Pfalz-Neuburg (1664-1732).

[131] NA SP 78/190/92, f. 273.

[132] NA SP 78/193/12, f. 45.

others;[133] but despite this a pro-Habsburg candidate, Philipp Karl von Eltz-Kempenich,[134] was elected in 1732. He supported Charles VI and fortified Mainz against the French in the War of the Polish Succession.

It is unlikely that Esterházy's visit to London with a relative of the Elector of Maintz was planned exclusively with the intention of their being made freemasons or for social purposes. They could have been initiated into freemasonry anywhere in Europe. But if one wished to communicate confidential information and to take part in sensitive discussions it were best carried out in person or through a trusted intermediary, preferably a relative. Given the political stature of the visitors and the context of the impending war in Europe, it is reasonable to assume that their objective was to seek tangible support for Austria against France, Spain and their allies. It is also likely that the visit would have been arranged through informal private channels since there are no relevant records in the State Papers, Domestic or Foreign.

There were reasons to be circumspect. The visit took place in the context of an impending continental war. French troops had been mobilised in the spring and early summer of 1733 and were being positioned along France's eastern and northern borders; and in August that year Russian forces entered Poland. Two months later France declared war on Austria and Saxony, and Spain joined with France to regain the territories it had ceded in Italy, both countries using the pretence of restoring Louis XV's father-in-law, Stanislaus Leszczyński,[135] to his throne in Poland. Notwithstanding

---

[133] NA SP 78/190/51, f. 145; SP 78/190/104, f. 299; SP 78/193/49, f. 161; SP 78/191/37, f. 99; SP 78/195/13 f. 28 et al. Also cf., for example NA SP 78/203/21, f. 35: Pelham to Delafaye, 3 May 1732.

[134] Philipp Karl von Eltz-Kempenich (1665-1743), Archbishop-Elector from 1732 to 1743.

[135] Marie Leszczyńska had married Louis XV in 1725.

Fleury's political preferences,[136] the anti-Habsburg faction in France was ascendant and combined with the French military who saw an opening to neutralise the risk of a Habsburg-aligned Duchy of Lorraine and remove it from Austria's sphere of influence.

The Habsburgs hoped that Britain and the Dutch Republic would support their cause but both were determined to remain neutral, at least nominally. Walpole's non-intervention was explained with the argument that the 1731 Treaty of Vienna, the Anglo-Austrian alliance, did not apply in these circumstances. But as Black notes, his unwillingness to support Austria was a function of the need to satisfy parliamentary concerns that Britain's national interests, and especially commerce and trade, would not be sacrificed on the altar of Hanoverian foreign policy. The Excise Bill crisis and the forthcoming elections also weighed on the Walpole administration and drove the expenditure of political capital away from Austria towards domestic issues.[137]

Notwithstanding Austria's entreaties, Walpole's position was that Britain would remain neutral. Despite a vocal minority in the Commons, a majority parliamentary vote in favour of intervention on Austria's behalf was unobtainable unless the Dutch ceased to be neutral, and perhaps not even then. Indeed, it was suspected that the United Provinces had negotiated their own arrangements with the French, an agreement to adopt neutrality in return for a guarantee that France would not attack the Austrian Netherlands.

The loss of trade and the prospect of higher taxes to fund war expenditure had less than limited support, and as Walpole expressed the position to Queen Caroline: 'Nothing could do the King so much disservice as engaging in war; first as the name of war was seldom acceptable in this country,

---

[136] Waldegrave wrote to Newcastle on 12 April 1733 that he believed Fleury would not engage in war 'even at the risk of being suspected of cowardice'. BL Add. MSS 32,871, f. 79.

[137] Jeremy Black, *The Collapse of the Anglo-French Alliance, 1727-1731* (Gloucester: Alan Sutton, 1987).

but that a war on account of a King of Poland was certainly what the nation could never be brought to think necessary or expedient; and as the elections were now coming on, the ferment in the country so great, and every circumstance that could blacken the Government so industriously improved, it is absolutely necessary for us to keep out of the squabble, and that the only part for us to take was to remain in an absolute state of inaction'.[138]

The relative anonymity of a London lodge offered a sphere in which to open discussions; and should they fail, the diplomatic fallout would be limited. Matters would be and were kept confidential, after all, Esterházy's name appears in only in a single uncensored press report.[139] Moreover, for Delafaye and Newcastle, the Duke of Suffolk's Head held other advantages: it was a staunchly Huguenot lodge with several government insiders among its members.

If it had been designed to garner overt support, Esterházy's mission was a failure. Triggered by the death of Augustus II, the Polish king, the War of the Polish Succession engulfed Europe. France and Spain supported the claims of Louis XV's father-in-law, Stanisław Leszczyński, as did much of the Polish aristocracy and Prussia. Austria and Russia favoured the Prince Elector of Saxony, Augustus III, the only legitimate son of Augustus II.[140]

With continental Europe in chaos and tens of thousands of troops engaged in Poland, the Rhineland and Italy, the British and Dutch attempted to intermediate to secure peace. A preliminary settlement was agreed in 1735. War eventually ceased and the settlement was ratified with the Treaty of Vienna in 1738.[141] Cessation of hostilities came at a high cost to

---

[138] Hervey, *Memoirs*, volume I, p. 258. Britain did however station a fleet in the Baltic.

[139] Esterházy returned to Austria to take up a formal position at the Habsburg court. He was subsequently ambassador to Naples (1750-52), and later achieved the rank of Field Marshal.

[140] He also held the titles of Grand Duke of Lithuania and Elector of Saxony.

[141] The Treaty was implemented after the death of the Duke of Tuscany, Gian Gastone de Medici (1671-1737).

the Habsburgs. Spain recovered its former possessions, Naples and Sicily, and France's price for accepting Augustus III as uncontested king of Poland was effective control of the Duchy of Lorraine. The territory was ceded to Stanislaw Leszczyński on the basis that following his death it would revert to France, assuaging French concerns that Lorraine would become part of the Habsburg Empire.[142]

Francis Stephen was compensated with the Duchy of Tuscany. His marriage to Maria Theresa took place in February 1736 but France and Spain's acceptance of the 1735 peace accord did not translate into supporting his election as Holy Roman Emperor on Charles VI's death. The crown went instead to Charles Albert, Prince-Elector of Bavaria,[143] the husband of Maria Amalia, Joseph I's younger daughter. Charles Albert was crowned Holy Roman Emperor and king of Bohemia, and with French and Spanish backing reigned as Charles VII until his death in 1745. Only after the Treaty of Füssen in April 1745, was it agreed that Francis Stephen would succeed. As crowned head of the House of Habsburg he co-reigned as Francis I, Holy Roman Emperor, alongside Maria Theresa.

Freemasonry's potency as a political tool appears to have declined in the late 1730s and 1740s. Horace Mann[144] wrote in 1739 that freemasonry had become so irrelevant that it 'was not even deemed a fault by the court of Rome'.[145] And Horace Walpole a few years later commented that 'the

---

[142] From France's standpoint, the 1731 Treaty of Vienna had undermined the Anglo-French accord. The threat posed by the Habsburg territorial expansion into Lorraine was existential and forced a response. It led to the 'Pacte de Famille', the Treaty of the Escorial and the War of the Polish Succession, pushing Austrian influence back from the French border.

[143] Charles VII (1697-1745), the son-in-law of Joseph I (Holy Roman Emperor from 1705-1711), was Holy Roman Emperor from 1742 until his death.

[144] Horace Mann (1706-1786), created 1st baronet in 1755, a career diplomat and long-standing British resident in Florence and envoy to the court of Tuscany.

[145] NA SP 98/42, 25 May 1739.

Freemasons are in so low repute now in England that one has scarce heard the proceedings at Vienna against them mentioned'.[146]

There were of course other views. When Lorraine was exchanged for Tuscany in 1738 Richmond wrote of his fear that 'the Pope won't approve of a Free Mason so near the Holy See'; and Newcastle, writing to Richmond and referring to Charles Fane, MP for Tavistock and Minister Plenipotentiary in Florence, 'Our Great Friend & Brother Mason', hoped that he 'will have little or no Difficulty in Tuscany'.[147]

The London press recorded the congratulations of the Grand Lodge of England to the duke on his wedding to Maria Theresa, noting that 'the Duke of Lorraine, having been made a Free-mason when in England, the Society has been pleas'd to send him their Compliments upon his Marriage with the Archduchess'. More to the point, the duke responded to Grand Lodge via his masonic mentor, Desaguliers, and 'on Thursday last, the Rev Dr Desaguliers deliver'd to the Society a very obliging Answer, on behalf of his Royal Highness'.[148]

[146] Horace Walpole to Sir Horace Mann, 4 May 1743 in *The Letters of Horace Walpole* (London: Richard Bentley, 1840), vol. 1, pp. 276-8.

[147] Timothy J. McCann (ed), *The Correspondence of the Dukes of Richmond & Newcastle 1724-1750* (Sussex Record Society, 1984), p. 18.

[148] *The Old Whig or the Consistent Protestant*, 15 April 1736.

Afterword

It is only prudent never to place complete confidence in
that by which we have even once been deceived.[1]

Espionage, Diplomacy & the Lodge examines a few of the many ripples that flowed from the decision to reconfigure English freemasonry and establish a grand lodge of English freemasons in London. Although described as the product of four founding lodges that came together in 1717 to create a structure for their mutual governance, the concept of a grand lodge was driven by a relatively small core of members of the Horn Tavern lodge, a group led by Desaguliers, Payne, Richmond and Delafaye.

Although the new grand lodge at first exercised influence over lodges established within the cities of London and Westminster, the self-determined expansion in its remit is evident from the near-immediate change of name to the 'Grand Lodge of England'. Within less than a decade Grand Lodge had positioned itself and was accepted as the legitimate governing authority for freemasonry and the principal force behind the movement's development elsewhere.

Freemasonry stood apart from the multitude of other clubs, associations and societies in eighteenth-century Britain, and was more than the product of the country's growing associational culture. Its inner circles included aristocrats and MPs, army officers, and well-known figures from the learned and professional societies; there were also strong links to the court.

But freemasonry's leaders not only endowed the organisation with social credibility; they also gave it a political purpose, a cause pushed forward and cemented by the publication of the 1723 *Constitutions*. A faux traditional history lauded the ancient antecedents of freemasonry, tracing its origins to Adam, 'our first parent', but more importantly the *Constitutions* rewrote the mediaeval *Old Charges* to incorporate latitudinarianism, religious tolerance,

---

[1] René Descartes (1596-1650), *Meditations on First Philosophy.*

which became an over-arching component of freemasonry. At the same time, freemasonry's mediaeval oaths were revised and updated to ensure that its members would swear to uphold the rule of civil law as enforced by the magistracy and judiciary, and abide by and respect parliamentary government and a constitutional, Hanoverian monarchy.

Freemasonry itself would become sacrosanct, with members agreeing to venerate the rulers and patrons of freemasonry; pay homage to the grand master and to his officers when duly installed; and confirm that it is not in the power of any man or body of men to make innovations in the body of freemasonry without the consent of grand lodge. The last restriction was introduced in the wake of the Duke of Wharton's attempt to hijack the organisation and turn it towards Jacobitism.

By the late 1720s, English freemasonry had become one of the most attractive clubs for the aspirational middling and gentry. Its more eminent lodges were headed by a litany of aristocrats from John, Duke of Montagu, one of the wealthiest men in England, to Thomas, Duke of Norfolk, Grand Marshall of England, and Lord Lovell, Sir Robert Walpole's wealthy political confederate. Its political, financial and social connections were an advertisement that presaged opportunities for influence and patronage, and in conjunction with a two-decades long press campaign the organisation was propelled to a position of pre-eminence in Hanoverian society, and across Europe and into the Americas.

But for its early rulers this was also a means to an end. In the two decades that followed the establishment of the new Grand Lodge, freemasonry's leaders were driven by a desire to protect and defend the political *status quo*. The constitutional crisis that accompanied and followed the Glorious Revolution may have led George I to succeed Queen Anne, but Hanover's grasp on the English, Scottish and Irish thrones was insecure and the threat posed by the exiled Pretender, father then son, and their allies in Europe, raised existential concerns that were at the forefront of eighteenth-century British politics up to and beyond the defeat of the '45 Jacobite Rising.

The same insecurities played on the tens of thousands of French Protestant refugees who had sought and found sanctuary in England. For the Huguenots, England remained a bulwark against the absolutism of France and Spain, and under the influence of men such as Delafaye and Desaguliers, English freemasonry would be positioned in the vanguard of its defence.

First Degree Tracing Board
Mid-Eighteenth Century

Appendix One

THE GRAND LODGE OF ENGLAND, SELECTED GRAND OFFICERS, 1717-1756

Year	Grand Master	Deputy Grand Master	Grand Wardens	Grand Secretary	Grand Treasurer
1717	Anthony Sayer	NA	John Elliot Jacob Lambell	NA	NA
1718	George Payne	NA	John Cordwell Thomas Morris	NA	
1719	J.T. Desaguliers	NA	Anthony Sayer Thomas Morris	NA	NA
1720	George Payne	NA	Thomas Hobby Richard Ware	NA	NA
1721	John Montagu, 2nd duke of Montagu	John Beale	Josias Villeneau Thomas Morris	NA	
1722	Philip Wharton, 1st duke of Wharton	J.T. Desaguliers	Joshua Timpson William Hawkins/James Anderson	William Cowper	NA
1723	Francis Scott, 5th earl of Dalkeith	J.T. Desaguliers	Francis Sorrel John Senex	William Cowper	NA
1724	Charles Lennox, 2nd duke of Richmond	Martin Folkes	Francis Sorrel George Payne	William Cowper	NA
1725	James Hamilton, Lord Paisley	J.T. Desaguliers	Col. Daniel Houghton Sir Thomas Prendergast	William Cowper	NA
1726	William O'Brien, 4th earl of Inchiquin	William Cowper	Alexander Choke William Burdon	Edward Wilson	NA

1727	Henry Hare, 3rd baron Coleraine	Alexander Choke	Nathaniel Blackerby / Joseph Highmore	William Reid	NA
1728	James King, 4th baron Kingston	Nathaniel Blackerby	Sir Joseph Thornhill / Martin O'Connor	William Graeme	NA
1729	Thomas Howard, 8th duke of Norfolk	Nathaniel Blackerby	Col. Hon George Carpenter / Thomas Batson	John Revis	NA
1730	Thomas Howard, 8th duke of Norfolk	Nathaniel Blackerby	Col. Hon George Carpenter / Thomas Batson	John Revis	Nathaniel Blackerby
1731	Thomas Coke, Lord Lovell	Thomas Batson	Dr George Douglas / James Chambers	John Revis	Nathaniel Blackerby
1732	Anthony Browne, 7th viscount Montagu	Thomas Batson	George Rooke / James Smythe	John Revis	Nathaniel Blackerby
1733	James Strathmore, 7th earl of Strathmore	Thomas Batson	James Smythe / John Ward	John Revis	Nathaniel Blackerby
1734	John Lindsay, 20th earl of Crawford	Sir Cecil Wray	John Ward / Sir Edward Mansel	John Revis	Nathaniel Blackerby
1735	Thomas, 2nd viscount Weymouth	John Ward	Sir Edward Mansel / Martin Clare	John Revis	Nathaniel Blackerby
1736	John Campbell, 4th earl of Loudoun	John Ward	Sir Robert Lawley / William Graeme	John Revis	Nathaniel Blackerby
1737	Edward Bligh, 2nd earl of Darnley	John Ward / William Graeme	Sir Robert Lawley	John Revis	Nathaniel Blackerby

Year					
1738	Henry Brydges, Marquis of Carnarvon	William Graeme	Lord George Graham / Capt. Andrew Robinson	John Revis	John Jesse
1739	Robert Raymond, 2nd lord Raymond	William Graeme	J. Harvey Thursby / Robert Foy	John Revis	John Jesse
1740	John Keith, 3rd earl of Kintore	William Graeme	James Ruck / William Vaughan	John Revis	John Jesse
1741	James Douglas, 14th earl of Morton	Martin Clare	William Vaughan / Benjamin Gascoyne	John Revis	John Jesse
1742	John Ward, Viscount Dudley & Ward	Sir Robert Lawley	Edward Hody / Samuel Berrington	John Revis	John Jesse
1743	John Ward, Viscount Dudley & Ward	Sir Robert Lawley	Edward Hody / Samuel Berrington	John Revis	John Jesse
1744	Thomas Lyon, earl of Strathmore	William Vaughan	William Graeme / Fotherley Baker	John Revis	John Jesse
1745	James Cranstoun, 6th lord Cranstoun	Edward Hody	Fotherley Baker / Thomas Smith	John Revis	John Jesse
1746	James Cranstoun, 6th lord Cranstoun	Edward Hody	Fotherley Baker / Thomas Smith	John Revis	John Jesse
1747	William Byron, 5th lord Byron	Fotherley Baker	Hon Robert Shirley / Thomas Jeffries	John Revis	John Jesse

Year					
1748	William Byron, 5th lord Byron	Fotherley Baker	Hon Robert Shirley Thomas Jeffries	John Revis	John Jesse
1749	William Byron, 5th lord Byron	Fotherley Baker	Hon Robert Shirley Thomas Jeffries	John Revis	John Jesse
1750	William Byron, 5th lord Byron	Fotherley Baker	Hon Robert Shirley Thomas Jeffries	John Revis	John Jesse
1751	William Byron, 5th lord Byron	Fotherley Baker	Hon Robert Shirley Capt. Thomas Jeffreys	John Revis	John Jesse
1752	John Proby, Lord Carysfort	Thomas Manningham	Hon James Carmichael Sir Richard Wrottesley	John Revis	John Jesse
1753	John Proby, Lord Carysfort	Thomas Manningham	Sir Richard Wrottesley Francis Blake Delaval	John Revis	George Clarke
1754	James Brydges, Marques of Carnarvon	Thomas Manningham	Fleming Pinckstan Arthur Beardmore	John Revis	George Clarke
1755	James Brydges, Marques of Carnarvon	Thomas Manningham	Hon Horatio Townshend James Dickson	John Revis	George Clarke
1756	James Brydges, Marques of Carnarvon	Thomas Manningham	James Nash Edward Joachim Boetefeur	John Revis	George Clarke

Appendix Two

The Members of London's Principal Huguenot Lodges

Solomon's Temple
1725 Membership Returns

Jean Theophilus Desaguliers	Master
Jaques Latouch[1]	Surveillant[2]
Jean Milxan[3]	Surveillant
Le bien Hon. Seigneur Carmichaell[4]	Dan. Grignion[5]
Pierre Bouchett[6]	Francois Guyot[7]
Elie Besthelott	Louis Buck[8]
Jaques Anderson MA[9]	David Lajonquiére[10]

---

[1] Also a member of the Red Lion lodge in Tottenham Court Road.

[2] Warden

[3] John Milxan (*d*.1756), a wine merchant trading with continental Europe. He lived in the Haymarket, west of Hemming's Row. His affluence and multiple business and social connections are underlined by his membership of at least two other French lodges: the King's Head in Pall Mall and the Swan Tavern in Long Acre.

[4] James Carmichael, 2nd Earl of Hyndford (*c*.1671-1737), a Scottish peer and member of the Horn Tavern lodge.

[5] Daniel Grignion (1684-1763), a fashionable clock and watch maker with premises at the King's Arms and Dial in Covent Garden, a short walk from Hemming's Row.

[6] Probably Pierre Bouchett, an auctioneer with premises at 5 Craven Buildings, close to Drury Lane.

[7] Francois Guyot [Guiot], a master glover of Grafton Street and a congregant at the Tabernacle, Leicester Fields.

[8] Also a member of the Red Lion lodge in Tottenham Court Road.

[9] James Anderson, *inter alia* author of the 1723 and 1738 *Constitutions*.

[10] La Jonquiére's name appears in the registers of the Savoy Church and Tabernacle, Leicester Fields.

Jaques Parmentier[11]
Laurenc des Grafiéres
Charles de L'Abelye

Federic Henoit Vertel Ec[r].[12]
Isac Thuret[13]
Israel Segalas[14]

It would be wrong to leave Solomon's Temple without commenting, perhaps speculating would be the more appropriate word, on the rationale for the presence of the only two non-Huguenot members of the lodge: James Anderson and the Hon. Seigneur Carmichaell, that is, James Carmichael, 2nd Earl of Hyndford.

Although both were members of the Horn Tavern, as was Desaguliers, this does not provide a convincing explanation of their presence at what was an otherwise French Huguenot lodge. It is however reasonable to believe that the lodge would have been intensely anti-Jacobite and it is this that may provide a superior explanation. James Anderson is known best as the author, or more properly the compiler, of the 1723 *Constitutions*. But what may be more important is his political leanings. There is evidence that he was avidly pro-Hanoverian and that he spied, informally or otherwise, for loyalist interests. His and his family's empathy towards the Hanoverians is outlined in a paper, 'New Light on the Life of James Anderson', by Sommers

---

[11] Jacques (or James) Parmentier (1658-1730), a well-known interior designer and decorator.

[12] Ec[r]. = Ecuyer = Esq.

[13] Isaac Thuret (or Thurett), was possibly a descendant, perhaps the grandson, of the French horologist Isaac Thuret (1630-1706). His son, Jacques (1669-1738), was appointed royal clockmaker to Louis XIV in 1694. Isaac Thuret is recorded in the *Register of Duties Paid for Apprentices' Indentures* on 1 February 1726 with an address nearby in St James's; he later moved to St George's Row in Knightsbridge.

[14] Israel Segalas (*d*.1735), one of London's better known gunsmiths; Solomon's Temple lodge met at his workshop on the corner of Hemming's Row.

and Prescott.[15] In particular, they point to the family's favourable treatment following the 1715 Jacobite Rising:

> During the '15, Aberdeen was a center of Jacobite agitation… With the failure of the rising there was a thorough-going purge of Jacobites and sympathizers. The effect on the fortunes of the Andersons was striking. When commissioners arrived in the city in 1716 for the visitation of schools and colleges, they 'did everything by information of the Presbyterian clergy and magistrates', because Episcopalians were plausibly suspected of being Jacobites. By the time they completed their inquiry, David Anderson [James Anderson's father] was one of the few academics neither censured or dismissed. Rather, that same year he was awarded an allowance by the synod of Aberdeen to repair and extend his house at the university.

Sommers and Prescott also note that David Anderson was later made a chaplain to George II with an annual stipend of £50, while James Anderson was selected to present the address from the Presbytery to the king and 'had the Honour to kiss his Majesty's Hand'.[16]

Anderson's possible spying on behalf of loyalist interests is suggested in the pamphlet *No King Sellers*, a response to *No King Killers*, a sermon written and published by Anderson in 1715.[17] The author accuses Anderson of informing on opposition interests: 'pick[ing] up Lies, which he may transmit to Aberdeen, there to expose such, as oppose his grim graceless Idol of Persecuting Presbytery'. To a certain extent everyone in upper and upper middling society in the early eighteenth century could be regarded as a spy. Whether one was an aristocrat or a clergyman, there was an expectation that matters of interest would be disclosed to an appropriate contact within

---

[15] Susan Mitchell Sommers & Andrew Prescott, 'New Light on the Life of James Anderson' (2016).

[16] NA SP 35/6 f. 57.

[17] Anon., *No King-Sellers*, (London: J. Roberts, 1715).

the administration, whether this was dinner party gossip or something more serious. Nonetheless, *Anti-Priapeiai ...or The Presbyterian Peezle*, another pamphlet, suggests that Anderson may have more been a more serious threat and confirms that opposition Tory and Jacobite interests in London were opposed to him.[18] The pamphlet satirised the Presbyterians and Anderson, then minister of the Presbyterian Church in Swallow Street near Piccadilly, who was believed to have caught 'the pox', any of several possible venereal diseases.

Like Anderson, Carmichael also came from a family of Scottish loyalists. His father, John, 1st Earl of Hyndford,[19] was sworn to the Privy Council in Scotland and in 1690 made a commissioner for the office of Lord Privy Seal. He was strongly supportive of the court interest in the Scottish Parliament and a regular attendee. His political standing is indicated by his appointment in 1690 as commissioner to the general assembly of the Church of Scotland where he represented the king, and his service on several important parliamentary committees included those covering church governance, trade and defence.

John Carmichael was created Earl of Hyndford, Viscount of Inglisberry and Nemphlar, and Lord Carmichael of Carmichael, in 1702, and was granted an additional pension of £400 as a reward for his loyalty. On Queen Anne's accession he was sworn a privy councillor and continued in office as secretary of state for Scotland, to which position he had been appointed in 1699. He was unsurprisingly in favour of the political coming together of England and Scotland, and was appointed to the commission that oversaw the Union. There is a possible connection between him and David Anderson, James Anderson's father. As chancellor of the University of Glasgow – he was appointed in 1692, Carmichael provided patronage to a number of

---

[18] Anonymous, *Anti-Priapeia: or, an answer to Priapeia Presbyteriana, or the Presbyterian peezle [sic]. In a letter from the General Assembly of Scotland, to their missionary at London, intercepted and paraphrased by Ille ego qui quondam* (London & Edinburgh, c.1720).

[19] Cf., Derek John Patrick, 'Carmichael, John, first earl of Hyndford (1638-1710)', *ODNB*.

Scottish academics at other Scottish universities, including Edinburgh and Aberdeen.[20]

James Carmichael succeeded to his father's titles in 1710. Albeit that his public life was in his father's shadow, Carmichael had nonetheless been sworn a Privy Counsellor for Scotland in 1704. He was a serving officer in the army and had acquired the rank of colonel of dragoons in 1706 and was promoted brigadier-general in 1710. His regiment, the Earl of Hyndford's Regiment of Dragoons, had been raised in 1702 to replace the Scots Greys who had left for Flanders. Its first colonel was his father, who passed it to his son in 1706.[21] The regiment was placed on the Irish establishment and was disbanded in December 1713 following the signing of the Treaty of Utrecht.[22]

Hyndford's zealous anti-Jacobite approach was obvious both before and in the wake of the failed 1715 Jacobite Rising, when he was one of the several Scottish Whig grandees who opposed what they perceived as the leniency shown to Jacobite sympathisers in Scotland, including members of

---

[20] Roger L. Emerson, *Academic Patronage in the Scottish Enlightenment: Glasgow, Edinburgh and St Andrews Universities* (Edinburgh: Edinburgh University Press, 2008), esp. p. 382.

[21] S.H.F. Johnston, 'The Scots Army in the Reign of Anne', *Transactions of the Royal Historical Society*, 3 (1953), 1-21.

[22] William A. Shaw and F.H. Slingsby (eds), *Calendar of Treasury Books, volume 27, 1713* (London: HMSO, 1955), pp. 476, 482. Daniel Defoe, one of Delafaye's many intelligence sources, knew the earl well having been employed on commission to purchase horses. He recommended Hyndford to Lord Harley as a potential commissioner to the general assembly of the Church of Scotland. Cf., Maximillian E. Novak, *Daniel Defoe: Master of Fictions. His Life and Ideas* (Oxford: OUP, 2003), pp. 381-2.

their own family.[23] He also corresponded directly with London warning of the 'thousand stories of the Pretender landing'.[24] But perhaps the most pertinent evidence for Hyndford's staunch Whig politics was that he was made a commissioner of police in Scotland, a position where loyalty was paramount and an association with Delafaye a virtual *sine qua non*. His was appointed in or before 1715, and remained in post until at least 1734.[25]

---

[23] Margaret Sankey and Daniel Szechi, 'Elite Culture and the Decline of Scottish Jacobitism 1716-1745', *Past & Present*, 173 (2001), 90-128, esp. 121-2. Also, GD220/5, National Records of Scotland, Hyndford's letters to Duke of Montrose 1714-16; and SP 54/11/44.

[24] NA SP 54/10/161 29 December 1715.

[25] NA SP 54/7/84, Earl of Hyndford, concerning commissions of police and petitioning for the payment of arrears due to him, 27 August 1715. Also 'Warrants for the Payment of Money', in William A. Shaw (ed), *Calendar of Treasury Books and Papers, Volumes 1 & 2, 1729-1734* (London: HMSO, 1897 & 1898).

The King's Head, Pall Mall
1725 Membership Returns

Mr Milxan	Master
Mr Sandys[26]	Warden
Mr Rading	Warden
Mr Lambert[27]	Mr Nicholls[28]
Mr Renier	Mr Richar
Mr Goodwin[29]	Mr Clark

---

[26] Possibly Richard Sandys (*d.*1732), a trader at the Blue Ball in Jermyn Street, a hundred yards to the north of Pall Mall, or his brother, Henry (*d.*1740 or 1743), an architect and decorator who lived nearby.

[27] Edward Lambert was one of London's leading confectioners at a time when the role of confectioner was held in high regard and commanded an elevated social status. He lived and worked almost next door to the King's Head, his premises being 'over against St Albans Street in Pall Mall'.

[28] Among the many men in London named 'Francis Nichols', the best know was the anatomist and physicist Francis Nicholls (1699-1778). Although in continental Europe for much of the early 1720s and living in London permanently only from around 1725, Nicholls was a frequent visitor from 1719. A possible masonic connection is that his sponsors at the Royal Society (FRS 1728) included William Rutty (1687-1730), a member of the lodge at the Bedford Head. Another Francis Nichols was the author and compiler of *The British Compendium*, a book detailing the titles, descent, marriages and issue of the nobility of England, Scotland and Ireland. It was published in three volumes in 1723. Nichols also wrote *Of the several degrees of gentry, and their precedency*, a work later incorporated into *The British Compendium*.

[29] Possibly Richard Goodwin, a haberdasher.

Mr Creek	Mr Flower[30]
Mr Favre[31]	Mr Guidon[32]

---

[30] Possibly Robert Flower (*d*.1735), a haberdasher.

[31] John Le Fevre [Lefebure], Foreign Secretary of the Post Office.

[32] Possibly Lewis Guidon (*d*.1742), a gentleman of St Anne's parish, Soho, or John Guion (*d*.1736), a master silk weaver, or Francois Guiott, a witness at the wedding that brought together the Richard and La Touche families. If the last, he was also a member of the Freemasons' Coffee House in New Belton Street.

The French Lodge at the Swan Tavern, Long Acre, Covent Garden
1730 Membership Returns

Mr John Oliver

Mr John Milxan	Mr Ezech. Varrene[33]
Mr Charles Raboteau[34]	Mr Elias Regnand [Regnaud][35]
Mr James Bernardeau[36]	Mr James Bousseau
Mr Daniel Simons	Mr Anthony Meymac
Mr Francis Mailliet[37]	The Rev. J.D. Agneaux[38]
The Rev. G. Cantier	The Rev. J.P. Stichelin[39]
The Rev. Daniel de Beaufort[40]	T.P. Duvall
Pierre Macculloch	Mr John Combecrose[41]
Mr James Demars[42]	Mr William Read

---

[33] Ezekiel Varenne (*d*.1740), a prominent apothecary who lived and worked in St James's.

[34] Charles Raboteau, a merchant and member of the French Church at West Street. He was later a governor of the Middlesex Hospital. Among his fellow governors was Elias Regnaud (see below), also his brother-in-law.

[35] Elias Regnaud (*d*.1760), a successful and well-known merchant.

[36] James Bernardeau (*d*.1753), a highly fashionable 'razor maker at the Pistol & L. in Russell Court, Drury Lane'.

[37] Francis Mailliet (*d*.1756), a master tailor, of Greek Street, Soho.

[38] Rev. Jean Joseph d'Agneaux, minister of La Patente, Soho, from 1718 until at least 1733.

[39] Rev. John Peter Stehelin (*d*.1753), minister of the French church at Hammersmith. Elected FRS 1739.

[40] Rev. Daniel Cornelius de Beaufort (1700–1788), the seventh child of Count Francis de Beaufort, chancellor to the Prince of Lippe-Detmold.

[41] John [Jean] Combecrose (*d*.1774), an apothecary and from 1755-60 a director, governor and benefactor of l'École de Charité Française de Westminster, the charitable French Protestant school founded in 1747.

[42] James [Jacque] Demars [de Mare] (*d*.1748), a master carver and gilder.

Mr Gabriel Gernier[43]

Mr John Massia

Mr Isaac Blanchard[44]

Mr John Mercadie

Mr Stephen Demainbray[45]

Mr Isaac Micheaie

Mr Thomas Hall

---

[43] A probable relation of 'Mr Gernier of Pall Mall', a prominent apothecary.

[44] Isaac Blanchard, a master lace weaver and haberdasher.

[45] Stephen Demainbray (1710-1782), scientist and astronomer, he lodged with Desaguliers at nearby Channel Row when attending Westminster School.

Prince Eugene's Head Coffeehouse, St Albans Street, St James's
1732 Membership Returns

Mr Lewis Mercy[46]	Master
Mr Lanse[47]	Warden
Mr Protin[48]	Warden

Mr Friard[49]	Mr St Jean
Mr Helot[50]	Mr Vincent La Chappelle[51]
Mr Duboys	Mr Moquet
Mr Lundier	Mr Noiree
Mr Laroche[52]	Mr Dubuis
Mr Staiman	Mr Levat
Mr Figniere	Mr Delahaye[53]
Mr Dumoulin	Mr Donlowis
Mr Debat	Mr Demere

---

[46] Lewis Mercy (*c*.1695-*c*.1750), a virtuoso musician.

[47] Possibly the 'Frère de Lansa' who translated *The Entered Apprentice's Song* and *The Master's Song* into French for inclusion in Louis-François de La Tierce's *Histoire des Francs Maçons*. He also published a collection of Masonic songs in French.

[48] Noel Protin (*d*.1747), a peruke or wig maker.

[49] Charles Augustus Friard (*d*.1755), another wig maker, also of Hanover Square. Secretary of the lodge: 'Le Frère Friard, Sécrétaire'. He signed the 1733 approbation to La Tierce's French translation of Anderson 1723 Constitutions, published as *Histoiries Obligations et Statuts de la tres venerable confraternité des Francs-Macons* at Frankfurt-on-Main in 1742.

[50] John Helot, a master watchmaker; a member of the Horn Tavern and King's Arms lodges. Not the chemist John Helott (1685-1766). Although Helott was elected FRS in 1740, proposed by Richmond and seconded by Hans Sloane and Martin Folkes, he worked and was resident in Paris in the early 1730s.

[51] Vincent La Chapelle (*c*.1700-1745).

[52] John Laroche (*c*.1700-1752).

[53] Possibly Charles Delafaye.

Mr Webber

Mr Jo Duboys

Mr Savigney[54]

Mr Coustos[55]

Mr Barby[57]

Mr Ball

Mr Morin

Mr Vigne

Mr Therry[56]

[54] Probably John Fessier Savigney, a razor maker who lived and worked in St James's. Classified advertisements indicate that he had premises in Pall Mall and a second outlet on the corner of nearby Gerrard Street.

[55] John Coustos.

[56] Probably Laurence Thare of George Court, St James's, the proprietor of a sedan chair hire business.

[57] John David Barbutt, Secretary to the Post Office.

POSTCRIPT: LONDON'S OTHER HUGUENOT LODGES

The Lodge of St George de l'Observance, No. 148, was warranted in August 1736 and met at the Sun in Fish Street Hill. It moved to the Bell in Nicholas Lane in 1740 and to the Bell in Eastcheap in 1742. No membership returns were submitted to Grand Lodge. The lodge was erased on 28 April 1775 but restored a year later on 24 April 1776. It was erased again on 7 April 1784 but reinstated on 17 November the same year. It was erased for a third and final time in February 1794.[58]

The Old French Lodge, No. 190 in the 1740 list, now Lodge of Unity, No. 69, was constituted on 13 April 1742 at the Hoop and Grapes in Greek Street, Soho. It moved the following year to the nearby Hoop and Grapes in Coventry Street. There are no surviving membership records prior to 1780, at which point the members were predominantly English.[59]

A 'French lodge', No. 254, was constituted on 14 December 1754 at the Crown Tavern, Great St Andrew's Street in Seven Dials, Covent Garden. The lodge was erased in 1830. According to Lane's *Masonic Records*, the lodge was originally named 'The French Lodge', then the 'Ancient French Lodge' and finally 'Loge des Amis Reunis'. It merged with Loge l'Egalité, No. 380, in 1785 and adopted the name 'Loge de l'Esperance' in 1799. There are no extant membership records or minutes prior to 1781.[60]

Another 'French Lodge', No. 331, was constituted on 29 January 1765 at the Old Bell Savage in Ludgate Hill. The lodge relocated to The Fountain at Ludgate Hill in 1766, and to the Horn Tavern, Doctor's Commons, in 1769. It was erased in 1775.

Knowledge of London's four other eighteenth-century French lodges is equally sparse. L'Immortalité de l'Ordre was constituted on 16 June 1766

---

[58]   Cf., Lane's *Masonic Records*.

[59]   Ibid.

[60]   Ibid.

and met at the Crown and Anchor Tavern on the Strand; it appears as No. 376 in the 1755 list. Lodge L'Esperance was warranted in 1768 as No. 434 and met at the Turk's Head in Gerrard Street, Soho. It merged with Loge des Amis Reunis in 1799. Loge Parfaite Egalité Lyonesse, No. 464, located at the Three Old Tongues in Pearl Street, Spitalfields, was warranted in 1774 and erased in 1780. Loge de l'Egalité, No. 469, was warranted in 1785. In 1787 it moved from the Coach and Horses in Frith Street, Soho, to the King's Head in nearby Gerrard Street; it moved again three years later to the King's Head in Grafton Street before merging with the 'Ancient French Lodge'.

Appendix Three

THE VILLEROY-COUSTOS LODGE, PARIS

The Members of the Lodge, 1736-7[1]

d' Aunillon (Abbé)

Bataillon

de Bauclas

Baur, J.C.

Beccaria, Janee Francoe

de Bertouch, R.

Boisseau

Bontems

de Bousch (Baron)

Bruguier, Pierre

Bulow, V.

Cave, H.M.

Coustos, Jean

de Czapski, (Comte)

Danicus, Enricus

Demeure, Philibert

de Dever, D.

Driver

Dudzeele, D.

Du Mont (Le Chevalier)

Dune de Sardegne

Farsetti, Philippe

---

[1]   Taken from *Lodge Minutes and Signature Book*, Bibliotheque Nationale, Paris, Joly de Fleury collection, 184, ff. 132-46. The members are listed alphabetically. Cf., *AQC*, 92 (1979), pp. 116-8.

de Feuillas

da Fletto, Giusepino

Fremant, J.P.

de Gatterburg [poss. Katerbourg], (Comte)

Géraudly, Claude

de Görtz, (Baron)

Gosselin, Jean Philippe

Gray, Laurent

de Gualtieri

Guignon

Hanker, Henry

de Hastrel, (Le Chevalier)

Jeliote

Klein, Jean Herman [poss. Hörman]

Krafft, Johann Daniel

de Lagerie

Le Breton, Thomas Pierre

Le Tourneur

de Liebentantz, M.G.

Lubormirski, J., (Prince)

Maille, Guillaurne

Manne, Carlino

de Meiners

Mellavitz

Michault

Naudot, Jaque Christophe

Naudot (le fils)

Paris de Meyzieu

Pasquier de la Haye

Pescheur

de Plessen

Quineau, Edward

Rey

Ricaud

De Royaucourt

de Scheffer, (Baron)

Sguiano

de Swirby, (Comte)

Tamm, Gaspard

Villemain

de Villeroy, (Duc)

Weiss von Fürstenfeld, Joseph Theodore

de Wendhausen, (Baron)

de Wendhausen, (Baron, le cadet)[2]

de Wind

The spectrum of nationalities includes some twenty-eight Frenchmen; seven Swedes; thirteen Austrians or Germans; six who were or may have been English (Messrs Cave, Coustos, Driver, Gray, Quineau and Scriver); and two from the United Provinces. Other nationalities, including Italian, are also represented.

The lodge minutes dating from 18 December 1736 to 17 July 1737 were seized in a police raid and are now held in the French National Library. Coustos was master until 17 February 1737 when the Duc de Villeroy was installed, and lodge meetings were held at the Ville de Tonnerre, Rue des Boucheries, St Germain, every second Tuesday. The lodge met on some twenty-two occasions and apart from the first two meetings the minutes were signed by all those present.

The lodge worked in French and contained numerous influential figures. Baron de Görtz, for example, was the eldest son of Charles II's chief minister, one of the chief architects of Sweden's repeated attempts

---

2   The baron's younger brother.

to overthrow the Hanoverians in Britain and Ireland and install James Stuart. The German-born Johan Christoph Baur, a Lutheran, provided banking and intelligence services to Louis XV; he later became deputy grand master of France.[3] Count Czapski, a Polish aristocrat, was cousin to Marie Leszczynska (1703-1768), who was married to Louis XV. Prince Stanislaw Lubomirski (1704-1793), a hereditary Prince of the Holy Roman Empire and another Polish nobleman, was Grand Marshal at the court of Augustus III. Count Carl Fredrik Scheffer (1715-86), a Swedish diplomat and politician, was subsequently grand master of Sweden (1753-74).[4]

The presence of Niels Krabbe DeWind, Denmark's ambassador to Paris, and Carl Adolph von Plessen, a colleague at the Danish Embassy in Paris, is of particular significance. Louis XV was seeking to pry Denmark away from its alliance with Britain and establish a pan-European anti-Hanoverian alliance involving Sweden, Denmark, Prussia, Spain and France.

Among others listed, Philippe Farsetti was a diplomat at the Venetian Embassy in Paris; Claude Jaquier de Géraudly attended the French court as the royal physician and dentist; Jean-Daniell Krafft, a leather merchant originally from Hamburg, founded what is thought to be the or one of the first lodges in Germany in 1737 and in 1743 became grand treasurer of the Provincial Grand Lodge of Lower Saxony; and Thomas Le Breton, a banker and goldsmith, was at this time also master of the lodge *Au Louis Argent* in Paris, a lodge constituted under an English warrant, No. 90, in 1732.[5]

Lastly, the lodge included a number of musicians: Jacques-Christophe Naudot (c.1690-1762), a flautist and composer; Jean-Pierre Guignon

---

[3] Schuchard, *Emanuel Swedenborg*, pp. 205 & 340.

[4] Scheffer was subsequently installed as a Knight of the Royal Order of the Seraphim and a Commander of the Order of the Polar Star, Swedish chivalric orders created by Frederick I.

[5] Lane's *Masonic Records*.

(1702-74), a leading violinist and composer; and Pierre Jelyiotte (1713-97), a fêted tenor. Their presence validates the affluence of lodge members; musicians and actors tended to join lodges either at the behest of their patrons for whom they would play in lodge, or in search of patronage.

Appendix Four

THE MEMBERS OF THE FIRST GRAND CHARITY COMMITTEE

Member	Lodge	Rank
John, Duke of Montagu[1]	Horn	GM
Earl Dalkeith[2]	Rummer	GM
Lord Paisley[3]	Horn	GM
J.T. Desaguliers[4]	Horn	GM, DGM
William Cowper[5]	Horn	DGM, GSec
Sir Thomas Prendergast[6]	Horn	GW
Brook Taylor[7]	Bedford Head	WM
Col. Daniel Houghton[8]	Rummer	GW, WM
Major Alexander Harding[9]	Horn	WM
Thomas Edwards[10]	Horn / Crown	WM
Giles Taylor[11]	Bell	WM

[1] John Montagu, 2nd Duke of Montagu (1690-1749), GM 1721/2.

[2] Francis Scott, 5th Earl of Dalkeith (1695-1751), GM 1722/3.

[3] James Hamilton, Lord Paisley (1686-1744), GM 1725/6.

[4] J.T. Desaguliers (1683-1744), GM 1719, DGM 1722/4, 1725/6.

[5] William Cowper (16..-1740), DGM 1726/7, GSec 1723/6, JP.

[6] Sir Thomas Prendergast (bap.1702-1760), GW 1725/6.

[7] Also a member of the Court of Governors of Bridewell Royal Hospital.

[8] Col. Daniel Houghton, GW 1725/6, JP.

[9] Also written as 'Hardine'. JP. WM of the Horn while Richmond was GM.

[10] A barrister (either Lincoln's Inn or the Middle Temple).

[11] A barrister at the Inner Temple, JP, a governor of the Bridewell Royal Hospital.

| William Petty[12] | Swan | WM |
| William Richardson[13] | Dolphin/Bull's Head | WM |

---

[12] Possibly Sir William Petty, an ancestor of the 1st Marquess of Landsowne. Cf., Edward Walford, 'Berkeley Square and its neighbourhood', in *Old and New London: volume 4* (London: Cassell, Petter & Galpin, 1878), pp. 326-38.

[13] Probably William Richardson (1698–1775), curate of St Olave's Southwark (1723-6); a governor of the Bridewell Royal Hospital.

Selected Bibliography

SELECTED PRIMARY SOURCES

Bodleian Library, Oxford

    MSS Rawlinson

British Library, London

    The Burney Collection of Seventeenth & Eighteenth-Century Newspapers

    Add MSS 28893-900, Add MSS 35585-36139, Add MSS 23782-91, Add MSS 32686-33067 passim and Add MSS 37366-97 passim.

    SP Domestic

    SP Foreign

British Parliamentary Papers

    Board of Trade and Plantations, Journals

    Calendar of State Papers, Domestic

    Calendar of State Papers, Colonial Series, America and West Indies

    Calendar of Treasury Books and Papers

    History and Proceedings of the House of Commons

    House of Commons Parliamentary Papers

    House of Commons, Journals

    House of Lords, Journals

    Report from the Committee of Secrecy (1742)

    Report from the Secret Committee on the Post-Office (1844)

    Statutes of the Realm

    Report of the Committee of Privy Councillors appointed to inquire into the interception of communications (1957)

Cambridge University Library, Cambridge

    Cholmondeley (Houghton) Correspondence

Huguenot Society of London

    William & Susan Minet, *Livres des Conversiones et des Reconnoissances faites a L'Eglise Francoise de la Savoye, 1684-1702* (London, 1914).

- Register of the Church of Hungerford Market, later Castle Street, London (London, 1928).
- Registers of the Church of Le Carre and Berwick Street (London, 1921).
- Register of the Church of Rider Court, London, 1700-1738 (London, 1927).
- Register of the Church of St Martin Orgars with its History and that of Swallow Street, (London, 1935).
- Registers of the Churches of The Tabernacle Glasshouse Street and Leicester Fields, London 1688-1783 (London, 1926).
- Registres des Eglises de la Chapelle Royale de Saint James, 1700-1756, et de Swallow Street, 1690-1709 (London, 1924)
- Registres des Eglises de la Savoye de Spring Gardens et des Grecs 1684-1900 (London, 1922).
- Registres des Quatres Eglises du Petit Charenton de West Street de Pearl Street et de Crispin Street (London, 1929).

Susan Minet, Register of the Church of the Artillery, Spitalfields, 1691-1786 (London, 1948).

- Registers of the French Churches of La Patente de Soho, Wheeler Street, Swan Street & Hoxton, also The Repetoire General (London, 1956).

Institute of Historical Research Publications

Cecil Headlam, *Calendar of Sate Papers Colonial, America and West Indies*

K.H. Ledward, *Journals of the Board of Trade & Plantations*

Joseph Reddington, *Calendar of Treasury Papers*

William Shaw, *Calendar of Treasury Books*

William Shaw and F.H. Slingsby, *Calendar of Treasury Books*

Library & Museum of Freemasonry, London

The Minutes of the Grand Lodge of Freemasons of England, 1723-1739 and 1740-1758.

Masonic Constitutions, Minutes & Miscellaneous

James Anderson, *The Constitutions of the Freemasons* (London: John Senex & John Hooke, 1723).

- *The Ancient Constitutions of the Free and Accepted Masons.* Enlarged Second Edition. (London: B. Creake, 1731).
- *The new book of constitutions of the antient and honourable fraternity of free and accepted masons,* (London: Caesar Ward and Richard Chandler for Anderson, 1738).
- *The Constitutions of the Ancient and honourable fraternity of Free and Accepted Masons,* revised and enlarged by John Entick, (London: J. Scott, 1756).

Eugenius Philalethes (prob. Robert Samber), translated from the French of Harcouët de Longeville, *Long livers: a curious history of such persons of both sexes who have liv'd several ages, and grown young again* (London, 1722).

W.J. Songhurst, *The Minutes of the Grand Lodge of Freemasons of England 1723-1739*, *QCA* Masonic Reprints, volume X, (London: QC, 1913).

London Metropolitan Archives, London

Legal and Property Records

Middlesex Sessions' Papers - Justices' Working Documents

Old Bailey Court Cases

Quarter Sessions of the Peace for Middlesex and Westminster

Westminster Pollbooks

Westminster Ratebooks: Property Values of Westminster Electors

Westminster Sessions' Papers - Justices' Working Documents

National Archives

Wills Proved at the Prerogative Court of Canterbury

National Records of Scotland

Hamilton Papers

The Sackler Archives of The Royal Society

A True and Exact List. London, 1725.

The Historical Register. London, 1726.

The True State of England. London, 1734.

Francis Atterbury, *Letter to a Convocation Man* (1697).

- *English Advice to the Freeholders of England* (1715).
- *An argument to prove the affections of the people of England to be the best security of government* (1715).

Nathaniel Blackerby, *The Speech of Nathanial Blackerby* (London, 1738).

John Byrom, *The private journal and literary remains of John Byrom* (Manchester: Chetham Society, 1854-7).

Martin Clare, *Youth's introduction to trade and business* (London, 1720).

John Coustos, *The Sufferings of John Coustos ... in the Inquisition at Lisbon* (London: Coustos, 1746).

Daniel Defoe, *An Account of the Swedish and Jacobite plot* (London, 1717).

- *A Short View of the conduct of the King of Sweden* (London, 1717).

John, Lord Hervey, *Memoirs of the Reign of George II* (London: John Murray, 1848).

Tim Hitchcock and John Black (eds), *Chelsea Settlement and Bastardy Examinations, 1733-1766* (London: London Records Society, 1999).

J.F. Lampe & B. Cole, *British Melody or the Musical Magazine* (London: B. Cole, 1739).

Christopher Layer, *The Whole Proceeding upon the arraignment, trial, conviction and attainder of Christopher Layer* (London: Buckley, 1723).

John Macky, *A Journey through England* (London, 1714).

- *Memoirs of the secret services ... during the reigns of King William, Queen Anne, and King George I* (London: Spring Macky, 1733), 2nd edition.

John Mottley, *A survey of the cities of London and Westminster, borough of Southwark, and parts adjacent* (London: J. Read, 1733-35).

Wiliam Monk, *Lives of the Fellows of the Royal College of Physicians* (London: William Monk, 1861).

M.H. Port (ed), *The Commissions For Building Fifty New Churches the Minute Books, 1711-27, A Calendar* (London: London Record Society, 1986).

William Smith, *A Pocket Companion for Freemasons* (London, 1735).

John Strype, *A Survey of the Cities of London and Westminster* (London, 1720).

Philip, Duke of Wharton, *The Life and Writings of Philip, Duke of Wharton* (1732).

A list of the names of the members of the Amicable Contributor for insuring
houses against loss by fire, at Angel-Court on Snow-Hill, September 29,
1714 (Andover: Gale ECCO, 2010) (reprint).

SELECTED SECONDARY SOURCES

Institute of Historical Research Publications
   A History of the County of Middlesex
   Survey of London
   J.C. Sainty, *Office-Holders in Modern Britain*
Oxford Dictionary of National Biography
Proceedings of the Huguenot Society of London
Quatuor Coronati Lodge, No. 2076
   AQC, 1886-2016

SELECTED BOOKS

David C.A Agnew, *Protestant Exiles from France* (London: Reeves & Turner,
   1874).

James Anderson, *The Constitutions of the Freemasons* (London, 1723).

Toby Barnard, *A New Anatomy of Ireland: the Irish Protestants, 1649-1770* (New
   Haven, CN: YUP, 2004).

J.V. Bennett, *The Tory Crisis in Church and State 1688-1730: The Career of Francis
   Atterbury, Bishop of Rochester* (Oxford: OUP, 1975).

Jeremy Black, *The Collapse of the Anglo-French Alliance, 1727-1731* (Gloucester:
   Alan Sutton, 1987).

  • *The English Press in the Eighteenth Century* (London: Croom Helm, 1987).

  • *Culloden and the '45* (New York, NY: St Martin's Press, 1990).

  • *Parliament and Foreign Policy in the Eighteenth Century* (Cambridge:
    CUP, 2004).

  • *Parliament and Foreign Policy* Cambridge: CUP, 2004).

  • *Great Powers and the Quest for Hegemony* (London: Routledge, 2008).

- *Trade, Empire and British Foreign Policy, 1689-1815* (London: Routledge, 2007).

Abel Boyer (ed), *The Political State of Great Britain* (London: J. Baker, 1711-40).

Brendan Bradshaw & Peter Roberts (eds), *British Consciousness and Identity. The Making of Britain, 1533–1707* (Cambridge: CUP, 2003).

Charles Carlton, *This Seat of Mars: War and the British Isles, 1485-1746* (New Haven, CN: YUP, 2011).

John Childs, *The British Army of William III, 1689-1702* (Manchester: MUP, 1987).

Peter Clark, British Clubs and Societies 1580-1800: The Origins of an Associational World (Oxford: OUP, 2000).

William Coxe, *Memoirs of the Life and Administration of Sir Robert Walpole* (London: Cadell & Davies, 1798).

Eveline Cruickshanks, *Political Untouchables: The Tories and the '45* (New York, NY: Holmes and Meier, 1979).

Eveline Cruickshanks & Howard Erskine Hill, *The Atterbury Plot* (London: Palgrave Macmillan, 2004.)

P. Deane and W.A. Cole, *British Economic Growth, 1688-1959* (Cambridge: CUP, 1969), 2nd edn.

Hugh Douglas, *Jacobite Spy Wars: Moles, Rogues and Treachery* (Stroud: Alan Sutton Publishing, 1999).

Richard Eason, *The last of their line: The Bible Clerks of All Souls College, Oxford* (Oxford: All Souls College, 1976).

Kenneth Ellis, *The Post Office in the Eighteenth Century* (Oxford: OUP, 1958), p. 65.

R.J.W. Evans & Peter H. Wilson, *The Holy Roman Empire, 1495-1806: A European Perspective* (Leiden: Brill, 2012).

William Bragg Ewald Jr., *Rogues, Royalty and Reporters, The Age of Queen Anne through its Newspapers* (Boston, 1954).

Michael FitzGerald, *Ragged London: The Life of London's Poor* (Stroud: The History Press, 2011).

Joseph Foster, *Alumni Oxonienses, 1500-1714*, (Oxford: James Parker & Co., 1891).

Paul S. Fritz, *The English Ministers and Jacobitism between the Rebellions of 1715 and 1745* (Toronto: University of Toronto Press, 1975).

P.N. Furbank & W.R. Owens, *A Political Biography of Daniel Defoe* (London: Pickering & Chatto, 2006).

William Gibson, *Religion and the Enlightenment 1600-1800: Conflict and the Rise of Civic Humanism in Taunton* (Oxford: Peter Lang, 2007).

John Graham, *A History of Ireland from the relief of Londonderry in 1689, to the surrender of Limerick in 1691* (Dublin: William Curry, 1839), pp. 75, 83, 372.

Robin Gwynn, *Huguenot Heritage* (Brighton: Sussex Academic, 2001), 2nd revised edn.

•   *The Huguenots of London* (Brighton: Sussex Academic, 1998).

Philip H. Highfill, Kalman A. Burnim, Edward A. Langhans, *A Biographical Dictionary of Actors, Actresses, Musicians, Dancers, Managers & Other Stage Personnel in London, 1660-1800* (Carbondale: Southern Illinois Press, 2006).

Jonathan Israel, *Conflicts of Empires: Spain, the Low Countries and the Struggle for World Supremacy* (London: The Hambledon Press, 1997).

Margaret C. Jacob, *Living the Enlightenment: Freemasonry and Politics in Eighteenth-Century Europe* (Oxford: OUP, 1991).

•   *The Radical Enlightenment* (Lafayette, LA: Cornerstone, 2006).

Susan Jenkins, *The Patronage and Collecting of James Brydges, 1st Duke of Chandos (1674-1744)*

(Farnham: Ashgate Publishing, 2007).

David Kahn, *The Codebreakers* (New York, NY: MacMillan, 1967).

Norma Landau, *Justices of the Peace 1679-1760* (Berkeley, CA, 1984).

John Lane, *Masonic Records 1717-1894*: http://www.hrionline.ac.uk/lane/.

Paul Langford, *A Polite and Commercial People: England, 1727-1783* (Oxford: OUP, 1998).

William Lee, *Daniel Defoe: His Life and recently discovered writings* (London: John Camden Hotten, 1869).

Karl Maria Michael de Leeuw, Jan Bergstra (eds), *The History of Information Security* (Amsterdam, NL: Elsevier, 2007).

John Locke, *Two Treatises of Government* (London, 1689).

John Macky, *Memoirs of the secret services* (London: Spring Macky, 1733), 2nd edition.

Earl of March (ed.), *A Duke and his Friends* (London: Hutchinson & Co., 1911), pp. 156-8.

Paula McDowell, *The Women of Grub Street: Press, Politics, and Gender in the London Literary Marketplace 1678-1730* (Oxford: Clarendon Press, 1998).

Alan Marshall, *Intelligence and Espionage in the Reign of Charles II, 1660-1685* (Cambridge: CUP, 1994).

Norman Milne, *Libertines and Harlots* (Bath: Parragon Publishing, 2014).

William Minto, *Daniel Defoe* (New York, NY: Harper & Brothers, 1887).

Paul Kleber Monod, *Jacobitism and the English People* 1688-1788 (Cambridge: CUP, 1989).

Paul Monod, Murray Pittock and Daniel Szechi (eds), *Loyalty & Identity, Jacobites at Home and Abroad* (Basingstoke: Palgrave MacMillan, 2010).

John Noorthouck, A New History of London (London, 1773).

Rosemary O'Day (ed), *Cassandra Brydges, Duchess of Chandos, 1670-1735: Life & Letters* (Martlesham: Boydell & Brewer, 2007).

Bernard Porter, *Plots and Paranoia: A History of Political Espionage in Britain 1790-1988* (Abingdon: Rourtledge, 2016).

Hastings Rashdall, *The Universities of Europe in the Middle Ages* (Cambridge: CUP, 2010).

John Richetti, *The Life of Daniel Defore* (Oxford: Blackwell, 2005).

Marsha Keith Schuchard, *Emanuel Swedenborg, Secret Agent on Earth and in Heaven* (Leiden, NL: Koninklijke Brill, 2012).

Romney Sedgwick (ed), *The History of Parliament: the House of Commons 1715-1754* (Martlesham: Boydell & Brewer, 1970).

Scott Showerby, *Making Toleration: The Repealers and the Glorious Revolution* (Harvard, Mass.: Harvard University Press, 2013).

Jacob Soll, *The Information Master. Jean-Baptiste Colbert's Secret State Intelligence System* (Ann Arbor, MI: University of Michigan Press, 2009).

Ian K. Steele, *The English Atlantic, 1675-1740:An Exploration of Communication and Community* (Oxford: OUP, 1986).

Jonathan Swift, *Travels into several Remote nations of the world by Lemuel Gulliver* (London: Charles Bathurst, 1742).
- *The Works of the Rev. Jonathan Swift* (London, 1801), vol. 13, pp. 353-4.

Daniel Szechi, *1715:The Great Jacobite Rebellion* (New Haven, CN:YUP, 2006).
- *Letters of George Lockhart of Carnwath, 1698-1732* (Edinburgh: Scottish History Society, 1989).
- *The Jacobites. Britain and Europe, 1688-1788* (Manchester: Manchester University Press, 1994).
- (editor) *The Dangerous Trade: Spies, Spymasters and the Making of Europe* (Dundee: Dundee University Press, 2010).

Mark Thompson, *The Secretaries of State 1681-1782* (Oxford: Clarendon Press, 1932).

Edward Walford, *Old and New London* (London: Cassell, Petter & Galpin, 1878).

Richard M. Ward, *Print Culture, Crime and Justice in 18th-Century London* (London: Bloomsbury, 2014).

Henry Benjamin Wheatley, *Round about Piccadilly and Pall Mall* (London: Smith Elder, 1870).

Henry Benjamin Wheatley, Peter Cunningham, *London Past and Present* (Cambridge: CUP, 2011) (reprint).

Sir William Yonge, *A list of the Colonels, Lieutenant Colonels, Majors, Captains ... of His Majesty's Forces on the British Establishment...* (London: House of Commons, 1740).

SELECTED JOURNAL ARTICLES & THESES

Robert P. Barnes, 'James VII's Forfeiture of the Scottish Throne', *Albion*, 5.4 (1973), 299-313.

Jeremy Black, 'Hanover and British Foreign Policy 1714-60', *English Historical Review*, 120.486 (2005), 303-39;

- 'British Foreign Policy in the Eighteenth Century: A Survey', *Journal of British Studies*, 26.1 (1987), 26-53; 'Fresh Light on the Fall of Townshend', 29.1 (1986), 41-64;

- 'Interventionism, Structuralism and Contingency in British Foreign Policy in the 1720s' *International History Review*, 26.4 (2004), 734-64; and

- 'British Neutrality in the War of the Polish Succession, 1733-1735', *International History Review*, 8.3 (1986), 345-66.

Rae Blanchard, 'Was Sir Richard Steele a Freemason?', *PMLA*, 63.3 (1948), 903-17.

George L. Cherry, 'The Rôle of the Convention Parliament (1688-89) in Parliamentary Supremacy', *Journal of the History of Ideas*, 17.3 (1956), 390-406.

- 'The Legal and Philosophical Position of the Jacobites, 1688-1689', *Journal of Modern History*, 22.4 (1950), 309-21.

John Childs, 'The Sales of Government Gazettes during the Exclusion Crisis, 1678-81', *English Historical Review*, 102.402 (1987), 103-6.

K.R.P. Clark, 'Defoe, Dissent, and Early Whig Ideology', *Historical Journal*, 52.3 (2009), 595-614.

David Connel, 'Recently identified at Burton Constable Hall: The collection of William Dugood FRS—jeweller, scientist, freemason and spy', *Journal of Historical Collections* (2009) 21.1, 33-47.

H. T. Dickinson, 'The Eighteenth-Century Debate on the Sovereignty of Parliament', *Transactions of the Royal Historical Society*, 26 (1976), 189-210J.

A. Downie, 'Swift and Jacobitism', *English Literary History*, 64.4 (1997), 887-901.

Paul S. Fritz, 'The Anti-Jacobite Intelligence System of the English Ministers, 1715-1745, *Historical Journal*, 16.2 (1973), 265-289.

P.N. Furbank and W.R. Owens, 'Defoe, the De la Faye letters and Mercurius politicus', *British Journal for Eighteenth-century Studies*, 23 (2003), 13-9.

• 'The Myth of Defoe as 'Applebee's Man'', *Review of English Studies*, n.s. 48.190 (1997), 198-204.

William Gibson, 'An eighteenth-century paradox: the career of the Decipherer-Bishop, Edward Willes', *Journal for Eighteenth-Century Studies*, 12.1 (1989) 69-76.

Mark Goldie, 'John Locke's Circle and James II', *Historical Journal*, 35.3 (1992), 557-86.

Janetta Inglis Keith Guite, 'The Jacobite Cause, 1730-1740: The International Dimension', unpublished PhD thesis (Hamilton, Ont.: McMaster University, 1987).

Philip Haffenden, 'Colonial Appointments and Patronage under the Duke of Newcastle, 1724-1739', *English Historical Review*, 78.308 (1963), 417-35.

D.W. Hayton, 'The Stanhope/Sunderland Ministry and the Repudiation of Irish Parliamentary Independence', *English Historical Review*, 113.452 (1998), 610-36.

J.M. Hintermaier, 'The First Modern refugees? Charity, Entitlement and Persuasion in the Huguenot Immigration of the 1680s', Albion, 32.3 (2000), 429-49.

Geoffrey Holmes, 'The Sacheverell Riots', *Past and Present*, 72 (1976), 55-85.

Gerald Howson, *Thief-Taker General: Jonathan Wild and the Emergence of Crime and Corruption as a Way of Life in Eighteenth-Century England* (Oxford: Transaction Books, 1985).

J. R. Jones, 'James II's Whig Collaborators', *Historical Journal*, 3.1 (1960), 65-73.

Norma Landau, 'Indictment for Fun and Profit', *Law and History Review*, 17.3 (1999), 507-36.

- 'Country Matters: The Growth of Political Stability a Quarter Century On', *Albion*, 25.2 (1993), 261-74.

Patrick McNally, 'Wood's Halfpence, Carteret and the Government of Ireland, 1723-6', *Irish Historical Studies*, 30.119 (1997), 354-76.

Geraldine Meroney, 'The London Entrepôt Merchants and the Georgia Colony', *William and Mary Quarterly*, 25.2 (1968), 230-44, esp. 235.

Lotte Mulligan and Glenn Mulligan, 'Reconstructing Restoration Science', *Social Studies of Science*, 11.3 (1981.

P.B. Munsche, 'Review: The Justice of the Peace, 1679-1760', *Eighteenth Century Studies*, 20.3 (1987), 385-7.

Andrew Pink, 'A music club for freemasons: Philo-musicae et -architecturae societas Apollini, London, 1725–1727', *Early Music* (2010) 38.4, 523-36.

J.H. Plumb, 'The Elections to the Convention Parliament of 1689', *Cambridge Historical Journal*, 5.3 (1937), 235-54.

- 'The Growth of the Electorate in England from 1600 to 1715', *Past & Present*, 45 (1969), 90-116.

Suzanne Joy Podhurst, *The Scriblerians Uncensored: libel, encryption and the making of copyright in eighteenth-century Britain and Ireland* (Unpublished PhD Dissertation, Princeton University, 2012).

Dorothy MacKay Quynn, 'Philipp von Stosch: Collector, Bibliophile, Spy, Thief (1611[sic]-1757)', *Catholic Historical Review*, 27.3 (1941), 332-44.

Nicholas Rogers, 'Money, Land and Lineage: The Big Bourgeoisie of Hanoverian London', *Social History*, 4.3 (1979), 437-54.

Pat Rogers, 'The Waltham Blacks and the Black Act', *Historical Journal*, 17.3 (1974), 465-486.

J.C. Sainty, 'A Huguenot civil servant: the career of Charles Delafaye, 1677–1762', *Proceedings of the Huguenot Society*, 22 (1975), 398–413.

- 'The Secretariat of the Chief Governors of Ireland, 1690-1800', *Proceedings of the Royal Irish Academy*, 77.C (1977), 1-33.

Lois G. Schwoerer, 'Locke, Lockean Ideas, and the Glorious Revolution', *Journal of the History of Ideas*, 51.4 (1990), 531-48.

Romney Sedgwick (ed.), *Lord Hervey's Memoirs* (London, 1931), vol. III, p. 12.

R. Shackleton, 'Montesquieu's Correspondence', *French Studies*, XII.4 (1958), 324-45. Original at Goodwood, Box 36, bundle IX.

Robert B. Shoemaker, 'The London Mob in the Early Eighteenth Century', *Journal of British Studies*, 26.3 (1987), 273-304.

Scott Sowerby, 'Group Hunting: Religion, Politics, and Ideology in Later Stuart Britain, 'Historical Journal', 58.4 (2015), 1191–204.

- 'Forgetting the Repealers: Religious Toleration and Historical Amnesia in Later Stuart England', *Past and Present*, 215 (2012), 85–123.
- 'Opposition to Anti-Popery in Restoration England', *Journal of British Studies*, 51.1 (2012), 26–49.
- 'Of Different Complexions: Religious Diversity and National Identity in James II's Toleration Campaign', *English Historical Review*, 124. 506 (2009), 29–52.
- 'Tories in the Whig Corner: Daniel Fleming's Journal of the 1685 Parliament', *Parliamentary History*, 24.2 (2005), 157–201.

Thomas P. Slaughter, 'Abdicate' and 'Contract' in the Glorious Revolution', *Historical Journal*, 24.2 (1981), 323-37.

James R. Smither, 'The St. Bartholomew's Day Massacre and Images of Kingship in France: 1572-1574', Sixteenth Century Journal, 22.1 (1991), 27-46.

W. A. Speck, 'The Orangist Conspiracy against James II', Historical Journal, 30.2 (1987), 453-62.

Larry Stewart, 'A Meaning for Machines: Modernity, Utility, and the Eighteenth-Century British Public', *Journal of Modern History*, 70.2 (1998) 259-294.

- 'Public Lectures and Private Patronage in Newtonian England', *Isis*, 77.1 (1986), 47-58.

Raymond Turner, 'The Excise Scheme of 1733', *English Historical Review*, 42.165 (1927), 34-57.

 • 'The Secrecy of the Post', *English Historical Review*, 33.131 (1918), 320-7.

John Wells and Douglas Wills, 'Revolution, Restoration, and Debt Repudiation: The Jacobite Threat to England's Institutions and Economic Growth', *Journal of Economic History*, 60.2 (2000), 418-41.

A.C. Wood, 'The English Embassy at Constantinople, 1600-1762', *English Historical Review*, 40.160 (1925), 553-61.

THE OLD
STABLES
PRESS

● Oxfordshire ●

Printed in Great Britain
by Amazon

18926039R00182